Jennifer

Much Cure

from Grana

Christmas 1971.

SYBIL THORNDIKE CASSON CH, DBE (1931)
24.10.1882 — 09.06.76
2 Dtrs & 2 Sons

M. Lewis Casson

Sybil, 1969

SYBIL THORNDIKE CASSON

by

ELIZABETH SPRIGGE

With a Foreword by
Dame Sybil

LONDON
VICTOR GOLLANCZ LTD
1971

ISBN 0 575 01341 9

Printed in Great Britain by
The Camelot Press Ltd., London and Southampton

In memory of
LEWIS CASSON

Dear Sybil, you were never one
Who went on acting when the play was done.
A public friend, a very private wife,
A star not only of the stage but life.

A. P. Herbert

ACKNOWLEDGEMENTS

MY WARM THANKS to Mr Russell Thorndike for so generously allowing me to quote *The Letters from America* from his own biography of his sister and to use material from his book *Children of the Garter*. And to Mr J. C. Trewin for kindly letting me draw freely from his biography *Sybil Thorndike*.

My gratitude also for permission to quote from their works to Miss Enid Bagnold, Mr Richard Church, Mr Basil Dean, Mr Christopher Fry, Sir Alan Herbert, Mr Michéal Mac Liammóir, Mr J. B. Priestley, The Lady Stocks, Mr Leo Underwood, Mr Emlyn Williams; to Lady Epstein for permission to include a photograph of the Epstein portrait-bust and to the Earl of Snowdon for allowing the reproduction of his photograph of Dame Sybil in *The Family Reunion*. Also to the Trustees of the copyrights of Dylan Thomas for the quotation from his poem.

To Mr and Mrs John Casson, Mr and Mrs Ian Haines (Mary Casson) and Mr Christopher Casson for their valuable contributions, to Miss Ann Casson for her letters about playing Saint Joan.

Special thanks for their editorial help to Dr Rosamond Gilder, Director in America of the International Theatre Institute, Mrs Enid Foster, Librarian of the British Drama League, Miss Freda Gaye, former editor of *Who's Who in the Theatre*, and to Miss Margaret Webster.

And for untold bounty in the way of hospitality, interviews and letters to:

Mr Frith Banbury, Dr E. Martin Browne, Sir Hugh Casson, Mr Randal Casson, Mr Gordon Chater, Sir Alexander and Lady Clutterbuck, Mr Billy Cotton, Mrs des Voeux, Mr Geoffrey Dunn, Dame Edith Evans, Mrs Marjorie Forsyth, Sir John Gielgud, Miss Mary Glasgow, The Rev. Canon A. T. Goodrich, Mr Nicholas Hannen, Mr Lionel Harris, Miss Wendy Hiller, Mr Jo Hodgkinson, Mr Malcolm MacDonald, Mr Michael MacOwan,

Mr Raymond Mander and Mr Joe Mitchenson, Mrs Mark, Miss Sybil Morrison, Miss Nora Nicholson, Lord Olivier, Mr and Mrs Dan O'Connor, Mr Reece Pemberton, The Rev. Canon H. J. Powell, Mr. J. B. Priestley, Miss Henzie Raeburn, Miss Margaret Rawlings, Mr Owen Reed, Sir Ralph Richardson, Mr and Mrs Clive Robinson, Mr Hugh Ross Williamson, Miss Athene Seyler, Sir Michael and Lady Turner, Mrs Ingaret van der Post, Miss Irene Worth.

It has proved impossible to trace the name of every photographer whose work has been used to illustrate the book. My thanks both to those acknowledged in the List of Illustrations, and to those who perforce remain unacknowledged.

E. S.

CONTENTS

LIST OF ILLUSTRATIONS

FOREWORD

YES, I HAVE always wanted to write a book about my life because I have found it so exciting, and I was specially encouraged when still fairly young to read Benvenuto Cellini's thrilling memoirs. He thought that everyone should write an account of their living and working, for "There's no life that's dull," he said, "no life without some sign of growth, and a thing grown or growing always holds some excitement." So everyone should tell a tale of themselves before they pass off to the Beyond. This laudable promise I made to myself, but it was pushed into the background —what with work and then marriage and such-like thrills. It was Lewis who through the years egged me on to do this thing which was already in my mind: he said it would get a lot of things off my chest which were worrying me. "Never mind if it's never published," he said, "that doesn't matter. Take it like a confession, it will calm you down and make you much easier to live with." So again I thought about it, but how to find the time?

Not a line did I write till I was sixty years old, thinking that now life was practically over, what with grown-up children and their progeny coming along so pleasantly and regularly. But at sixty life became even more full, and no writing was done. At sixty-five I started again to put a few words and thoughts together, but I found myself going back to the beginning again, because heredity is such an absorbingly enlivening study, so I never got beyond the great-uncles.

Then world tours came along, besides lots of new plays at home, so that I said, "Oh, it's too much! I can't be bothered with my idiotic life when 'there is throats to be cut and works to be done . . . so Chrish sa' me, la.'" I shoved the whole thing out of my mind and felt completely happy, although publishers were worrying me, but of them I took no notice.

Then one day Elizabeth Sprigge happened along. I'd known her for some years since she was running the Watergate Theatre at Charing Cross. She said, "Could I help you with your auto-biography? People are wanting it, you know." I felt saved. "Oh, *you* do it," I yelled at her, "like the angel you are, and leave me to get on with my life and work."

Now, I had read some of her biographies, Gertrude Stein and Strindberg and others, and had enjoyed them tremendously, and here was my chance to get rid of my responsibility and think no more about my tiresome self. But it didn't turn out that way at all. Elizabeth put me through searching examinations, with Lewis interfering a great deal. We all thoroughly enjoyed our-selves and Lewis and I had lots of fun remembering things of old—in fact, there are few things more pleasant than reliving one's past life, even rows and difficulties. After Lewis went I became a bit tired of myself. In fact, I felt I didn't want to hear my name or see my face again. I think Elizabeth understood this, but actually one can't help being interested in one's life and doings, so I was lured into talk and began once more to enjoy the search into the past. And now the book is done, and of course Elizabeth has made me out far more important than I am, for she is a generous friend and sees few faults where there are many.

And now, glory be, for the next ten years, when I shall be nearly a hundred years old, I need not think about myself at all, but only about Lewis and the children and the grands and great-grands, and lovely friends and what a pleasant upheaving life I've had, and so on to the unknown and exciting future. I know that more than half of what I wanted to say has had to be scrapped, darling friends fobbed off with a line or not mentioned—not Elizabeth's fault—it's just that I'm a bit overcrowded.

So let the circus go on with gratitude for an adventurous life—for husband, family, friends, work and a sympathetic biographer—and "all shall be well . . . all manner of things shall be well".*

Sybil Thorndike Casson

* Julian of Norwich.

PREAMBLE

AND SO THIS autobiographical biography came to be written with, on my side, great happiness and pride at being entrusted with the work, and also great diffidence, for I saw from the beginning how impossible it would be to convey the full quality of the book's subject to all its readers.

Contemplating her portrait before the sittings began, I visualised Sybil Thorndike chiefly as the actress whom I had watched for nearly half a century playing that astonishing variety of roles, from those terrifying harpies of the Grand Guignol to the beauty and serenity of the later parts, not forgetting a full measure of mirth. Of course I already knew that Sybil Thorndike was a tremendous human being and one who, in Gertrude Stein's words, was "loving being" to the full, but it is only during these precious years of sharing in her memories that I have glimpsed the high, wide vista of her personal mountain range.

Often, when I arrived in the morning for one of our sessions, Sybil would be at the piano playing Bach, "the nearest thing we have to God Almighty", performing with the skill of a musician who loves her art and has never neglected to practise it however much else there was to do. "Actors aren't as dedicated as musicians," she says, and Sybil Thorndike is a dedicated person. Or else, as I approached the door, she would be singing. Scarcely an hour of her everyday life passes without some snatch of song, and this pursuit, allied to her sensitive reading aloud of poetry, both in public and in private, and particularly to Lewis Casson, has made her voice grow ever more melodious with the passing of the years.

So now I cannot think of Sybil Thorndike without thinking of music and of poetry, of human love and love of God. If this sounds gushing let me declare at once that it is *not*. Sybil has sometimes teased me about being such a stickler for accuracy. "It's near enough," she would say, "what does it matter if I lie a bit?"

And I would answer: "That's O.K. for you artists, but not for the wretched biographer." So to the best of my ability I am telling the truth about Sybil. Anyhow, she's not someone to gush over, and if I ever hear anybody describing her as "sweet" I blench. Sweet, no! Even Sybil's love has a touch of astringency.

To this day she lives every moment twice over. I remember Lewis Casson saying to me: "One of the things that makes Sybil's life so difficult for her is that she can never say no. The diary may be blank when she agrees to help but however full it is by the time the day comes, she keeps her promise."

Yes, all her life Sybil Thorndike has kept her promises, as we can now so clearly see.

ELIZABETH SPRIGGE

PART I

CHAPTER I

FOREBEARS

SYBIL THORNDIKE'S GRANDFATHER was a certain Daniel Thorndike, who was commissioned in the Artillery at the time of Waterloo but never saw active service, although he attained the rank of general. Various portraits of him made an early impression on Sybil, and when she was very small she used to play with the lacquered papier-mâché pots which he made himself to house the gum-arabic used for dressing his carefully rolled whiskers. She remembers, too, playing with his duelling pistols, which were kept in her father's dressing-room.

The General, who lived in Bath, was also a successful amateur actor and musician, playing several instruments, notably the flute. He married early, a beautiful young girl of the Faunce family, by whom he had two children; but while they were still very young, one Sunday morning when her husband was in church, his wife eloped to Australia with her lover, the namesake of the famous playwright, Dion Boucicault. This was a terrible blow for the General, not only to him personally, but to his family pride and his sense of propriety. This first wife was never mentioned again, not even to her children, and in due course the General obtained a divorce. Years later he married again, this time Isabella Russell, Sybil Thorndike's grandmother, a woman many years younger than himself and well suited to his temperament, for, although she was vivacious and took her part in family theatricals and musical entertainments, she was at the same time correct, religious and obedient. By her the General had four sons and one daughter. The first two boys died in infancy, the third was Arthur John Webster, Sybil Thorndike's father, and then came Francis, and finally Isabella.

The General's home was run on the strict lines of a godly Victorian household, the whole family and all the servants gathering for morning and evening prayers, with the General reading from the Scriptures in the "sonorous mouthed diction", as Sybil calls it, which is a characteristic of the Thorndikes. Arthur would have liked to be a soldier, as his father was, but he was allowed no say in the matter—he was destined for the Church. As, even in childhood, he had always had a strong religious bent, he was easily reconciled to his father's decision— soldier of England or soldier of Christ seemed much the same thing to him.

He showed no particular brilliance at school or at St John's College, Cambridge, but was a good all-rounder who enjoyed mastering difficulties and whose vitality, combined with his good looks and amiability, made him popular with tutors and fellow-students alike. Besides the imaginative mystical sense that had continued to develop, he was keen on sport, playing tennis with enthusiasm and rowing for his college—only missing a place in the Cambridge crew by being a few pounds underweight.

His best friend at college was John Alcott Bowers, whose sister Agnes Macdonald, known as 'Donnie', sometimes came up to visit her brother. She was a good pianist, and used to accompany Arthur in his rendering of such songs as *The Devout Lover*, *To Anthea* or Tosti's *Farewell*. Young Thorndike found her extremely attractive, but at these first meetings she was not particularly impressed with him. Nevertheless, Donnie was destined to become Arthur's wife, and the mother of Sybil Thorndike.

Donnie's father, also John Alcott Bowers, was a very different kind of grandfather from General Thorndike. The family lived in Elgin, the small town in northern Scotland, where his father was the postmaster, and the boys became local postmen and tended the sheep in the surrounding meadows. John was quiet but very ambitious, and during his hours of shepherding he read studiously and taught himself a measure of mathematics. With some difficulty he persuaded his father to apprentice him to an engineering shop

in Aberdeen. Here he did extremely well, and when one day he
heard a couple of men say that they would give twenty pounds
to anyone who could find a flaw in a certain machine and put it
right, he at once volunteered to do so. He got the twenty pounds,
and immediately shipped himself as an apprentice in a boat bound
for Southampton. Here "he somehow squirmed himself", as
Sybil puts it, into the Royal Mail Line, which later became the
Union Castle, and ended up as head consulting engineer.

He married Betsy Alcott, whose family lived at Portchester in
Hampshire. She bore him three sons—John, William and Ted—
and three daughters—Adela Fanny (known as Sam), Agnes
Macdonald and Belle, who died young. All three sons became
parsons, "very large-scale parsons, all extraordinary preachers".
The eldest, Sybil's Uncle Jack, became Archdeacon of Gloucester
and finally Bishop of Thetford, achieving the possibly unique
distinction among bishops of having as his memorial a laughing
likeness. "The plaque in the choir of Norwich Cathedral portrays
his jolly face with a broad grin." Apparently he made his congregation so happy, telling funny stories even in the pulpit,
that it was impossible to conceive of a solemn memorial to him.

They were highly unusual, these Bowers brothers. Willy and
Ted both did well at Oxford, but according to their niece they
should have been actors, not parsons. Ted was particularly
brilliant, but he could not keep out of debt, and presently his
father settled his affairs, gave him a sum of money, and sent him off
to America, where he married a Canadian girl and ended up as a
dignitary of the Episcopal Church in Texas. Uncle Willy was
most extraordinary, "something of a genius but not saintly at all".
He had a gift for making money by gambling on the Stock
Exchange, and if he wanted anything for his church or his parish
he would go off and have a fling, and come back with the cash for
the new candlesticks, or whatever was needed.

He was a highly exciting, theatrical preacher, and his church at
Gillingham, in Kent, was packed each Sunday with sailors and
men from the dockyard.

"It was a sight I'll never forget," Sybil says, "a whole

congregation in a state of emotion, tears pouring down their faces, Uncle Willy making them laugh and cry as he wished. In the vestry afterwards he'd catch hold of one and say, 'Well, how did it go? I got 'em, didn't I? Not a dry eye in the place!' I used to think it humbugging, so I believe did Father, but it wasn't, it was drama—it was a stage performance. He thought my father dull and pious because he couldn't use the same method, and they never really hit it off.

"I can remember certain meal-times when Uncle Willy and my mother would get all worked up with hymn tunes. 'Come on, Don!' he'd shout at her, conducting with his knife and fork, and off they'd go at the tops of their voices—*There is a Fountain Filled with Blood* or *Hark, the Glad Sound!*—we children enjoying it all like an entertainment, Father not too happy at the mixture of hymns and rowdiness, and Uncle Jack, the Bishop, being very sweet and amused, but really siding with Father. Mother, who after all was Willy's sister, was really his kind—madly dramatic—she ought to have been on the stage, although she had a strong religious streak too.

"Willy's stories were jam for us children. He'd repeat the point at least six times, laughing with a boisterousness that had us nearly in hysterics. He too went to America, but he came back and finished his days in Bethnal Green, beloved by all the barrow boys, who thought his church was the real thing."

But this, of course, was many years later. After their first encounter, in Cambridge, Arthur and Donnie did not meet again for some years. When he came down from Cambridge, and was preparing for ordination, Arthur lived for a time at Bere Regis in Dorset. Thomas Hardy remembered him as "a beautiful fair-haired lay-reader who used to be in and out of the cottages with great diligence and persistence, with a Bible under his arm." Later he and his friend John Bowers became fellow-curates at St Mary's Redcliffe in Bristol. John was married by now, and Donnie was staying with him and his wife. There was a festival procession in the church, and, as the choir passed their pew singing *Onward Christian Soldiers*, Donnie whispered to her sister-in-law, "Louie, I could marry that man walking with Jack"—almost the same words that Donnie's daughter, Sybil, was to write to her brother Russell Thorndike when she first saw Lewis Casson.

Louie whispered back, "That's Arthur Thorndike, and he's coming to supper."

His hair had grown darker, and he was even more beautiful than in the Cambridge days. Donnie had not recognised the young man whose songs she used to accompany, but now she was captivated. Arthur found her as enchanting as ever—she had lovely blue eyes and a gay, smiling face—and it did not take him long to propose, Donnie sweeping away all his scruples by assuring him that they could easily live on half the income that she discovered him to have.

And so three months later, in 1881, Arthur and Donnie were married, and went to Barley, near Welwyn, moving to the parish church of Gainsborough in Lincolnshire for Arthur's senior curateship, just in time for their first child to be born there on October 24th, 1882. She was baptised by her father Agnes Sybil.

CHAPTER II

CHILDHOOD

(1882–1900)

As a child Sybil used rather to resent having been born in Gainsborough, where her father was only a curate, instead of in the cathedral town of Rochester, where her brothers and sister were born, after their father had attained the dignity of a minor canon. It was his singing voice, Sybil says, which got him the canonship, for music was a necessary part of this office. Arthur Thorndike would, in fact, have been quite content to remain a curate all his life; he was not at all ambitious. He liked to spend his spare time playing the cello, and he was also very skilful with his hands, and as a hobby would make miniature chests of drawers out of cigar boxes, or carry out other feats of carpentry. "Your father enjoys making silly little three-legged stools and useless things," Mother would say to us. "He hasn't any ambition to get to the top of the tree."

But his wife certainly thought that he should be a bishop, if not an archbishop. This strong desire of Mrs Thorndike's to see her family gain laurels continued in respect of her children, and particularly Sybil.

Although she spent only the first eighteen months of her life in Gainsborough, Sybil feels that this must account for her "innate love of the northern counties and curates", and she is reminded to this day of her birthplace whenever she smells new-mown hay. "Ah, Gainsborough!" she will exclaim, breathing in that fragrance. "My strongest sense, I think, is my sense of smell—I often remember places that way." She also recalls sorrowfully from this period a wax doll which she took to bed and which melted under her, but all the rest of her childhood memories—and her memory is remarkable—are of Rochester, "where Dickens lived, and the stones both here and in Chatham speak of him to this day". In fact the Thorndikes lived at No. 2, Minor Canon Row, where the Reverend Septimus Crisparkle had resided, and Sybil and Russell, as children, pictured him as their father, and thought that Dickens must have taken his likeness and put him into *Edwin Drood*. After all, were they not both minor canons, both beautiful, good singers and fine swimmers?

Thus the children grew up with great affection and respect for Charles Dickens, although this did not prevent them from smashing up their father's precious bust of him one day, having become convinced that it was Dickens's ghost and that it was haunting them.

Russell was born in Rochester a few months after the move there, and Sybil remembers attending his christening when she was two years old, dressed in a green velvet pelisse and a leghorn hat. "I still get the feel of that velvet mixed with the lovely musty cathedral smell." She was rather ashamed of her baby brother for yelling so lustily during the ceremony.

"Church bells, always church bells, our lives run by the cathedral chimes. I think this must have given me my feeling for life in the church and cloister—in fact, one of my first ambitions was to be a nun in the winter and a gleaner in the summer."

The cathedral provided the whole background to their lives, for not only were the family activities conditioned by their father's manifold duties as a minor canon, but their mother too was deeply involved in his work. She brought to this her exuberance and sense of fun, which made church life endlessly exciting for the children, and prevented her husband from becoming too fanatical a religious.

"In a way we were brought up in the tough side of the Church," Russell Thorndike comments. "I remember tremendous quarrels between the High and the Low at tea-parties."

From a fine pianist Mrs Thorndike had developed into an excellent organist, and she played and sang beautifully and with great ease—music was as natural as breathing to the whole family.

Acting was equally natural to the children—Sybil Thorndike has really never been able to imagine anybody unable to act. From their earliest days she and Russell would lean out of the nursery window and watch their father and the "cathedral dignitaries swooping by with gowns flapping" from the daily Offices.

"Our first acting must have been imitating their walks—the two steps, then a run and a hop of Canon Cheyne, the great Hebrew scholar, and the Archdeacon, who always looked back at the corner with a sort of *plié*, and a chuckle and a twinkle of the eye, very often a wave too—never dreaming that the two innocent little faces peering down from the window were intent on getting their imitation of him up to standard. The two other minor canons were rather frivolous, and had occasional tickings off from the elder dignitaries in consequence—such nice young men they all were, always so jolly to us. About one, Minor Canon Livett, the Precentor, we felt a sort of jealousy, as he had a very beautiful face and was a fine musician, and we felt that he was a kind of rival for Father, whom of course we knew to be perfect in every way. There was no rivalry between themselves—these nasty feelings were only in us.

"We felt all these dignitaries showed up badly against Father, who had a walk that was vigorous and lively, and we used to think he could fly, for his gown gave him the appearance of having wings. We felt the others didn't know how to use their costumes like Father, who when he put on a surplice and stole really looked as if he were a priest of ancient days and had charge of an Ark of the Covenant.

"Then there was our beloved Dean Hole of roses and preaching fame; his great stature, magnificent lion-like head and splendid voice fitted into our childish imaginations. His first visit to our home in Minor Canon Row was an event; Mother fell for him immediately, and so did we, for he asked us if we knew what a tip was, we said we didn't, and he gave us half-a-crown each and said that was a tip—naturally we adored him."

Mrs Thorndike and Dean Hole became great friends. She used to find mechanical toys for him—a little fiddler who danced, and tiny clowns that turned head over heels—and the children would have the fun of watching the Dean sitting on the deanery floor playing with them. Mrs Hole was a beautiful woman whose uniform was a shady hat and gardeners' gloves, for the famous rose-garden was chiefly her work, and the children felt that it wasn't quite "her" when they saw her in her elegant Sunday best.

Then there was Canon Jelf, who made Sybil and Russell feel that his old house and garden in the precincts were as much home as their own house. There were several Jelf children of about their own age—Kitty, who was Sybil's best friend, and remained so until her death a few years ago, and Phil and Gordon, who were Russell's special pals. They formed themselves into a gang with "Jelfs and Thorndikes for ever" as their motto, and got up to endless pranks, although they had to beware a little of Canon Jelf, who was the very pattern of a saintly Anglican priest. Luckily he had a sense of fun and was not too severe so long as the children behaved themselves properly in church, and did not make a game of holy things. The Thorndikes were the transgressors in this respect, and were often a menace to the vergers when they used the crypt for their games, hid under the choir stalls, or scattered quantities of torn-up paper from the nursery window to represent a snowstorm. Nevertheless, in spite of their constant reprimands the vergers remained their friends. The young Thorndikes were always playing church.

"We held long services with boots, tennis rackets and tall hot-water cans for congregation; we were very ritualistic, and bobbed and genuflected far more than was necessary. We both preached—I, in advance of my time, a potential Maude Royden—but Russell was the star turn, making up texts like

'The Indian horses gallop in sin, so do the Indians also', from things we had misheard in the cathedral."

On one occasion, after they had gone with their father to a very High church where he was taking duty, they even played at High Mass. They did this very thoroughly; they discovered a real altar frontal in the box-room, Russell wore an Indian table-centre as a cope and a tea-cosy for a mitre, they took the bell off their father's bicycle for sacramental use, Sybil imitated the sound of the organ—she had rigged one up with handles of knives for notes—while at the same time singing a Gregorian chant, and Russell celebrated Communion with biscuits and a bottle of cough mixture.

This time it was their father who discovered and admonished them, which they thought most unfair, as they had been performing the service very devoutly. Needless to say they had no notion of blasphemy, any more than they imagined that they were being irreverent when they used sacred places for their games.

"The cathedral was our playground, our home, our scenes for plays and romances, and it was our own milieu—we had no reverence, we knew and loved it too well."

They had a great contempt for "holy-bobs", people who made a show of being pious, and they did not feel that Sunday was special, except that exciting things were more apt to happen on this day.

"I remember a neighbour passing our window on the way to the cathedral. I was all dressed up ready for matins, and playing with a doll. 'Fancy you playing with a doll on Sunday, you naughty little girl,' she said. 'I shall have to tell your father.' I put out my tongue and called out, 'Father lets me. He *likes* dolls on Sundays.' "

Religion, in fact, like music and drama, was as natural to the Thorndikes as breathing, and they loved the services.

Canon Thorndike, 1908

Mrs Thorndike

The Little Sailor

The four Thorndikes

"We knew all the hymns by heart, and I sang at the top of my voice. Mother used to poke me if I sang too loud. All the functions, too, were an excitement, whether it was confirmation, socials, ordinations and bishops coming with *The Church's One Foundation* and cold chicken to follow—all was a thrill for us."

Forbidden to play at Christian worship, Sybil announced to her brother, "We'll just have to go over to Baal," whereupon they stripped to the waist, armed themselves with paper-knives, and sang at the tops of their voices the chorus from the *Elijah, Baal, we cry to Thee!*

This time their father failed to admonish them; he simply dissolved in helpless laughter.

The Jelfs did not take much part in these religious games, although they were at the heart of the other acting activities, and they also ganged up with the Thorndikes to persecute the "street cads", butcher and grocer boys, and such like—"horrid little snobs we were"—and as sleuths to track down various inhabitants of the precincts, thus preventing the murders and burglaries they were sure would have been committed otherwise.

"Acting was with us always," but the young Thorndikes' first experience of a stage came when a play was performed in the Jelfs' drawing-room, in which the Jelf and Thorndike children had small parts as fairies and elves. This whetted their appetites, and it was not long before they had rigged up a splendid stage on a disused bed in the attic. They labelled their plays, "A play for much crying", "A play that is very frightening", "A play where you can scream with laughing as much as you like", in order to make sure that the reaction of the audience was the right one. The servants were their favourite audience, because they were less apt to criticise the use to which various household objects were put in the performances.

In many of the plays "killings" predominated, and looking back Sybil wonders how this instinct came to manifest itself in such young children. But even with them, she thinks, the acting-out of evil feelings worked as a kind of catharsis. All the

Thorndikes, except Arthur, had quick, strong tempers; they were fierce arguers, but quarrels or scenes were rare and never violent.

Another aspect of life had by now opened up for Sybil—school. Before she was quite five she began to go each morning to the Miss Rivetts' school, where Miss Fanny taught general subjects and Miss Hattie music, and where, as soon as he was old enough, Russell joined her.

Naturally, considering her home life, Sybil excelled, especially when called on to read aloud. She had splendid people to emulate. Her father used to read Shakespeare and poetry to the children, and the beauty of his voice never failed to thrill his listeners, old or young, while Mother Don Don, who had no particular use for Shakespeare or the poets, read them stories.

"And she read like a play. Oh, we were thrilled when Mother read to us as children, because she always read with such conviction."

And then there were the music lessons. In these too Sybil was advanced for her age, but on one occasion she fell into disgrace because she could not remember the lines and spaces of the staves, and was thus discovered to be playing her piano exercises by ear and not reading the piece at all. This was considered deceit, and her shame was all the greater because a little boy six months younger than herself could read the notes with ease. In later years he became a popular theatrical agent, but Sybil Thorndike never forgave him for disgracing her. She sobbed all the way home because she felt that she had "let Father down". This was a tremendously strong and restraining feeling in those early days, for she adored her father.

On the whole these first school years were enjoyable, but one memory stands out painfully to this day—that of seeing a boy caned, and hearing his cry and the whack of the cane on his hands and back. The small Sybil was "horribly frightened" and shocked, and from that day hated and despised physical chastisement. Street fighting was common at this time and was something to be avoided on one's daily walks, but this did not offend Sybil as did anyone hitting another in cold blood or as a punishment. As she grew older this feeling grew into her hatred of war, and her contempt for the idea that one could do something wicked and call it righteous if it was against an enemy.

Sybil was ten and Russell eight when their parents took them to a real theatre for the first time. This seems strange to Sybil now, when she considers how her own children have lived in the theatre from infancy, and how her father loved the theatre and almost idolised Henry Irving. The play was *The Private Secretary* at the Chatham Opera House, and the children had not imagined that anything in the world could be so glorious and so funny.

Two changes now came into their lives, the birth of their sister Eileen in 1890 and then, as Mr Thorndike had been made vicar of the largest parish in Rochester, the move to St Margaret's Vicarage. This thrilled Sybil and Russell. Their new home was a fine, spacious house on top of a hill, and the two large nursery windows looked over the garden and a couple of steep fields, across which they used to race down to the River Medway. The attic provided them with rooms where they were allowed to move the furniture around—which they endlessly did—and to carry on with their acting. Before long, however, they had even more scope, for they were given permission to do their plays in the parish room, attached to the vicarage. They were annoyed that they were not allowed to use the baby in their plays, but by the time she was three she proved a very useful extra.

By now Sybil and Russell were separated in their studies, Russell at his preparatory school, while Sybil, from the age of seven, had gone to the newly-built Rochester Grammar School for Girls. She was rather proud of being at such an up-to-date place and was full of good resolutions, but she was not a very successful scholar, because there was so much else to interest and excite her. Scripture lessons were wonderful, for the mistress who taught this subject had a true vocation, and made the Old Testament as lively as any adventure story. Then there was the Shakespeare class, which of course she enjoyed. For this subject, too, she had a fine teacher with a real love of language who read with great emotion. Sybil used to go home and do passages from

Julius Caesar to Russell in her teacher's thrilling voice—with great effect, she felt. Although the idea of history interested her, she did not find it easy to learn, for the history teacher frightened her. Nevertheless, she recognised and admired the calm detachment of a scholar, a quality which has always held a fascination for her. Her form mistresses were strict disciplinarians, and she was constantly having to make excuses for work not done. Noughts, noughts, noughts for every lesson, and terrible rowings which reduced her to tears, for again she felt that she was "letting Father down". But her misery never lasted long. "Rejoice not against me, oh mine enemy, when I fall down I shall arise." That was her motto, and arise she did.

Years later, when she was already a well-known actress, one of her former school-teachers wrote this description of her:*

"A wistful-eyed, small-featured little face comes before me, framed in straight-parted hair—the face of a child who is looking out into the future. Her questing expression asks what it is that she has to do some day somewhere. I see her among all the class-mates that don't mean much to her, learning the dull school-lessons that don't mean anything to her, listening rather wearily to the teacher who means even less. Such was Sybil Thorndike at the age of twelve. The writer remembers no other girl in that particular class, but little Sybil attracted one even then by the characteristics of the artist, and the impression of an isolation in which she perhaps already felt a longing for self-expression . . . "

Fortunately for Sybil, she was able to do a certain amount of acting at school.

"A great moment came when our form was called on to give a public performance of *Julius Caesar*—and I was cast for Brutus. 'Here's your great chance,' Russell said. 'It's a pity your face is so red. You ought to be pale with short hair.' So childish of him, I felt. If I *thought* Brutus I'd *be* Brutus, and the

* Name of journal and date of article unknown.

audience, if it had any sense, would realise that. The performance went off with a dash. I was applauded even more than
Antony, and Mother was told I was cut out for the real
theatre."

Another favourite activity was dancing. At the time that
Sybil started going to the grammar school, her mother and a
Mrs Langhorne started a dancing class. The instructress was a
wonderful teacher, and although she was very strict most of the
children enjoyed the class.

"What a company of exhibitionists we were! Two daughters
of Captain, later Admiral, Holland* were the best executants,
but another girl and I ran them pretty close, for the four of us
were chosen to do a tambourine dance before the Duchess of
Teck, mother of our beloved Queen Mary, when she came
down to open a big bazaar in the Corn Exchange. I'm afraid I
let the side down, for we danced this wild Spanish dance with
verve and fire, and were highly applauded and presented to Her
Royal Highness, but imagine my dismay when Dean Hole
remarked, 'I particularly liked this little girl who showed such a
charming red garter.' That was me, and we'd been specially told
to wear black garters to match our black stockings. Everyone
laughed, but I was horribly ashamed."

Mother Don Don, who accompanied the dancing lessons, played
dance music with tremendous verve—Sybil says she has never
heard any person or any band play it so well, and she looks back
to the swift whirling dances of her girlhood with nostalgia.

"Even the waltzes, though smooth, were swift. We all did
wild dances when I was young. Men had to take two or
three collars to a party as the exercise was so strenuous, and
we girls got more and more excited, and in spite of our tight
stays we were far more vigorous than the freer bodies in the
present-day dance hall. The end of a ball was always a gallop,

* Rear-Admiral Swindon C. Holland.

and at the finish we were all dropping with heat and exhaustion. Wonderful, and worth it."

But the art which had by now really captivated Sybil—and for ever—was piano-playing. She was studying both the violin and the piano at school, but it was only to her piano lessons that she gave herself wholeheartedly.

"I was lucky in my teachers, and even if then I did not wholly profit by them I now see what they planted in me, and I did work. When I was eleven I was sent to play at a London concert. I'd performed at school concerts and got away with it finely, encores and all. Acting came to my aid in this, for whenever I appeared on a platform I pretended I was a great pianist, and sometimes that air and belief carried me further than my prowess as a performer. This Steinway Hall concert was a different thing altogether. Hayden Coffin was the singer, and for the first time my pretence of being a great pianist failed me. I was absolutely petrified. Hayden Coffin was wonderfully kind to me. Seeing me shaking with fright he took me to peep through a chink at the audience. 'Play to that nice old man in the front row and don't think of anyone else,' he said, and I did just that and it helped me. I had to take an encore. Hayden Coffin kissed me and said, 'Little Miss Paderewski—splendid.' I was congratulated warmly and my teacher and Mother were delighted, but nerves really were playing havoc with me. I do not think any child should be made to suffer such nervousness as I did at performances. Perhaps it was a sign that this was not the profession I should have chosen, passionately as I loved the piano."

At this period Russell intended to be a parson—a bishop, no less. He liked singing and had a good voice, and on the strength of this their Bishop, Dr Randall Davidson, later Archbishop of Canterbury, wrote to Sir Walter Parratt to find out when there would be a voice-trial for St George's Chapel, Windsor. There proved to be one very shortly, and Mrs Thorndike and Sybil made Russell

Rosalind

Sybil aged 13

The first recital

practise for hours on end to improve his chances of becoming a
St George's chorister.

"How Sybil worked at me! She used to make me get up
about five o'clock, with a wet sponge, and say, 'Come and do
oratorios.' "*

And she gave him this parting advice:

"Whatever you do, don't forget to put on a holy-bob face.
I shall be praying for you all day, and I shan't practise at all."†

When he got home he found her on her knees, her room
clouded with incense. She had burnt two shillings' worth of
fumigating pyramids for his success, and this had been achieved.

In her Preface to *Children of the Garter*,‡ Russell Thorndike's
book about St George's, Windsor, Sybil recalls her brother as
"an odd little boy", giving himself airs and graces about proces-
sions and royalty at Windsor, while she herself squatted on the
floor, "little Miss Socialist even in those days", shouting, "What
about the starving poor?"

All the same, she immensely enjoyed her visits to Windsor
to see her brother—they were an added richness to her life. So
much to see, and so much music and such interesting people.
Sybil and Russell missed one another greatly, and their reunions,
when holidays came, were ecstatic. Sometimes they all went to
Cornwall or Devon for a holiday, which was a great treat, for,
although she hated other sports, Sybil liked to swim.

When she was thirteen, Mrs Thorndike thought she ought to
have more sustained professional training as a pianist and more
time to practise, so she took her for an audition at the Guildhall
School of Music where she herself had studied, and where a
German professor, Herr Francesco Berger, was famous for his
success in producing virtuoso performers.

Sybil wrote at once to Russell at Windsor:

* Russell Thorndike: *Sybil Thorndike* (Thornton Butterworth, 1929).
† *Sybil Thorndike*.   ‡ Rich and Cowan, 1939.

"Darling Russell,

"It's over, and I'm a pupil at the Guildhall School of Music. Mother took me up yesterday. We got to the School at ten minutes to eleven, and there was a most glorious noise going on, millions of pianos and violins and singing all going on at once, I felt awful quirks. The porter at the door was an awfully nice man, very like a verger and just as interested in everything. I was taken, and Mother too, into Professor Francesco Berger's room—he's a most fascinating person. Lots of pupils, about five of them, were sitting on chairs against a wall under a picture of Bach, and one of Wagner opposite, and a girl called Gertrude Meller, older than me, awfully pretty, and a tiny waist, well, she was playing some Chopin thing. Oh! Russell, I'll never be able to play like her, she's glorious, she can lift her hand higher than her head and it always comes down on the right note, and all the time she looks as if it's awfully easy. I sat and shivered on my chair. Mother made me feel worse by saying, 'Now don't be shy,' and then Prof. Berger said, 'Now, let's see what this little girl can do.' So I played a lot then, all without my music. I felt after the beginning I was getting on finely, then he stopped me and laughed and said, 'Very nice, little girl, very nice, you've got some feeling.' Then he turned to Mother and said, 'She has no technique at all; she must give up everything and work at technique.' Mother said, 'Yes, she shall,' and I said, 'Oh yes' too; then he said I must give up the violin— oh! I was glad, Russ, and that I must give up games, everything I do with my hands except the piano. I was gladder still then. I do hate tennis and cricket and all the things you and the Jelfs want me to play, and now I needn't ever again—and that I was to practise three hours a day and then I might possibly be able to play the piano in a few years—I'm so happy I don't know what to do . . . Goodbye, angel, I wish there was nothing but Shakespeare and piano, I do loathe lessons so unless they are to do with plays . . ."

So now Sybil left school and had a room downstairs instead of in the attic, for which Mrs Thorndike provided a Liberty wallpaper with a frieze of tulips. Her aunt Isabella gave her her own grand piano, and an upright was also put in the room so that Sybil and her mother could play duets together. Mrs Thorndike was eager for her daughter to make a name as a pianist.

"I didn't care twopence whether I made a name or not. Mother was so ambitious. She hadn't been able to fulfil any of her own ambitions, so she worked it all off on me. I loved her, but she was terribly critical—oh, she was awful over the piano, because she was such a clean, lovely player herself, and every time I messed up anything she'd jump right down bang on me.

"After my first term I wanted to know more of harmony and counterpoint. I had met Professor Ebenezer Prout, already a very old man, on the stairs one day.

" 'What are you doing, little girl?'

" 'Piano, sir.'

" 'Well, you play a Bach Prelude and Fugue every day, and nothing will go wrong with you.'

"And so I have all my life!"

Her other lessons Sybil now shared with the children of Arthur Thorndike's churchwarden, Fred Smith, a lawyer and several times Mayor of Rochester. One day each week she went to London for her piano lesson, and every day she had to put in four to five hours of practising. The regime was extremely strenuous. She was wakened by her alarm clock at five and plunged into a cold bath, which her father said would be good for her, "and which I accepted as a sort of discipline suited to a nun, which in my piano-self I fancied myself to be". Two and a half hours' practice until breakfast, then over to the Smiths' house for lessons until one. Home for dinnner, out for a walk with the Smiths and the governess, always speaking French, an hour's practice in their house, more lessons, home at five o'clock and more practising after that.

"On Saturdays I stopped being an overworked young student and became a little girl again. I used to dress my darling pug-dog up in baby clothes and do all kinds of ridiculous things. Our play-room then was a cellar in the Smiths' house, and those children too remained our friends for ever."

The governess, Miss Brockbank, was an excellent teacher, and she developed Sybil's interest in history and geography. Even the hated hour of needlework was made tolerable for her by Miss Brockbank's reading from such books as *The Conquest of Peru* and *The Conquest of Mexico*.

Theatricals continued, and this led to some difficulties in term time, but even Herr Berger had to let her off practice when she was needed for a charity performance. Mrs Thorndike had started an amateur company to do musical comedies with the help of Claude Aveling, Registrar of the Royal College of Music. He took a great interest in Sybil's career as a pianist, but always told her that she would finish up in the theatre.

The small Eileen had been followed in 1894 by another little boy, Frank. Sybil was a good elder sister to these children; she was very fond of them, and although she did not in general enjoy teaching she taught them music from their earliest days. She had also been teaching in the Sunday school since she was ten years old.

"Mr Berger has given me a ticket to hear Jenny Hyman* play," she wrote to Russell. "She is only ten or eleven, and has a lot of bushy black hair. I think she is a Jew, because she looks interesting like they always do, and she played Beethoven gloriously. I felt very despondent, Russ, I can't ever be like that, and I'm years older—nearly fourteen—so even with work I can't catch up—but still you never know. I *might* be able to. I'm to play at an afternoon recital at Madame Berger's drawing-room next week, it's the first time Mr Berger has let me play to people. I feel awfully frightened . . . Mother is buying me a green velvet frock from Liberty's. I don't think I shall play nearly as well as if I could wear my everyday dress. I do hate

* Later Professor at the Guildhall School of Music. She remained a friend of Sybil's all her life.

clothes, I wish we could live in combinations. You could have them dark so they'd look better."

Although she dresses beautifully Sybil has never given much thought to everyday clothes, though naturally she is interested in stage costume—an inherent part of any character.

It was about now that their aunt Isabella and the senior curate decided to give Sybil and Russell a treat and took them to see *Julius Caesar* at His Majesty's Theatre, one of the most thrilling experiences of their early years. The theatre itself was a revelation to them.

"Beerbohm Tree knew how to run a theatre! Flunkeys in white wigs and scarlet coats. You *felt* you were going to see a show."

The call of the trumpets in the overture quite unnerved her. Every part of her body ached, and sometimes during the play tears ran down her face. She was completely transported. She knew now that acting and plays, particularly Shakespeare, would always be dominant factors in her life, but she had never considered the stage as a possible profession. She was going to be a pianist.

So the rigorous regime continued, with Sybil working eight or nine hours a day at her music and taking Sir Walter Parratt's advice, "Now mind, every day, my dear, you play an old piece so that you never forgot what you have learnt in the past."

During one school holiday Canon Thorndike took duty in Brighton, and going to High Mass there made Sybil's passion for High Church blossom.

"Father Ross was wonderful! Of course Russell and I fell madly in love with him, and from that moment we were the most ardent Anglo-Catholics you could possibly have. I mean, we bowed to practically every word, and crossed ourselves. Mother was so pleased at my virtue that she gave me a lovely enormous crucifix to hang over my piano, and I dedicated myself to the Lord and to the piano."

By the time she was sixteen she had already had a few professional engagements—small ones, to accompany some singer and
play a solo, at about a guinea a time. These concerts were mainly
in private houses, but even so she was in an agony of nerves every
time. Her only comfort was the earning of these few odd guineas,
for she felt that it was high time she began to be self-supporting.
Her professor now suggested another means of earning. He
thought that it would be good for her to take a few piano-pupils.

"Oh, I loathed them! I loathed them like poison, I've got
no gift for teaching at all. I've got infinite patience with
myself, and not one grain with anybody else."

Not surprisingly, the young pupils were terrified of her.
The next move in her career was her first piano recital.

"Of course this gave me a kick. We took the biggest hall in
Rochester, the Corn Exchange, and it was packed with people,
all come to hear this little what-d'you-call-it genius, which I
wasn't at all."

Sybil was supported by Mr Jacoby, the violinist, with whom
she had often played before. They opened the recital with a duet,
after which Sybil gave a long programme of Chopin, Schumann
and Bach. She was warmly applauded, and everybody told her
that she was "going places". Yet she had been as tortured by her
nerves as ever, and was only able to get through the recital by
her old trick of pretending to be a great pianist. One listener
spotted this—Claude Aveling, who had produced so many of the
Thorndike musicals and had written one play, *Princess Zara*,
with music by Arthur Somervell, in which Sybil had played the
leading part. He came round at the end of the recital and said,
"I could see you putting on the airs of a fine pianist. It came off
well, but you're not a pianist, you're an actress."

To show him how wrong he was, and to prove how right she
had been in her choice of a profession, Sybil now persuaded her
parents to allow her to stop her other lessons and concentrate

entirely on music. She gained an exhibition and a small scholarship at the Guildhall, which helped with the fees and increased her self-confidence. All that was needed now, she felt, was to practise incessantly and overcome her nervousness.

She had been overworking for several years, and this strain, combined with the nerves which made her unconsciously tense her muscles, now began to manifest themselves physically. She had none of these troubles when acting, which she continued to do, however busy she was, for this was her relaxation. The trouble began with a few twinges in her left wrist, which after a while she mentioned to her professor. He said it was probably "piano cramp" and advised her to see a doctor, who told her to wear a wrist-strap and to stop playing for a while. This she did, but as soon as she began to play again the pain came back.

"I feel utterly and entirely wretched!" she wrote to Russell. "Everything I've been working for has stopped. I shall never be a pianist. When I do octave passages, Russ, it's torture, and I never was good at octave passages. De Pachmann worked fourteen hours a day for two years, so I read last week—once this wrist gets well, I'll do that."

One thing that helped through this period of depression was Russell's move to the King's School in Rochester. His voice was breaking, so, much to his regret, he could no longer be a St George's chorister, although Sir Walter Parratt sent for him to sing at Queen Victoria's funeral. Soon after this—to Sybil's dismay, because she knew that their father had always wanted his elder son to go into the Church—Russell told her that after all he did not want to be a parson but a writer.

At about the same time Arthur Thorndike was offered the living of Aylesford, which he had for a long time hoped for, because of the beauty both of the place and of the church and vicarage. There was no undue sadness at leaving Rochester, for Aylesford was only seven miles away, so the Thorndikes did not lose touch with their friends or the cathedral, and they all fell in love with their new home, perched on a hill in a cluster of old houses above the winding Medway and the ancient bridge. Sybil found the countryside a solace to her troubled mind, and best of all were her afternoon walks with her father, visiting parishioners and going on Sundays to a neighbouring hamlet, Pratling Street, where she used to enjoy playing for evensong on a little American organ. All this she found a delightful relaxation.

"You've got to have tea in every cottage," her father told her. "Never mind how bad it makes you feel, you've got to have tea when it is offered."

He had often taken Sybil into the worst slums in Rochester, and she was greatly perturbed by the conditions in which she saw the very poor to be living. Her father did not seem to notice these at all—it was people's souls that interested him.

"Mother didn't care if their souls were saved or not. She loved all those people—she didn't go down as Lady Bountiful, she was their pal, and it was the drama of it all that she enjoyed. Hearing about the husbands coming home and beating their wives, or seeing all the family slops thrown out of the window, 'Oh, my dear, how awful!' she would exclaim, but it was I who really minded. That was the beginning of my Socialist feelings, though I didn't know there were such people as Socialists. There were Liberals, and Liberals were beyond the pale. Father was a staunch Conservative, and Mother was a Conservative because it would never have occurred to her that one could be anything else! We taught our dog a trick—put a bit of sugar on his nose and said, 'Gladstone!' and he wouldn't touch it. Then we said, 'Salisbury!' and he'd gobble it up with joy."

On these walks with her father, whom she still loved more than anyone else in the world, Sybil and he used to have long religious discussions. She had developed a serious interest in philosophy and religion. It was from her cousin, Basil Bowers, that she first heard about Greek philosophy, and she was greatly impressed by the

Student's History of Philosophy which he gave her, and which opened her mind to a whole new continent of thought. Now she had had a further adventure in this realm. On her journeys in the train to London for her music lessons, she had met a young science student who lent her books by such exponents of the theory of evolution as Darwin, Huxley and Herbert Spencer. She remembers to this day the excitement of reading Grant Allen's *The Evolution of the Idea of God*, and from Huxley she discovered that there was such a philosophic attitude as "agnosticism". She discussed these new ways of thinking with her father, and although he questioned the wisdom of her reading such books he did not forbid her to do so, and his mind was soon set at rest by finding that her exploration of these, to him, atheistic ideas did not in the least diminish her allegiance to the Church.

Eileen and Frank now had a governess to teach them, but Sybil still superintended their musical education. Eileen was keener on acting than on music, and of course there was plenty of scope for this—acting for parish entertainments was going on as vigorously as ever—but Frank loved his piano lessons, and as soon as he was old enough he began to learn the 'cello and accompanied Sybil to the Guildhall School of Music for his lessons. By now these two were fast friends.

Just before she was eighteen Professor Berger thought that it was time for Sybil to give another piano recital in Rochester. This was a much more ambitious affair. She played a trio with Henry Such, the violinist, and his brother the 'cellist, both fine artists, and followed this with a long solo programme. Once again she was tortured by nervousness, and afterwards the pain in her wrist was agonising, but everyone, including the press, said how well she was developing, and so on she went, in spite of the pain, practising and playing in halls and private houses and still taking a number of pupils at home.

"Then one day the doctor said to me, 'I think you ought to stop for a year and not do any piano-playing.' Well, at that the bottom dropped out of my world. I thought I'd die. But Russell, always to the fore, said, 'Why don't you chuck it

altogether—you can still play for fun—and come on the stage?
Let's go on the stage together.' "

This was a surprising development, for, although they had
always acted together so much, Russell was eager to become a
writer and Sybil was constantly urging him to write religious
plays. She had an idea then that the stage was a very immoral
place. In any case she could not bear the idea of giving up her
music, so for a while she went on struggling, in spite of the pain
and the frustration.

"Then one day I realised it was over, and I said to Russell,
'All right, if I can't be a professional pianist I'll still play for
my own joy, and I'll go on the stage with you, if you're
still keen.' But I really could have committed suicide if I'd
been brave, I was so miserable."

But not for long. Deep down the sense of failure and the heart-
ache remained, but the relief from pain, and the thought that
she need not take any more hated pupils, buoyed her up. Her
new career with Russell would be a tremendous adventure.
How they would act!

CHAPTER III

LETTERS FROM AMERICA

(1900–1905)

THE FIRST PERSON Sybil and Russell told about their momentous decision to go on the stage was their mother. It was something of a shock to her, because Russell was working hard to get into Cambridge and his parents still hoped that he would enter the Church, while Sybil had been adamant about continuing her musical career, in spite of her nerves and her wrist and the declarations from all sides that she was a born actress. However, they did not waver, and, since their mother was by nature as impetuous as her children, it did not take long to persuade her that this was the best course for them. And when their father was told of the plan he too threw himself wholeheartedly into the problem of finding out the best way for them to start their stage career. Not only did he himself love the theatre, but he saw a certain affinity between working in it and working in the Church. In each profession you had to learn how to get inside other people's minds and hearts.

Training schools for professional actors were then rare, although Beerbohm Tree was shortly to found the Academy of Dramatic Art (made Royal in 1920), which was followed two years later by Elsie Fogerty with the Central School of Speech and Drama. Before this, acting had simply been taught within the theatre companies themselves, but as early as 1896 Ben Greet* had founded an Academy of Acting off the Strand, which had a large room at the top known as the Bijou Theatre. It was understood that students who reached a sufficiently high standard in

* Later Sir Philip Ben Greet.

their training would be sent out for their first professional engagements with one of Ben Greet's touring companies.

When the young Thorndikes found an advertisement of the Academy of Acting they and their parents quickly decided that it was the right place for them to train. Ben Greet, then in his mid-forties, had already achieved great distinction as an actor and actor manager, particularly in the field of Shakespeare. It was he who started the famous open-air performances in Regent's Park as early as 1901, and long before that he had formed the Woodland Players to tour the country with those of Shakespeare's plays most suited to a pastoral setting. He had also recently joined William Poel in the revival by the Elizabethan Stage Society of the fifteenth-century morality play *Everyman*.

The Thorndikes had seen him act in the theatre at Chatham and thought him splendid, and Sybil in some mysterious way had discovered that he was "keen on Church", so Mrs Thorndike wrote to the Ben Greet Academy, and it was arranged that she and Sybil should have an interview with Frederick Topham, the principal of the Academy, as Ben Greet himself was touring in America.

"So up I went with Mother. Oh, I looked such a sight! I put on a veil, God knows why! We climbed up the stairs—it was in Bedford Street in an awful room high up on about the fourth floor. And there was that little man, Fred Topham, a wonderful principal and a brilliant old actor. 'Well, would the girl like to do something for me?' he said, and then he gazed at me and added, 'No, I don't think I'll bother her to do anything—she looks as if she can act.' And I said, 'Of course I can act, I've acted since I was four. Anybody can act, it's the easiest thing in the world.' "

Mrs Thorndike told Fred Topham that her son also wanted to join the Academy, and back they went to tell Mr Thorndike that both children had been accepted. Years later, in an article about her then famous daughter, Mrs Thorndike wrote:

"I think the real secret of my children's happy youth lay in the fact that my husband and I 'let them alone'. We did not try to force any career, any mode of life, on any of them. They were allowed to build up their own personalities, with our mature judgment always to be called on when necessary.

"It was a delight to us that they all chose the stage as their profession, although we had suffered with Sybil when wrist delicacy forced her to give up the idea of making a career as a pianist.

"But if one or all of them had chosen other professions we should have found no fault. Their lives were theirs to live, and our part was to act merely as their guides to what was beautiful and good and most to be desired."

So in the autumn of 1903, when Sybil was nearly twenty-one, she and Russell entered the Ben Greet Academy. In spite of their self-assurance about acting, the talent of some of their fellow-students—there were about twenty-five of them—impressed the Thorndikes, and Fred Topham laughed in a friendly way at their cocksureness, and told them that they might learn to act properly in time if they worked very hard. In fact, they both made great progress, and were given many interesting parts to play, although to Sybil's annoyance Fred Topham thought that she was cut out for character parts and comedy, but not for tragedy.

"I *can* do tragedy," she burst out to Russell later. "I'm going to be a tragedienne."

Russell replied that it would be a great bore to have to be so solemn and soulful, to which she retorted, "Tragedy is something much bigger than solemn. Solemn just makes me laugh. And as for soulful, I *hate* soulful. But *tragic* I know about, and that's what I'm going to be."

So for two terms the young Thorndikes worked very happily at the Academy, and generally managed to go to the theatre once a week, standing in the pit and gallery queues and waiting at the stage-door to see their favourite players come out. They also studied together at home, and Sybil found that she could play the piano without much pain if she did not do so for too long at a time.

At the end of their third term Ben Greet returned from America, and the pupils gave a performance of Pinero's *The Cabinet Minister*, Sybil playing the leading part of Lady Twombley, a woman of about forty, with Russell as her husband, Sir Julian. He was given the leading part because he could play the flute—and play it well enough to play it badly.

"It was all great fun," Sybil says, "and mine was a lovely comedy part. Pinero came and talked to us, and when the show was over Ben Greet said, 'I'll take the girl to America. The boy's too young—I'll give him something to do in one of our English companies.' Then he turned to me, 'Would you like to come to America with me?' I thought, 'America, how gorgeous!' 'Yes, I will,' I said. 'When do we start?' And he said, 'Here, here, half a minute! You've got to discuss it with your parents.' "

There was a great deal of discussion during the next few days, but Sybil was determined to go, and soon swept away all objections. She was to sail on August 24th, and meanwhile she and Russell were to play small parts in Ben Greet's Company of Pastoral Players. It was a fine company, with Matheson Lang as leading man and Helen Haye and Hutin Britton as leading ladies, and with them also were Nigel Playfair and May Martyn, later to become his wife. At Downing College, Cambridge, on June 14th, 1904, Sybil gave her first professional performance as Palmis in *The Palace of Truth* by W. S. Gilbert, and on the same evening she "waltzed on" as the Green Fairy in scenes from *The Merry Wives of Windsor*. Four days later the Pastoral Players performed *My Lord From Town*, a comedy by H. M. Paull.

The tour continued in pastoral settings for about six weeks. Living meagrely in digs made the young Thorndikes feel they really belonged to the profession, and they revelled in their new life. The only flaw for Sybil was that she had such small parts. "I couldn't understand why I wasn't given more leads." This faith in her own talent did not prevent her from sincerely admiring the actresses who were playing the leads—from the beginning she has been unfailingly generous about her fellow-players, and truly grateful for any help that they gave her.

At the end of this agreeable tour came the preparations for the trip to America. Sybil was in a state of wild excitement; she had always wanted to travel, and now the world was opening its doors to her.

Although she was twenty-one, she was very young for her age. Fortunately she and Ben Greet's niece, Daisy Robinson, who was two years her senior, had become friends. Daisy had already had a good deal of experience of stage life, and the two mothers made many plans for their daughters to live together during the American tour and help one another in their new experiences.

"I was raw, absolutely as raw as could be. Nobody could be innocenter than I was. Russell told me later that my parents had discussed whether they ought to tell me the facts of life. Fancy the facts of life at twenty-one! I simply didn't know them. Anyhow, they decided I'd be all right and told me nothing. Why I didn't get into the most awful fandangles I don't know, because I could fall in love so easily with anybody who looked actory and exciting."

Sybil was so carried away by the prospect of the adventure ahead of her that she hardly had time to grieve about leaving her beloved home and family—anyway, it was a very jolly send-off at Euston with Ben Greet and all the company there, two of whom, Eric Blind and Frank Darch, she already knew from the pastoral tour, and Russell bringing along "a lot of actory-looking people" from his current tour to impress her. But once the train had steamed out into the night she and Daisy dissolved into hopeless sobs, until Ben Greet came into their compartment and said, "Well, you two little duffers, what are you crying for? Go and eat some sandwiches and then go to sleep."

All through the American adventure Sybil wrote to her family constantly—very often a joint letter to her parents and Russell. The first one ran:

"I've never felt so excited in my life—it's glorious. We all bundled out early in the morning at Glasgow and then went by train to Greenock, where we saw our ship, *The Numidian*. It's a lovely morning; the ship doesn't look very large, I suppose she's all right; she's not as big as the ships Uncle Jim sends off—but we've just had the best breakfast I can remember. B.G. paid for Daisy and me, 'for luck,' he said—wasn't it decent of him? Heavenly bloaters with soft roes, tons of toast and tea and marmalade. B.G. said, 'Is this your usual appetite? Because you'll have to be careful not to get fat.'

"Goodbye, angels, there are such a lot of people surging about and the mail will have to go . . . I'm awfully happy and terribly excited, and we are to swot fearfully hard, and I'm sorry if I've ever been in beastly tempers, I never mean it, and I'll write a bit every day. Hug darling little Turvy* for me. I expect he'll miss me—Goodbye, lambs,

"Yr loving Sybil."

It was a very rough voyage, taking fourteen days, but the leading lady, Constance Crawley, was very kind to Sybil, and once she was well she did not waste a moment.

"I've loved every minute of it except the seasick bit. Ben Greet told me the other day that it was going to be very hard work, and was I a quick study? I said, 'Yes, awfully quick,' and he said, 'Well, you'd better learn everybody's parts, because you never know when you may have to go on.' So I'm starting on *Hamlet* because I know all *Twelfth Night* and a good bit of *As You Like It*. I learn parts first thing after breakfast, when I've had a good walk round the deck—there's Eric Blind and Frank Darch always to go walks with . . . A fancy-dress ball was on last night. The company did an entertainment too. Scenes from *Twelfth Night*; they let me play Curio, and I also played the accompaniments for anyone who sang. They all act very well, I'm going to too when I get going—Daisy is awfully nice—and she's a very good critic and tells me lots of things I do wrong which is a great help."

* Sybil's pug-dog.

Then came the first letter from America:

"We saw New York early in the morning. We passed
Nantucket lighthouse late at night, and all the Americans sang
their patriotic songs. I wish you'd been there, Russ, we'd have
bawled out *The British Grenadiers*, wouldn't we? I did bawl
them out inside myself, and I told Eric Blind I was singing
God Save the King as well, and he said, 'Splendid, let's sing it
out loud,' and we did, and all the English people joined in,
and a lot of the Americans too, which I thought very jolly of
them. My dear, the skyscrapers are marvellous, I think they
look beautiful and the statue of liberty is splendid. You feel
that every nation can come to America and earn their livings
and have adventures and not worry any more. I suppose
England does that too, only when one is in a country one
doesn't realise it quite the same.

"We took ages going through the Customs. The man who
turned my trunks upside down said, 'Got any nOOOO
clothes?' I said, 'Every single thing in my trunk is new.' Then
he looked at my hats and said, 'Say, are these your nOOOO
Sunday hats? I guess you look dandy in the one with scrambled
eggs on it'—he meant my buttercup one. Then Ben Greet
came and said we'd got to play a pastoral of *As You Like It* and
Twelfth Night on Long Island next Saturday, so we must rehearse tonight. Isn't it lovely starting work at once—hardly
even waiting to unpack. Well, we went in cabs to a sort of
hotel lodging-house on 6th Avenue, Daisy and I and Ben
Greet. I'm glad Daisy is here, she makes me think things are
real and ordinary, I can't help feeling it's all a dream."

And so the tour began, but in spite of her many small parts
Sybil found time to keep her promise and write pages home every
day.

"The first pastoral is over, and I did enjoy myself. We
played *12th Night* at night. I played a lady-in-waiting to
Olivia—a fearfully uncomfortable dress—very tight in the

waist and an Elizabethan collar that pricked. I don't think it looked very nice, though I managed the skirts all right—my hair isn't tidy enough for Elizabethan. Ben Greet said I looked like a rag-bag—he said it under his breath on the stage—it wasn't very encouraging . . . And now what do you think, Father, you'll be awfully jealous. We are going to Niagara..."

"We've seen it! and we're on the train now going to Chicago, and I feel rather like the child in the Stevenson poem about 'the stars going round in my head'—and I wish I could find some new adjectives, I've used up all the wonderfuls and marvellouses, so when I say them about Niagara you must multiply them by a hundred and sing them like the chorus in the *Messiah*—*Wonderful, Counsellor*, the *Mighty God*, you know the one I mean—*that* will make you realise, if you shout it. Going down the street at Niagara Falls (it's a town, you know), just an ordinary street, with shops and people with quite ordinary faces buying, you hear a dull roar. It gives you an awful queer feeling as if something was waiting to jump out on you. I couldn't speak, I was feeling so terrible. It was rather like the feeling before Caesar makes his entrance, and you feel you won't be able to bear it. We saw a huge cloud, and it was spray, just imagine, going up twice as high as the Falls— and then the roar got more and more awful, and we saw Niagara! I've never wanted you all so much in my life. I'm sure it's far better for people than church, because you don't *believe* in God—you know it, Niagara makes you know it. It makes all those books I read with Bulbrooke*—Huxley, Grant Allen and Darwin—all seem rather footling, though I always feel there's more in Darwin than church people say, but I daresay they've all seen Niagara now from where they are, in Purgatory, Heaven or Paradise or wherever you say they are, Father, and are sorry they said such definite things on earth, though I *like* definite people, even if they contradict themselves next day—what does it matter, anyway? . . . Oh! Niagara, how gorgeous it all is. I wish I didn't get so hungry. This

* The young student she had met in the Rochester–London train.

Niagara day has made me worse. I ate three fried eggs with bacon to match for lunch and everything else corresponding. I saw B.G. look at me very reproachfully and I said to myself, 'I swear I won't eat another meal today because I must get to look more poetical.'. . . Goodnight, angels, I'll never forget Niagara—never—

"Yr loving Sybil.

"P.S. Later. Had an enormous meal. Thoroughly enjoyed it. Two helps of everything and hoped B.G. wouldn't notice. As B.G. walked out of the dining-car he said, 'Old fat Syb'. It made me feel rather depressed."

In Pittsfield Sybil met Mrs Love, a friend of Ben Greet's who was very musical, and being able to "talk piano" with her was a great comfort.

"You know, Russ, I always feel a bit of a rotter to have deserted music, though in a way it was taken out of my hands. I feel I ought to have gone on teaching those pupils that made me in such a temper—you see, acting is absolute pleasure all the time, you never have that awful agonising feeling that you won't be able to do things that you get when you are working at music . . . With the stage it's *being* something that counts. Of course you have to learn how to speak with lots of voices and walk with lots of walks and you have in a way to practise doing real life things well—like we used to practise tumbling down the stairs without hurting ourselves—but with music you feel as if you were suddenly let loose into a vast world, and you've got to conquer every tiny little bit of it before you can even start to be at all . . . Somehow or other Mrs Love drew it all out of me how I felt about shirking music and living only happily, and she was very wise about it all. She said that the acting art was different because you don't employ an artificial medium (sounds good that, doesn't it?). She means you don't have to learn a new language like notes and strings, but she says if I look at it properly it's just as hard—that the medium I use is myself, and I must make myself as perfect as I want to

make notes and strings, and, Russ, not only walking and dancing, moving and speaking beautifully, but mind too, and oh!
dear, I have been such an ass, I did get so bored with school—
and learnt precious little. There's French—well, look at what
I know of that—nothing. Anyway, I've bought myself a French
and a German grammar in Pittsfield and Mrs Love is helping
me with both . . . Oh! and I'm getting a bit of piano done every
day and I keep a little manuscript-book to do bits of harmony
and counterpoint in."

"We're in Chicago. Everyone told me it was going to be
awful—it's not—it's lovely—very noisy, but I don't mind noise.
Ben Greet took Dai and me to see *Romeo and Juliet*. My dear,
it's a marvellous play. I can't *tell* you what I felt during the
Balcony Scene. You know how love bores me—well, it
wouldn't if it was like *Romeo and Juliet*. Oh! I'd love to play
Juliet.★ That potion scene—but I don't suppose anyone would
want me to, I don't look tragic, romantic, do I? How I wish
I did."

"Oh! *Everyman* is fearfully difficult. I can't imagine anything
worse than getting the giggles when you're playing an abstrac-
tion—but I shall think holy-bob thoughts all the time and save
myself from destruction!"

After this came five days going west, Sybil greatly enjoying the
nights on the train, and the days passing very quickly, what with
studying languages, learning parts, talking to friends and gazing
out at the landscape.

"I shan't write much now as Beatrice† has to be got into my
head—she's great fun—but I'm afraid I prefer all the men's
parts. I hope I'll be a man in my next incarnation. Oh! and
that reminds me. Agnes Scott‡ is a great reader of Mrs Annie

★ Sybil never did play Juliet, and later on would not have wanted to. "I've
never really liked love parts."
† *Much Ado About Nothing.*   ‡ A member of the company.

Besant and modern American writers who call it New Thought, and she has talked to me about it. I find it very interesting, Russ. Father, even you couldn't fail to be entertained by Mrs Besant's book called *Karma* and one called *Reincarnation*. I was so enchanted with *Reincarnation* that I could hardly go to sleep . . . And the other complication is Christian Science, of which you've never heard. I'll explain it all some time. America seems full of thrill."

On, then, across the prairie, Sybil enjoying every moment of the days and nights on the train, imagining herself an explorer and a pioneer, and continuing to write pages home about exotic cowboys, herds of buffalo and little prairie dogs, while ahead loomed the mountains that she had always so longed to see, and which proved to be more glorious than any anticipation. And at last down out of the snows into California among the orange and lemon groves. "You can't imagine the glory of it. It's the smell of the air—something the sun does to the air— it's sort of intoxicating."

The first play they gave here was *Hamlet*, unabridged, in the Greek Theatre at the University in Berkeley with a number of "corduroy students" walking on and having small parts—"I rather like Shakespeare in American accent". During the rehearsal Sybil, who was playing a Court lady, disgraced herself by bursting out laughing, having overheard some whispered joke while Ben Greet was in the middle of one of Hamlet's long soliloquies. In general jokes tended to bore her, so this was a piece of sheer bad luck, but Ben Greet was furious and called her a "giggling schoolgirl". "I feel all disgraced and most miserable," she wrote to Russell. However, the thrill of *Hamlet* soon put everything else out of her head. She found Mrs Crawley wonderful as Ophelia, and looked forward to playing the part herself one day, "but of course it's Hamlet I'm longing to do". She saw that Russell was more likely to get a chance at this part than herself, "as you are a male and so is Hamlet, but really he's not more male than female—he's everybody who has got something they want to do and keep failing."

After the performance of *Everyman* in San Francisco they went to Chinatown, and Sybil had her first experience of Chinese theatre, which greatly impressed her.

"Do you know, Russ, it made me realize more and more how foolish it is to try and make an audience deceived into thinking they are seeing actual life—I don't believe the theatre is made for that at all, any more than sculpture or painting is actual . . . You don't want actual life, you want a more concentrated thing, a life that you don't see really because eyes are not clear and hearing not acute—in the theatre your senses must be sharpened, and with that you've got to have a child's mind that will believe dreadfully seriously in it, and yet at the same time know it's playing."

In San Francisco a man who took Daisy and Sybil to a fair tried making love to them in turn, and Sybil wrote to Russell:

"It made Dai laugh, and it made me laugh too when he said things to her, but when it started with me I really couldn't bear it—finally, he said to me, 'You ought to have been a boy, you haven't got the instincts of a girl,' and I said, 'No, I haven't. I wish I was a boy, and tonight I wish I was a boy more than ever . . .' Oh dear me, I feel so relieved to think I won't ever marry, I couldn't stand anyone saying 'in love' things to me all the time. I shall adopt lots of children, and you and I will live together, Russ, won't we? —much more fun than lots of hateful people married to you."

When, after some weeks travelling down the coast of California, they reached Stockton, Sybil got what she called her "great chance". Mrs Crawley was unwell and Sybil played Viola, loving *being* Viola, and was delighted by the good notice in the local newspaper, which did not know that the part had been played by an understudy. "Ha! ha! now my foot is on the ladder truly and really."

In Los Angeles she played Nerissa, this time because Daisy

was ill, and then they moved on to Santa Barbara, where she greatly enjoyed swimming in the spacious baths on the front, the weather being deliciously warm although it was now mid-winter. The highlight of this stand, for her, was the visit to the Spanish Mission and being shown over the monastery—"all the allowable parts, that is". Ben Greet gave the monks two boxes for *Everyman*, assuring the Superior that it was a religious service and not really a play at all. The cast was very much surprised when at the appearance of Death all the monks burst out laughing, until it was explained to them that in mediaeval times Death was often a comedy character, and the monks were just being mediaeval—like the play.

Sybil's only sorrow was that Daisy was now seriously ill and could not travel with the company to San Diego. When they returned to Santa Barbara she was in hospital having her appendix out, and Sybil was very unhappy about her and wished that her mother could be sent for.

One night during this second visit to Santa Barbara she had an interesting psychic experience. She was feeling very unhappy—she had fallen in love with Eric Blind, who was sweet to her but treated her like a child—and she wrote a long letter to her father. When she read it through she found that it expressed little of what she wanted to convey to him, so she tore it up and went to bed, saying, "Oh, Father, Father, I hope you'll understand!" She heard later that at about four o'clock the following morning —which, allowing for the difference in transatlantic time, would have been just the hour when she spoke to him—her father at home in Aylesford had been wakened by the call, "Father! Father!" He had at once woken Mrs Thorndike, saying, "I believe Sybil is in some trouble. I've just heard her calling me."

It was now, in Los Angeles—through Eric Blind, in fact—that Sybil discovered in poetry a new intimate joy "like music", and learnt a great deal of Browning and Shelley, being quite carried away by the *Ode to the West Wind*, "the most sweeping thing I ever read", a feeling she has never lost. He also introduced her to the poetry of Walt Whitman, which was a revelation.

"I always see America through Walt Whitman's poetry. Perhaps that's why I love it so much."

It is astonishing what an amount Sybil read, and how she managed to go on with her French studies and to play the piano whenever there was one at hand, when, on top of rehearsals and acting, there was always so much to see. She found the north of California, with its great redwood forests smelling "something like Father's 'cello", even more wonderful than the south. "I like the feeling of the north always—there's something fascinating about tropics, but for real living give me north and nippy air and autumn smells."

From Seattle she wrote, "We're rehearsing *The Star of Bethlehem*. I'm playing the old drunken wife of the shepherd Mac, a filthy old creature." Sybil loved this mediaeval shepherd drama, "a lovely dancy play, taking the whole Christmas story like a child's story, which of course the Church does", but what she enjoyed most was playing "a real low vile part. I find I haven't been low for a long time, it was beginning to get on my nerves always being such a perfect lady". Sybil was also the voice, using a high treble, of the Archangel Gabriel. "How the boys in the company used to jeer! 'Old Syb an Archangel.' I could have killed them."

She was lyrical in her description of the next part of their journey—up the Puget Sound to Victoria—and, to add to the general excitement, early one morning in the bows of the ship Frank Darch proposed to her. "Laugh! We both laughed till I thought we'd wake the whole shipload." Anyhow, to the great amusement of all the company they declared themselves engaged, although they knew very well that the engagement would not last more than a few days, as indeed it did not.

Christmas was spent in Vancouver—"It's beastly, beastly, hateful, hateful being away on Xmas Day, but there it is—if one wants to travel one mustn't grumble"—and then they turned south again, and were soon once more performing at the University in Berkeley.

"Well, of all things! I *have* played a part in *Hamlet*, and a

Young Sybil

Young Lewis

Medea, 1920

Grand Guignol, 1920–1922

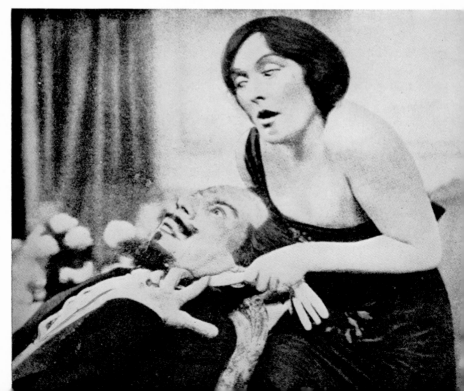

most unexpected one. About half an hour before the play began B.G. said, 'Syb, go and put on a beard and make yourself look like a murderer and play Lucianus, nephew to the King.' I said, 'I don't want to put on a beard, I'll be much better making a face.' He said, 'You can make a face too, if you like, but you'll not look like a murderer without a beard,'—so no help for it—*how* I loathe spirit-gum, and how can men drink whisky?—a black beard I put on. You'll not believe it, but Ben Greet said he'd got a new man to join the company—and Mr Crawley after the show said, 'Was the funny little fat man who played the murderer joining—he was rather odd but if suited might be clever'—and it was me. I did feel such an ass, but I really rather enjoyed it—Oh! they did all laugh after when they knew it was me."

Occasionally Sybil's high spirits deserted her again:

"In the train. We have just left the most horrible place, San Diego. I was miserable all the time and I still feel ill. Agnes Scott stayed up all night last night with me, I had such terrible things happening in my head, and my bales of cotton nightmare."

Ever since childhood Sybil had had a terrifying dream, when she was ill or troubled, of walking down a sort of alleyway between bales of cotton, and her feet getting tangled in cob-webby stuff and an awful noise growing louder and louder. She still occasionally has this dream.

By the time they reached Colorado she was feeling her happy self again, and the Rockies were mountains enough even for her. She was deeply disappointed not to see the Grand Canyon, but she enjoyed the long trip through the Middle West, playing many different small parts on one-night stands. At Kansas City Mrs Crawley had a fall half-an-hour before a performance of *Everyman*, so at last Sybil's wish to play a tragic role was fulfilled. She had played Beauty and Kindred and the Angel, but she had not rehearsed or officially understudied the long part of Everyman himself. However, with her extraordinary memory, and her total absorption in each play she took part in, she frequently memorised the whole thing, so when Ben Greet asked her if she could go on and do it, she did—with a little trepidation (she admired Constance Crawley's performance enormously), and great enjoyment. To her delight, after the performance Ben Greet congratulated her and said that he did not see why, if she worked hard and kept thin and managed not to look too healthy, she should not play tragedy. Her round face and rosy cheeks, her good appetite and exuberance, were both an inconvenience and a constant surprise to her. In her innermost being she felt that she was truly a tragedienne. As she wrote to Russell, "Mine is really a vicar's wife's face—it's tragic for me too, the way I want to do all things my face doesn't fit." Sybil has never recognised her own beauty: the fine structure of her features, the poetry of her sea-blue eyes and the expressiveness of her mouth.

Mrs Crawley's accident gave her the chance of playing many leading parts. She could not have too many roles, and has never wanted to play the same part, however good, for long.

It was an adventure to live each of these characters in turn—to *be* Everyman summoned by Death to give "a reckoning" before God, to *be* the mirthful Beatrice. It was all the most wonderful experience, not only coming to understand and portray so many different human beings, but getting to know and to love so much language. Words in a way compensated for the loss of music in her life, and the rhythm both of poetry and prose grew ever more important to her.

One side of theatre that she never thought much about was the audience; she was simply concerned with the play, and let the audience take it as they would. It was difficult, for instance, for her to wait for a laugh; unless reminded she would go spontaneously straight on.

And so to Chicago again and up into Canada, still often doing one-night stands, until at last, after nearly a year away, the Ben Greet Company sailed for home. Mr and Mrs Thorndike met her at Tilbury, but in spite of her intense joy at seeing them, and of being back in her much-loved home, she at once announced that in a month's time she would be off to America again.

"And this time Russell is coming with me."

CHAPTER IV

THE LION HOUSE
(1905-1908)

ON THE WAY to New York with Russell, Sybil fell into conversation with a man whose face she liked. She told him that it was a pity he couldn't be a king, as he was exactly like her image of Rudolf Rassendyll. He turned out to be Woodrow Wilson, then a professor and President of Princeton University, and he and the young Thorndikes became fast friends. On this tour the Ben Greet Players visited several universities, which Sybil and Russell found particularly enjoyable, and otherwise played far and wide, with many adventures, including an encounter with a bear. At the invitation of Woodrow Wilson they gave a number of performances at Princeton, during which the Thorndikes stayed with the Wilsons, and it was here that disaster befell Sybil. Once again the play was *Everyman*, and she was acting the part of Good Deeds, dressed as a nun. She had just reached her last speech—

> All earthly things is but vanity:
> *Beauty*, *Strength* and *Discretion*, do man forsake,
> Foolish friends and kinsmen, that fair spake,
> All fleeth save *Good Deeds*, and that am I.

—when a piece of fluff blew into her throat. She was speechless.

"I woke up the next morning and I couldn't make a sound. I was in agony. Ben Greet said, 'Well, you've got to go on somehow,' and of course I was determined to. So I invented a voice for myself, an entirely false voice. And they all said what a fine contralto voice I had—but it was false, and for three months I played in the open air on an invented voice, which was simply hell for any actor ever to have done."

Russell was extremely worried and plied her with gargles and inhalations, but Sybil's voice, long overworked, grew steadily worse. Ben Greet, whom all his actors loved and revered, was impatient of any ailments or other interruptions to his company's work, and in spite of Russell's protests Sybil went on playing all her parts, often two performances a day, in a low growl. Russell took her to see a specialist in Philadelphia who told her that she must stop work at once, but she refused to give up, and Ben Greet encouraged her in this. At last, on Russell's insistence, he and Sybil sailed for home.

Sybil was taken for a consultation with one of King Edward's medical advisers, Sir St Clair Thomson, who looked at her throat and was appalled to learn how she had been using her voice with the vocal chords in such a condition—they were covered with nodules. He told her gently that he feared she might never be able to speak on the stage again. This was really a moment of despair for Sybil; for the second time she would have to give up her chosen profession because of a physical disability. In a hoarse croak she asked Sir St Clair if there was any chance of curing her voice, and when he saw how stricken she was he told her that if she could be absolutely silent for six weeks he would tell her then if there was a hope of recovery.

"He said, 'Take a notebook, and for six weeks don't speak a single word. Can you do that?' And I croaked, 'Of course I can.' And do you know, that silence was one of the most wonderful experiences of my life. I always loved silence after that. I used to go for long walks with my dog, I read poetry and practised the piano for hours, and I prayed, oh God, how I prayed—and it was oh God! I went to church with Father every morning, but I never spoke a word, and after the first week I hardly wanted to write anything down, except when I met some of the villagers on my walks and they spoke to me. Then I pointed to my notebook and wrote my little answers down.

"It was rather awful seeing Russell off, going back to join the Ben Greet Players in America without me, but of course I was with Mother and Father and they were full of sympathy. It was then that the countryside, which I had always loved, became something specially wonderful to me—like silence and solitude.

"And after six weeks, in fear and trembling, I went back into Sir St Clair Thomson's room, and he looked into my throat and found that the growths had completely disappeared."

He told Sybil that she must have the constitution of an ox and praised her perseverance, and she spoke to him in a normal voice that sounded most peculiar to her—she had half-expected to hear the growl to which she had grown accustomed. Sir St Clair told her that she must be careful of her new voice and get it into trim, and sent her to a man who gave her some excellent vocal exercises which she still does every morning to this day. A further month passed and then, determined to work again, she took a room in the flat of her old friend, Ethel Cunliffe, who lived in a workman's dwelling opposite Lambeth Palace. The Archbishop, whom the Thorndikes had known when he was Bishop of Rochester, and his wife were most kind to Sybil, and the palace garden was a great solace to her, for she sorely missed the country.

Ethel Cunliffe was a prison visitor, and many discharged women prisoners came to the flat. They greatly interested Sybil. But looking for jobs was a depressing affair. After a few abortive attempts to find work through managers, she asked the advice of Nigel Playfair, whom she had met in the first pastoral tour before she went to America. He gave her an introduction to the lately formed Play Actors Society, and she was at once given the part of O Chicka San in *His Japanese Wife*, and then, as her American accent was unusually good, that of an American girl in a farce called *The Marquis*, performed at the Scala Theatre one Sunday in February 1908.

How little did she suspect that this evening would have a

momentous effect on her whole career—indeed, on her whole
life; for Bernard Shaw was in the audience. The following day
she had a note from Nigel Playfair: "Shaw saw your ridiculous
play last night—liked you very much—says you might do as
understudy for Candida. Come along quick and read the part."

Sybil had played Dolly Clandon in *You Never Can Tell* in
her early days as an amateur actress, but beyond this she knew
little of Bernard Shaw. She was captivated by him the moment
they met. Shaw had just turned fifty. He was tall and lean, as
always, with a white face, light blue eyes, his hair and beard red,
and his speech and manner most exhilarating.

"Shaw said, 'I want you to read Candida to me.' And I
thought, this is jam, this is easy as pie after Shakespeare, and I
put everything into it—Lady Macbeth, Rosalind, Beatrice,
everything. And Shaw rocked with laughter, I mean he nearly
rocked the roof off, and when I'd finished he said, 'Splendid,
my dear young lady. You'd better go home, see if you can
marry a nice young man, have several children and do all the
housekeeping, and then I'm sure you'll be a very good Candida.
But you'll do for the understudy.' "

He said this so charmingly, with such a twinkle in his eye, that
Sybil was not downcast. It was wonderful to be understudying
Ellen O'Malley with her friends Nigel Playfair and his wife,
May, both in the cast, and also to be given the lead—a lovely part
of a very young woman, Molly—in *The Subjection of Kezia*,
the curtain-raiser by Mrs Havelock Ellis. And later, when Sybil
thought over what Bernard Shaw had said, she came to understand the wisdom of his words—that to achieve good *acting*
one must be widely and deeply experienced in *living*.

Bernard Shaw was unfailingly kind to her, told her to sit
beside him at rehearsals, and talked to her continuously about
acting. He told her that there was something about her which
reminded him of Janet Achurch, who had created the part of
Candida in the first performance of the play by the Stage Society
at the Strand Theatre in 1901. Shaw must also have seen how much

Sybil Thorndike resembled his own description of Candida—
her "serene brow, courageous eyes, and well-set mouth and chin
signifying largeness of mind and dignity of character". He told
Sybil to watch Ellen O'Malley closely, "She's a beautiful actress
and will teach you a lot," and Sybil watched and drank in every
word Shaw said to her or to the cast.

"He was a better actor than any of them, and he knew the
exact tune of every line he wrote. It was like a musical score.
I can remember the musical score of *Candida*—every intonation that he wanted to get—away from accepted English
sometimes because his Irish had a more amusing sound."

Candida was to go on tour under the auspices of Miss Horniman,
whose own company was shortly to become famous at the Gaiety,
Manchester, as the pioneer of repertory theatre in England.
Annie Elizabeth Frederika Horniman, the daughter of a wealthy
Quaker, was a rebel from her childhood against the Victorian
middle-class conventional view of a young woman's life, and a
firm believer in the equality of the sexes. Only after years of
stubborn pleading had she been permitted, at the age of twenty-
one, to attend the Slade School of Art. Here she acquired a love
of art which remained with her always; more important, she met
fresh ideas, made interesting friendships and escaped from parental
tyranny. She paid her first visit to the Wagner Festival at
Bayreuth and saw several Ibsen plays, and Ibsen himself when he
was called on to the stage in Munich—all experiences which
made a lasting impression on her.

Her theatre career began in 1893 when her grandfather died,
leaving her a substantial legacy. She backed a season at the Avenue
Theatre* which included Yeats's *The Land of Heart's Desire* and
Shaw's *Arms and the Man*, directed by Florence Farr. These
productions were not financially successful, but history was being
made, for, besides giving the first public performances of Shaw's
plays and launching Yeats, outside the theatre was a poster
designed by a young artist named Aubrey Beardsley at which,

* Later the Playhouse, and then acquired by the B.B.C.

according to Miss Horniman, "even the cab horses shied", and inside the theatre Granville Barker was earning thirty shillings a week as an understudy.

Her interest in Yeats led to the founding of the Abbey Theatre in Dublin, which she subsidised for many years, and which inspired the work of Synge and other playwrights. Before long it had become one of the most famous theatres in the world. But at a time of growing nationalist feeling she remained a "foreigner" in Ireland and, because of this and more personal antagonisms, returned to England and started the Gaiety Theatre, Manchester. She would have preferred to launch her experiment in London, but failed to find a theatre there, and her meeting with Iden Payne influenced the choice of Manchester. Payne's cherished ambition was to launch a theatre in the provinces akin to Granville Barker's achievement at the Court in London, and Manchester was the obvious choice for such a venture. His contact with Miss Horniman turned his dreams into reality and she appointed him as her manager. The Midland Hotel Theatre was taken for a season in September 1907 and there, under the name The Manchester Playgoers' Theatre, the enterprise began.

The project had a good start and before many weeks had passed Miss Horniman had succeeded in purchasing the Gaiety Theatre. She could not get possession, however, until March 1908, so she arranged for the company to go on tour until their permanent home was available.

The tour started in Belfast, with the company from London playing *Candida* for half the week and the Manchester company playing *Widowers' Houses* for the remaining days.

Sybil wrote from Belfast to her brother in America:

"Darling Russ, I've seen a man I could marry—it's most absurd. His name is Casson, Lewis Casson . . . Well, I saw his photo first outside the theatre this morning and I thought, 'Now, there's a nice face. I like that man.' He's rather like Basil Bowers* only his face is more tidy; it looks strong and determined. I said to May Playfair, 'Who's that man?' and she said,

* Sybil's cousin, whom she had always admired and loved.

'That's Casson. He's a very good actor, but he's rather difficult to get on with. I like him all right. He's a socialist.' To-night we went to see *Widowers' Houses*, and I saw the bloke. He was playing the young man's part, and I liked him better than any young man I've ever seen on the stage because he spoke so fast that it woke you up and made you puzzle a bit, instead of going to sleep as a lot of actors who are highbrow make you."

She also told Russell how nervous the young Basil Dean, who was in the same digs as herself, made her feel with his sophisticated talk of the theatre. The next letter said:

"I met him—Casson—this morning. I was out with Nigel and May when we met him. They introduced me, but he only barked a sort of huffy how-do-ye-do to me and didn't speak another word to me. He wore a very shabby overcoat and a hat all down over his eyes like a tramp—he looks as if he would fight you if you gave him a chance, but quite suddenly something Nigel said made him laugh and his face looked quite different, and he's got a really lovely voice, very direct, and 'I mean every word I say and don't you forget it'."

The two companies now moved on to Dublin and there, one afternoon at the zoo, Sybil and May Playfair found Lewis Casson trying to hypnotise a large lioness.

After this meeting the three of them walked all round the zoo, Sybil trailing behind the other two and looking at the animals while they talked shop, which bored her. At last she said, "I'm going back to the lion house to look at the wolves." Lewis Casson said, "I'll come too," and May Playfair, who was worn out because Lewis Casson walked so fast, decided to go and have tea.

So there were Lewis Casson and Sybil Thorndike alone together in front of the wolves. They had a long conversation about animals and then they talked about other things, and he told her that he had been a schoolmaster, and she felt shy of him being so highbrow, but went on thinking how much she liked him and how she wished she were a boy so that she could have him for a pal.

She continued to write to Russell about Casson, and just before her letters reached him in America he picked up a photograph from Eric Blind's table—Eric Blind, with whom Sybil had thought herself in love—saying, "Who's this? This is the sort of man Sybil will marry." It was Lewis Casson.

The two companies now parted, to go on separate tours. When Sybil said goodbye to Lewis Casson she thought, "Oh, I really do like that man. If only he hadn't got golf clubs. I hate games like poison, and there's the only man I really think I might marry, and he's got golf clubs." When she left he gave her a beaming smile, and she thought, "He likes me too," and indeed she was right, for from the time of that first conversation in the lion house he was "very much taken with her". As he said:

"I met her first casually in the street in Belfast with the Playfairs. We stopped to talk, but Sybil stayed rather in the background so I noticed her eyes more than anything else. I didn't hear her voice at all during that occasion. I saw her play that night in a little sketch by Mrs Havelock Ellis. It was a simple part, but I was very much struck by her playing. And then we met in Dublin at the zoo. She was with May Martyn again, and I was in the lion house trying to tame a lioness when they came in. It's said that I've been trying to tame my lioness ever since. Anyway, after May had gone, Sybil and I had a real talk and I got to know her as a person rather than as an actress. When we left Dublin to go our separate ways, I remember very well seeing Sybil standing in the doorway of her dressing-room in a strong light, smiling her farewell. My early memories of her are a series of pictures."

A few weeks later Sybil found herself at the newly opened Gaiety Theatre, where she was elated to meet the famous Miss Horniman.

"I like her awfully on first acquaintance," she wrote to

Russell. "She looks as if she's stepped out of a mid-Victorian picture—tall and dignified and I think just a beautiful face, and she wears the most wonderful clothes, all made in the same mid-Victorian style of the loveliest materials—beautiful stuff that you'd only think of for curtains, and are surprised to see how well it furnishes the human body. She makes a real picture. I like seeing people looking as if they'd been painted by some-one—Miss Horniman looks that. She is a very enterprising woman. She spends most of her money on the theatre and lives very simply herself in a sort of bachelor way. I admire her, and would like to do what she is doing."

Sybil was engaged to understudy Candida and another long part, and when she went into the front of the house Lewis Casson was on the stage, rehearsing. He waved to her—to her great surprise, because, although they had had such a pleasant conversation in the lion house, he had not been exactly oncoming.

"Then he came down into the stalls and said, 'Look, I'm rather good at teaching people parts. You've got to learn these pretty quickly. Would you like me to help you?' So we went up on to the roof of the theatre and that's when we began to be friends, because we really discussed things on the roof while he was hearing me. We got covered with smuts, Manchester smuts, on that roof. And then he said, 'Do you like walking?' And I said, 'Oh, I love walking more than anything!' Thank goodness it turned out he didn't like games, in spite of those golf clubs."

So in the late spring of that year, 1908, Sybil Thorndike and Lewis Casson, and Charles Bibby and Hilda Bruce-Potter, both leading members of the Gaiety Company, went for long walks in the lovely country outside Manchester.

"Lewis and I always walked together and discussed every-thing. He told me such a lot, and I came to share his enthusiasm for Granville Barker."

Granville Barker, the actor, writer and producer, was then thirty-one, two years younger than Lewis Casson, and belonged to a circle of brilliant friends which included Gilbert Murray, William Archer and Bernard Shaw. He was at this time producing plays by Shaw, Ibsen and Galsworthy, as well as Gilbert Murray's translations from the Greek, at the Court Theatre, which under his influence had become the centre of London's theatre-minded intellectuals. Lewis Casson had been at the Royal Court Theatre from 1904, when the Vedrenne-Barker management started what was virtually a revolution in the theatre, and had moved with him to the Savoy, only joining Miss Horniman's Company in 1907, when Granville Barker's enterprise came to an end. Besides other parts, Casson had played Eglamour in *Two Gentlemen of Verona* for Barker, and the Messenger in Gilbert Murray's translation of *Hippolytus*.

He had developed an immense appreciation of Barker that was to influence profoundly his own work as a producer. Barker brought out the best in his actors, and expected creativity and brainwork in them all. He never treated the leading character as a star part in which the actor's personality was exploited to the detriment of the play. Every part, however small, had to be played to its full, and this too was part of the Horniman-Iden Payne policy. They were out to combat the star system and the prevalent long-run tradition. All this Lewis Casson talked about to Sibyl on their walks, and she wrote to her brother:

"Well, I'd like to see this man who everyone thinks is like God—no, more like Napoleon, I imagine—if he says a thing, all these highbrow actors say it's right . . .

"Casson's acting interests me—you're frightfully conscious of a brain, not so much that he's *become* the person but as if he was making *you* see the person and he was giving you suggestions—it's not the way I could work, but it's very interesting, and his speed is most exhilarating. I do detest people who if they're saying something either beautiful or important go three times slower in case you miss anything. By the time some of them have got to the end of a sentence you've forgotten the beginning and then you're lost. Casson speaks nearly as fast as you think."

It was not only about theatre, however, that Lewis Casson talked to Sybil Thorndike, but also about politics, the Fabian Society and social reform.

"Do you know anything at all about politics?" she wrote to Russell. "I don't, except that you're supposed to vote Conservative if you're respectable and be anything but a socialist. Well, most of these highbrows are socialists—full of 'the people'."

Lewis Casson also told her about the Women's Suffrage movement, took her to hear Mrs Pankhurst, whom she thenceforward greatly admired, and even persuaded her to take the chair at a suffragette meeting. Before long she found herself a member of the Women's Social and Political Union, casting aside the Conservatism she had taken for granted as "awfully dull", and finding that what Bernard Shaw and Lewis Casson told her was true—"thinking about life helps you to act". "Lewis became my mentor and my guide."

After three weeks Sybil's engagement in Manchester came to an end and she set off for home. Lewis Casson travelled to London with her and, finding that she had time before catching her train to Aylesford, invited her to tea in his chambers in Clifford's Inn. Here, most unlike herself, as she had always loathed mending of any kind, she sewed two buttons on his coat. He saw her off. "And I thought once more, 'Well, that's a nice pal.' But I really was very smitten, although I kept telling Russell that we weren't falling in love."

The Gaiety was now closed for alterations, and Lewis Casson arranged to produce *As You Like It* and play Orlando at his old college, St Mark's, Chelsea.* He invited Sybil to play Rosalind. This was wonderful enough, but by the same post she had an offer from Iden Payne to join the Gaiety Company again and

* Amalgamated with St John's, Battersea, in 1923.

play whatever parts were going—with Lewis Casson as the leading man. She joyfully accepted both invitations by return of post.

It was a wonderful experience actually to be playing with Lewis Casson, and she even got something of a thrill when she had to put his wig straight. After the performance she met some of his relatives for the first time, and was rather scared by them. "Very learned women they were." One sister, Elizabeth, was a social worker, later to become a doctor and introduce occupational therapy to this country, another was a schoolmistress, and one the wife of a schoolmaster. "They put the wind up me."

Sybil did several other pastoral plays with Lewis Casson, her old principal Fred Topham and Nigel Playfair. Then she and Lewis separated once more for further tours, meeting again in August on Brighton Pier. Sybil was playing Candida at last, her favourite part so far.

"Well, on Brighton Pier I could see he was really pleased to see me, and off we went to watch Doughty's Dogs. They were marvellous. Lewis was very tickled with them, and so was I. I adore performing dogs, they enjoy it so much. I never mind when it's dogs, because they have to be treated kindly or they wouldn't enjoy it."

After the dogs they swam together off the West Pier. Here is a conversation they had in the late autumn of 1968 about those early days:

Sybil: Marie Lloyd was swimming that day. She wouldn't dive, but I did—went flat with a smack that resounded all over the city.
Lewis: Our next meeting was in Birmingham. We went for walks in what is now Edgbaston, but was then real country.
Sybil: Do you remember the two trees, Lewis?
Lewis: Yes. Under the full moon.
Sybil: It was a harvest moon, absolutely wonderful. There were two trees that specially struck us, and whenever, later on,

we had rows—we both have fierce tempers—one of us would say "the two trees" and all would be peace again. On the way back you held my hand, which surprised me very much.

Lewis: And then it was a fish-shop in Exeter.

Sybil: Yes, and you said, "I saw your Candida last night. I made some notes and criticisms. Come and have some coffee and I'll go through the part with you." And you told me all my faults—Hilda Bruce-Potter came and had coffee too and she was simply furious, but I was pleased, because your criticism helped me. You said I was too bouncy and talked too fast. I was always being too bouncy. It was difficult for me to play Candida at first. I was so soaked in Ellen O'Malley's performance. Gradually I found my own. I love that play. The last speech is wonderful.

Lewis: We went on the river at Exeter and then you came to tea with Jules Shaw and me. The house stood on a bank and I climbed up a wrought-iron balcony—a very steep climb— to show how well I could do it. Soon afterwards I proposed to you.

Sybil: It was on the Friday at the café. And before that I had a beautiful pair of new gloves from you. I'd dropped one somewhere—*gloves* to go for a country walk!—and you'd taken the other.

Lewis: And then we met for lunch.

Sybil: But the morning before that, you came to the house where I was digging with Hilda Bruce-Potter just as I was coming down to breakfast. You had a baby with you.

Lewis: It was a little boy. He was crying, so I brought him in to see you.

Sybil: Afterwards Hilda said, "He brought that along just to see how you'd react." Well, it was a darling little boy and I love babies.

"Lewis Casson has asked me to marry him," she wrote to Russell the next day. "I'm so taken aback. He's never even called me by my Christian name. I didn't fall flat on my face when he proposed in the Kardomah Restaurant over coffee and toast, but the whole room spun round and so did the houses outside. So I suppose it means I shall marry him. I was too *bouleversée* to give him an answer then. On the Sunday we went to Early Service together, and then somehow or other we found that we were engaged."

As long as she can remember, Sybil has wanted to escape from life's confines, to "break the mould", as she puts it, when speaking with reverence and envy of the great explorers, whether in earthly or spiritual realms. It might be Sir Francis Young-husband or Sir Edmund Hillary or the astronauts, Euripides or Rabindranath Tagore, Teilhard de Chardin or even Jesus Christ himself: they are all "breakers of the mould" to her, and this is the quality which of all others she most admires. As soon as she met Lewis she knew instinctively that he too was an explorer—as he remained for the whole of his life.

Mr and Mrs Thorndike were slightly perturbed by the news of their engagement, and hoped that Sybil would give the matter rather longer thought, but she did not need to think further. She had imagined herself in love several times before, but this was her first adult love—she was now twenty-six—and she knew that she had given her heart away in the lion-house.

CHAPTER V

FOLLOWING THE GLEAM

(*1908–1909*)

RETURNING TO THE Gaiety in the spring of 1908, when the theatre was at last scoured and reconstructed to Miss Horniman's satisfaction, Lewis Casson played Provost in the daring opening production, in the Poel manner, of *Measure for Measure*. William Poel came up to supervise Iden Payne's production and played the part of Angelo. During the summer the company went on tour again, and when they visited Carlisle Sybil's father joined her to meet his prospective son-in-law. Mr Thorndike was pleased that his daughter was to marry a man with a background so akin to her own, and to Sybil's great joy he and Lewis became good friends at once.

"Our branch of the Casson family came from Seathwaite," Lewis explained, "on the borders of Lancashire and Yorkshire, and we are descended from the Reverend Robert Walker, always known as 'The Wonderful Walker', a famous worthy of the eighteenth century who was commemorated by Wordsworth and in a book by Richard Parkinson called *The Old Church Clock*.

"Walker's parish was extremely poor, and in addition to his work as a parson, which included running a village school in the church, he kept a small sheep farm, on the proceeds of which he raised a large family. My great-grandfather married his grand-daughter, moved to North Wales and founded one of the original slate quarries in Merioneth. This prospered and out of the profits the Casson Bank was founded. My father became a bank manager, managing the branch at Denbigh, the historic old market town in North Wales, where we—I was one of seven children—were brought up.

"We were thirty miles from the nearest theatre at Chester—occasional visits to the pantomime combined with visits to the dentist were all the shows we knew—and yet my early years, like Sybil's, were full of the theatre. My father was a well-known amateur actor when he was young, and I remember him reading *Macbeth* to us when we were very small. I played Orlando, in a shortened version of *As You Like It*, to family and friends when I was about six. From that sort of age my brother Will and I were always acting for family parties, and later on at the local infirmary and the asylum, and so forth. We also loved toy theatres. We hadn't any money to buy one, but we constructed a really elaborate little theatre for ourselves. I've always been good with my hands—liked making and mending things—and I love wood. I inherited this taste from my father, as well as my love of music.

"My father was not particularly interested in banking: his real passion was for the organ. Not only was he a fine organist, but he developed a fanatical interest in the instrument, and eventually devoted most of his mind and the family money to inventions concerning it."

"Yes, he built organs all over the world," Sybil added. "He had a perfect ear—he was a genius, really. I remember years later, when we were in America with John Drew and went to Salt Lake City and visited the big Temple there because it had a beautiful organ, the organist was very bored by us all—he didn't want to talk to a lot of actors. But when he heard Lewis's name he said, 'Are you any relation of Thomas Casson?' And when Lewis said that he was his son, the organist was absolutely thrilled. I was rather frightened of 'Taid-Taid' at first (that's what we called Lewis's parents—'Taid-Taid' and 'Nain-Nain', Welsh for grandpa and grandma), but we became great friends. Of course I was fascinated by his being so musical, and Nain-Nain was the most adorable, pretty little Welsh lady you could imagine. I loved her from the moment I saw her."

"She was the daughter of a sea captain," Lewis said, "part-owner of a schooner trading up and down the Pacific. Her mother spent the whole of her short married life—it was only four years—at sea, and my mother was born at Valparaiso. As a little girl she used to climb the rigging.

"My own career was a very mixed one. I was the second son, born in 1875, and I went to the Grammar School in Ruthin. In 1891 I left school and went up to London, where my father had recently started an organ business. I worked there at the bench for about six months, then the business collapsed, and I followed my brother Randal to the City and Guild Institute in South Kensington, both of us doing engineering and I chemistry as well. I was there for two years and during that time I became more and more convinced that where I ought to be was in the Church. Although my father was not a parson like Sybil's, religion—Anglo-Catholicism—was almost as integral a part of our family life as it was of hers. So I announced that I was going to be a priest, and as there was no money to pay for my training I took a post at St Augustine's Elementary School in Kilburn, and then went on to St Mark's College in Chelsea and later became a member of its staff.

"By this time—about 1896—my father had invented a new instrument which he named the Positive Organ; this was a small, more or less portable organ for use in village churches, and the invention prospered so well that my father induced me to go back and help him again in the organ trade. This I did for a further two years, but my father was no business man—he was always building some large organ at less than cost price—so the project failed, and once again I was faced with choosing a career. By now I had decided not to go into the Church, and having really been an actor all my life I went into the theatre.

"During my time at St Augustine's I had joined a dramatic society and played continually for them—the usual kind of plays published by French, but we also tried our hand at Shakespeare, and my very first production was *The Merchant of Venice*. It was at about this time that I met Charles Fry—

he was professor of elocution at a London organ school which eventually became the London Academy of Music and Dramatic Art. I also used to work for a society which sent people out to recite at public functions, and through this, and playing in a large number of Shakespeare plays for Fry, I met that splendid Elizabethan, William Poel. He had just discovered *Everyman*, and given it the moving production that has so often been reproduced—the only financial success he ever had, and even then his followers made more out of playing *Everyman* and Shakespeare according to his ideas than he ever did himself. I suppose he was in his late forties when I met him, but I thought of him as quite old. He peered at you with little twinkling eyes over steel spectacles, set well down on his nose, and he spoke with a queer interjection—'Ah rumptarrah'. He wasn't a great actor, but he was a great man of the theatre.

"Then I met Acton Bond, one of Irving's company, who liked my work. He recommended me to Poel's great disciple, Granville Barker, that genius of the theatre who was about to produce *Two Gentlemen of Verona* at the Court Theatre for J. H. Leigh. With no doubts at all now about what I should be, in spite of my family's disappointment I threw up everything else, became a professional actor, and had the privilege of playing for the Vedrenne–Barker management at the Court Theatre during most of its reign—the reign that established Bernard Shaw as a popular playwright. When Granville Barker left to go to the Savoy I went with him, but the season petered out and the enterprise came to an end. I then joined Miss Horniman's company in Manchester, and through this happy move met Sybil. Very soon our long partnership began, since when we have never ceased to argue, criticise, fight and enthuse on every phase and aspect of our beloved theatre."

One cannot overestimate the influence that William Poel and Granville Barker had on Casson's work. Sybil too counts Granville Barker as one of her most important masters, and she came later to have a great regard for William Poel.

"I never worked under him as Lewis did, but in my early years at the Old Vic he used to come down to see the productions, and he helped me with the phrasing of my lines. I remember going for a walk with him, he talking all the time about phrasing. Wonderful man."

William Poel advocated the platform stage, which Granville Barker used with great effect for his productions at the Savoy. He also called for a "rapid, highly coloured musical speech of great range and flexibility", a concept which appealed strongly to Lewis Casson, as a Welshman. And Granville Barker too had an inspired knowledge of how a voice should be used in the interpretation of a character.

Sybil noticed Lewis's captivatingly quick speech the first time she watched him act, and as a producer he never stopped urging his actors to work with their voices and attain a full expression of their lines. This preoccupation of Casson's with speech was, one might almost say, vented on his wife. Here once more they are conversing late in 1968:

Sybil: Lewis used to have more notes in his voice than anyone I've ever known—three octaves—and a wonderful ear. He has never stopped going on at me about my voice. Oh, how I had to work at it, and do still. I've got a lovely exercise I do every day when I read the leading article to Lewis in the morning. I try not to come down to the key-note until the very end of the article. To keep my voice up like Lewis in his Welsh fashion. Welsh is much more amusing than English. I have always found this practice very helpful, specially in reading poetry—not to go back to the home-note at the end of a verse, which is very boring. There are climaxes one can use, and keep the key-note for the finish. That's what the theatre needs most of all now—a fresh attitude to speech. Of course, some people get very interesting sounds—Larry,* for instance, and John Gielgud. But Gielgud's speech I wouldn't call ordinary English—ordinary

* Laurence Olivier.

English is very da-da-da, da-da-da, until you get tired of the same intonation.

Lewis: We have always been much more interested in the human voice, whereas the general tendency among actors has been towards décor and movement—depending on the eye much more than the ear. I suppose Irving was the great example of it, of playing chiefly for the eye.

Sybil: I never cared very much about décor. It rather bores me. It takes me away from the play. I like the words and the characterisation, I like a bare stage.

Lewis: I think I may have a certain reputation for being too much a director and not a producer, because I worry so much about the intonation and the phrasing of the speech— actually making the play live through the human voice. I think we both work on the conviction that the main thing to get over in the play is the author's emotion and the meaning that he is trying to get across, and this is far more important than any grouping and that sort of thing. Therefore I prefer, during rehearsals, to spend quite a lot of time, as Poel used to do, working round the table to get the general musical interpretation of the play right, before you start moving at all. Actors don't really like that very much, because they say they can never get ideas until they start moving.

I like as a director, as far as possible, to get the ideas of the actors themselves and mould them into what one is trying to do. You can generally take the actor's own way of saying the thing, knowing what he is trying to say, and make it much more vivid by increasing the pitch and range of his speech. The difficulty is that, as acting is so very realistic nowadays, you might almost say that what Sybil calls "da-da-da, da-da-da" is the proper way to speak. That if you are imitating the language of the drawing-room and the street, you have to follow that rather dull intonation. One of the things I have fought for in producing speech is to get away from that. It's the inner meaning of living that is a necessity, not the mere imitation of how you would speak in real life.

Sybil: Another thing is that everything else in the theatre these days has become symbolic in a big way, movement and everything much larger in size, but speech has got smaller. It's become very dull, without beauty, without phrasing, and it's the last thing people bother about as long as they can make it sound like the King's Road, Chelsea, on a Saturday afternoon.

Lewis: In fact the theatre ought to be setting an example of high-class speech—well, class is the wrong word, but really clear speech. Just as dancing and the ballet want good movement, perfect movement. Nobody would be allowed to sing badly in opera or to dance badly in ballet merely because people do that in real life. Even though you are playing broad Yorkshire, there is no point in playing to a London audience with a Yorkshire accent if they can't understand it. You can suggest the Yorkshire accent, but you must speak so that this particular audience can understand it.

Sybil: Absolute realism is what they are all working for. Absolute. I mean, they don't mind whether it is heard or not. You can't hear everything that's said in the theatre if you are sitting far back. One great alteration in the theatre since Ellen Terry's day, for example, is that actors now are much more interested in playing a character, and not using their own. An actress used to use her own personality and never go far away from it. One could see this in Ellen Terry's work. If she had gone away at all from her own—from what people thought of as her own—personality, she could have done extraordinarily exciting things. But she didn't because people wouldn't accept it. When a person has so much charm the public ask for the charm and don't want impersonations. Real impersonation isn't merely putting something on, it's extracting other personalities from inside yourself. And I believe that in them you can find more expositions of your own character. Bad, good, indifferent and all sorts.

After Carlisle the Horniman Company went on to Blackpool,

and here it was Mrs Thorndike who came to meet her prospective son-in-law. This was not nearly such an easy encounter for Lewis as that with Sybil's father. Mrs Thorndike was given to speaking her mind in no uncertain terms.

"You're not in the least the kind of man I wanted Sybil to marry," she complained. "I wanted her to marry somebody distinguished and have a salon."

Sybil demurred and Lewis defended himself and he and Mrs Thorndike had quite a fierce argument. Sybil was in despair, thinking that they would never be friends, and then suddenly, without the slightest embarrassment, Mrs Thorndike asked Lewis to lend her a penny to go to the ladies. They both burst out laughing, and by the time Mrs Thorndike returned she was more reconciled to the match. After all, Lewis Casson was very well bred and had a beautiful voice and remarkable good looks. About one thing, however, she was adamant. The young couple wanted to be married at the earliest possible moment "with the least possible fuss". Mrs Thorndike, on the other hand, was determined that her daughter should have a beautiful wedding that all the clergy and people of Aylesford and Rochester would enjoy. Before they parted she had won her point, and the date was fixed for December 22nd.

Sybil and Lewis returned to Manchester for the rest of the autumn season, and played together for the first time in Basil Dean's first play and first production, *Marriages are Made in Heaven*, a strange little tragedy about a Kentish farm-hand who is about to marry the girl he loves, when he is informed by his rival that she is his half-sister.

After this they acted together in a number of productions, one of the most important of which was *Hippolytus* in Gilbert Murray's translation. To quote Sybil again:

"*Hippolytus* is surely one of the most beautiful plays in the world; it has every quality that makes a great tragedy. I know rehearsing it and studying it for the first time was like being in a magic country, and one day, when Lewis had got the words and general shape of the play drilled into us, he told us that Gilbert Murray was coming for the next rehearsals.

"The following day we met Professor Murray, and as soon as he spoke to us I knew what Lewis had meant by saying I was lucky to be working under such a man. Lewis had known and admired him since first meeting him in 1904 during the Vedrenne–Barker management at the Court Theatre. He was very gentle and quiet, but he knew exactly the sort of effect he wanted to get, and by a word could put one on the right track. With everyone he seemed to give the keynote of the part in a phrase. He said to me, 'an opalescent dawn—that is how you must think and feel as Artemis', and anyone who has played the goddess will appreciate what he meant, although it is very difficult to bring it off in performance. Even then Lewis was the interpreter for me. Professor Murray said, 'Casson will show you how to do it—he moves and speaks like a Greek'."

Sybil needed this help, for she found it difficult to "get rid of anything personal", and both Gilbert Murray and Lewis Casson were perfectionists and hard to please. However, studying the play "made her know what she wasn't like", and in this spirit she approached the part of Artemis, "Virgin of God most High", standing aloft on a pillar and speaking to the dying Hippolytus words of immortal tenderness:

Artemis: With thee and loving thee, poor sufferer!
Hippolytus: Dost see me, Mistress, nearing my last sleep?
Artemis: Aye, and would weep for thee, if Gods could weep.

Gilbert Murray was then the most important interpreter of the great Greek plays that the English-speaking world had known, but there has been an unending controversy about the use of lyrical English verse in his translations. William Archer, praising them, observed, "Greek tragedy demands to be clothed in a formal decorative beauty scarcely attainable in English without the aid of rhyme",* and Professor Murray himself stated that "the wholeness" of the play was his first concern and that his translations were intended for "sustained and rapid action on the

* *Gilbert Murray, An Unfinished Autobiography* (George Allen & Unwin, 1960).

stage". He explained that rhyme served to mark the end of the line, which was never in doubt in the Greek iambics, and that Greek verse could scarcely ever be mistaken for prose.

The Cassons found Murray's handling of the inner stresses of the play and the mystery and significance of the Chorus an uplifting experience. Although he did not read his own work aloud dramatically, he was not averse to passionate delivery on the part of his actors. What he demanded of them was sincerity, and he preferred the Choruses spoken rather than sung, so that the words were not subjugated to the music. Professor Murray was, in fact, not musical, but he had a perfect ear for metre.

Gilbert Murray and his wife Lady Mary—who *was* musical and played the organ, and was also a champion of women's rights, so she and Sybil had much in common—remained close friends of the Cassons. Sybil worshipped Gilbert Murray, and she never failed to find his renderings of the many Greek tragedies in which she was to perform perfect to speak, perfect to act. Years later she wrote:

"The year 1908 was a rich one for me, for I met three men who profoundly affected my life. In the early spring, Bernard Shaw; a few weeks later Lewis Casson . . .; and in the autumn Gilbert Murray. In my own inside self these three are connected, and [Lewis Casson] helped to interpret for me the other two, whose works have since been a guidance and a light to lighten the darkness for us both."*

Russell came back from America, and he and his sister Eileen went up to Manchester to stay with Sybil and meet Lewis, and very much enjoyed watching the Horniman Company at work. It was a most stimulating time; besides the friendship of the incomparable Miss Horniman, with the oxidised silver dragon studded with opals always coiled about her neck, there were Iden Payne and the other members of the company, and Sybil and Lewis also came to know well some of the authors whose work they were performing—Charles McEvoy, Allan Monk-

* *Essays in Honour of Gilbert Murray* (George Allen & Unwin, 1936).

house, Stanley Houghton—and the Manchester critics, of whom the brilliant C. E. Montague was the leader. It was here too that they first encountered James Agate, with whom they were to have many violent disagreements and to remain close friends, for they have always found serious criticism interesting and stimulating.

"One critic whom I really did love was Robin Littlewood, who was one of the founders of the Critics' Circle and worked in Fleet Street for half a century. He gave me a great deal of encouragement in my early days. He understood the sensitivity of an actor and his eagerness to learn more of his art. Robin loved the theatre and his work for it more than he loved himself, and that is a very lovable trait."

As Christmas approached the company went off to play in Ireland. The last play on this tour was *Candida* in Cork, with Sybil in the lead and Lewis as the poet Marchbanks.

"That was the Saturday night, and Lewis and I were to be married at Aylesford on the following Tuesday, and we simply had to catch our train back to Dublin so as not to miss the boat. We reduced *Candida* to something like an hour, by sheer speed. People who came in a little late found we were in the middle of the second act.

"We went straight down to Aylesford, and on Monday there was a big to-do in the barn—Lewis making a fatuous speech about taking away 'the jewel of the village'. He met my brother Frank, a wild young thing of fourteen, for the first time, and they remained fast friends ever after. On the Tuesday morning, the morning of the wedding, Lewis and I went to Early Service together, and as we came out I remember him saying, 'I feel awful about taking you away from all this'. And I was crying. I felt, 'I can't bear leaving Aylesford, I can't bear to leave home.'

"And there we were—a bright frosty day—very cold. A real Christmas wedding, the church decorated with holly, and the two bridesmaids—my sister Eileen, now eighteen, and a young friend of hers—in white dresses and red cloaks and wreaths of holly. The village people had said, 'Can Miss Sybil drive to the church and then to the train in an open carriage so that we can see her?' Oh, it was so cold! My nose was as red as the holly.*

"Father gave me away, wearing his cassock. He looked so beautiful. His was the most lovely face I can ever think of. I adored him, and I do still. I often talk to him—I'm sure he's somewhere about. I had two bishops to marry me, the Bishop of Rochester and my uncle the Bishop of Thetford, and of course the other dignitaries were there too. There was a large choir wearing scarlet cassocks and Mother was at the organ. After the wedding we drove to the station with the village brass band walking in front of the open carriage. We had to stop so that I could make a speech to the villagers who were lining the road. I wasn't so cold then because Lewis had given me a beautiful squirrel coat and a toque to match, with a long blue feather in it. And so off we went—on what some people called 'a most boring honeymoon'."

Miss Horniman had given Sybil and Lewis a month's holiday, and this they spent first in a two weeks' tour in Derbyshire, joyously, to quote Lewis, "tramping in the blizzards and the snowdrifts, talking our heads off, thrashing everything out as we still do", and afterwards staying with Lewis's Uncle Randal and Aunt Lucy and his cousin Alec at their house, Bron-y-garth, at Portmadoc in North Wales. This is a square stone mansion, built at the turn of the century, with large windows letting in the lovely sky-water light on every side. The house is built on rock and set among trees in a bowl of mountains, with the river Glasllyn flowing beneath through a stretch of land not long before reclaimed from the sea.

---

* Sybil had had her beautiful embroidered white satin wedding dress made in Manchester, but Lewis firmly refused to buy any new clothes for the occasion. According to Russell Thorndike he simply said, "I shall wear my first act *David Ballard* for the wedding and my second act *Widowers' Houses* to go away in."

"I fell in love with Wales—really in love, like falling in love with a person. I had never seen intimate mountains before, and we faced them out of every window. Climbing Moel y gest, the small one just behind the house, became a favourite walk.

"I loved the house, specially the smell of the panelling in the big room, made out of local wood, and the piano and the books. Later Lewis inherited Bron-y-garth, but none of my family loved it as much as I did.

"Besides our walks we had a wonderful time, going to visit all the county. Very societyish she was, Aunt Lucy. And I sat up beside her in the carriage—an open carriage, if you please, in mid-winter—wearing my lovely squirrels and fairly fancying myself as Lady Gimcrack. Oh, it was gorgeous!"

The title of this chapter was suggested by Lewis Casson's superb reading from Tennyson's poem *Merlin and the Gleam*. These lines might be Casson's advice to a young actor:

> Not of the sunlight,
> Not of the moonlight,
> Not of the starlight!
> O young Mariner,
> Down to the haven,
> Call your companions,
> Launch your vessel,
> And crowd your canvas,
> And, ere it vanishes
> Over the margin,
> After it, follow it,
> Follow The Gleam.

So they were launched, their course already charted.

CHAPTER VI

FAMILY WAY

(1910–1914)

BACK THE CASSONS went to their first married home, digs in Didsbury, Manchester, to play repertory at the Gaiety Theatre and go on various tours in the north of England. One of the highlights of the season was Galsworthy's *The Silver Box*. Lewis had created the part of the magistrate's clerk in the original production at the Court Theatre three years before; now he was playing the magistrate, and Sybil had the part of Mrs Barthwick, "a lady of nearly fifty, well dressed, with greyish hair, good features and a decided manner". Galsworthy warned her that she would find the part difficult. She did not believe him, for she still felt that once she got under the skin of a character, however alien to her nature, there was no part that she could not play; but in this case she soon acknowledged that he was right. He wanted his actors and actresses to be more impersonal than most other playwrights did, and Sybil says that at one rehearsal she cried in despair, "I can't do it. It's too hard. Do you want me to take away everything that is *me*?"

"Yes," replied Galsworthy quietly. "If you would do that I think we shall get what I want. Shall we try again?"

Sybil did her best, for her self-confidence never prevented her from eagerly accepting advice and constructive criticism.

Galsworthy also surprised her by describing *The Silver Box* as comedy, for to her, whose socialist convictions were now as ardent as her husband's, and who had an innate compassion with suffering, the play appeared chiefly as a terrible indictment of social injustice, and the laughter that greeted the performance each night continued to amaze her.

She soon discovered, however, that the term comedy did not deny the play's strong element of tragedy and that, although Galsworthy tried to treat the social picture objectively, it was coloured by his passionate humanitarianism. *The Silver Box* took the Gaiety by storm, and the Cassons came to regard it as one of the few perfect plays.

Another older woman whom Sybil had recently portrayed with success was Lady Dennison in St John Hankin's *The Charity that Began at Home*, a "most admirable figure of combined good breeding and woolliness of mind". This great variety of parts delighted her, and with her remarkable memory she could learn them quickly and surely. To add to her happiness she had now discovered that she was "in the family way". She went on working for as long as possible, but when that summer the company did its first very successful season in London at the Coronet Theatre, Notting Hill Gate, she had reluctantly to retire and went back to the vicarage at Aylesford. When the season ended Lewis took a job with Lewis Waller, coming down to Aylesford at the weekends.

Most fortunately for Sybil, a few months later Mr Thorndike was given the living of St James the Less in Westminster, at the same time being made an honorary Canon of Rochester. The Thorndikes moved to the vicarage in St George's Square. The neighbouring parish to theirs was that of Father Olivier, Laurence Olivier's father, who at once became a friend of the Thorndikes. Sybil was able to have her baby at her parents' new home, and there, on October 28th 1909, John Casson was born.

Sybil had a very hard time. She and Lewis had looked forward with such deep joy to the arrival of their child, but she was not prepared for childbirth to be such appalling and prolonged torture. Grim and silent during these terrible hours, Lewis concentrated on inlaying with purple heart wood the beautiful writing desk which he had bought for Sybil in York market, and which she uses to this day. He appeared so remote that the servants even wondered if he were not unfeeling about his wife's ordeal, whereas he was in fact in agony. When at last the boy was born, there was great family rejoicing.

Lewis's engagement with Waller soon came to an end, and as he and Sybil had now left the Horniman Company there was a prospect of being very hard up. However, Lewis found a little work here and there, and Sybil's younger brother Frank, who was now starting his stage career, played a small part with his brother-in-law in a Sunday production.

Frank had all the fire and brilliance of the Thorndike family and shared to the full their adventurousness. Starting with those early days when he had gone with Sybil to the Guildhall School of Music, he had become an accomplished 'cellist, and then, at the age of thirteen, had been sent to boarding school in Oxford. He turned up one morning at Aylesford and announced that he was learning nothing and so he had run away. After this he went to day school in Rochester, but at the first possible moment followed Sybil, Russell and Eileen into the theatre. Before long Gerald du Maurier, after seeing him in *Vice Versa*, engaged "Master Frank Thorndike" for a part in *Alias Jimmy Valentine*, in which he was an outstanding success. This was a great joy, particularly to Sybil, who adored him—but all the family believed firmly in Frank's theatrical gifts.

The first part that Sybil played after the birth of her baby was Columbine in Chapin's touching little play *The Marriage of Columbine*—a Sunday night performance for the Play Actors' Society. Following this Charles Frohman, who had just started a London repertory company with Granville Barker and Dion Boucicault as producers, invited both Sybil and Lewis to join his company. Granville Barker and Lewis Casson were eager to work together again, and Sybil was delighted to have a chance of being produced by this great man.

"I remember Dion Boucicault saying, 'What salary do you want?' and my telling him I got £5 in Manchester. He said, 'You won't get that here'. So there we were—Lewis with £7 and me with £3. 10. 0. It was a fantastic repertory, with Irene Vanburgh, Lena Ashwell, Hilda Trevelyan and Lillah McCarthy as leading ladies—the salary list must have been enormous."

On the strength of this engagement the Cassons had taken a flat in St George's Square, two doors from the vicarage, which Lewis furnished chiefly by buying up derelict but often beautiful old pieces in York market and very skilfully restoring them.

Sybil was understudying and playing small parts. She attended all the rehearsals and learned more of her craft from watching Granville Barker direct and act. In that whimsical little play *Prunella* or *Love in a Dutch Garden*, written by Granville Barker and Laurence Housman, she played a tiny part, Romp, 'the jolly girl', one of the mummers, and Lewis was the statue of love, the part he had played in earlier productions, and in which many people still remember him.

For Sybil, the great experience of this play was watching Granville Barker showing Charles Maude* how to play the part of Pierrot.

"There's one of his gestures, Russ," she wrote to her brother, "that no one but God would have thought of—and things he does with his voice when he's showing people what he wants— things that not a single one of us can do. I shall go on practising and trying to do what he does and then one day, of course, he'll be directing a great national theatre in Trafalgar Square, and perhaps he'll want Lewis and me in the company, and I don't care if it's only to walk on, we'll be seeing such beautiful things."

Strange little parts in strange little plays—and then suddenly Sybil's luck changed. Dion Boucicault came up to her when she was in the wings in *Prunella* and said, "I've got a leading part for you". This was Maggie in *Chains* by Elizabeth Baker, a character after Sybil's own heart—that strong, adventurous young woman who is determined to break the mould of the suburban security-complex.

"If I were a man I wouldn't stay in England another week. I wouldn't be a quill driver all my life."

* Later the husband of Nancy Price.

Fortunately Lillah McCarthy did not want the part, so it was given to Sybil, and Boucicault worked very hard with her, which meant, as always, getting her to do less. "I do everything too much."

One particular friend at this time was the violinist Nikolai Sokoloff, who had been a friend of Russell's in America. He had spent some time with the Thorndikes at Aylesford, and he and Sybil had done some violin and piano recitals together in Kent. Later he became conductor of the Cleveland Orchestra, but his first conducting was for the Cassons at the Gaiety Theatre, Manchester.

Sybil was a success in *Chains*, and Charles Frohman, coming over to see his English repertory company, immediately invited her and Lewis, who had a small part in the play, to join him for a season in America.

Sybil was distraught. On one side was this excellent offer—not only of earning good money, when they were in such financial straits, but also of supporting John Drew, the American star, whose work they knew and admired, in his first-class company. On the other side was the appalling wrench of leaving their son John.

"I thought I'd die. Lewis didn't feel it quite as much as I did, because men *don't* feel leaving a child quite so much. I'd got a very nice little nurse, and Mother said she'd look after John at the vicarage. So we borrowed twenty pounds from Actors' Day Fund, and off we trundled. The in-laws, Nain-Nain and Taid-Taid, saw us off, and all the way to Liverpool I never stopped crying. I felt 'poor Lewis', but I couldn't stop. I was hysterical at the thought of leaving that baby—the first baby—and a baby meant the most awful lot to me."

The play was Somerset Maugham's *Smith*, and although she was not the star—he had written the play for Marie Löhr, and now Mary Boland was doing it—Sybil had "a very showy part" as an adventuress, with some good scenes with John Drew. And not only was he "angelic", but Charles Frohman gave her all kinds of wonderful hints as to how to play an adventuress and manage her hobble-skirt.

Before they left New York, after a most successful run, for an extensive tour of the country, Frohman had made the Cassons an offer.

" 'Look,' he said, 'I'll make Sybil a star, and you can play every year, three months in New York, and then go on the road.' And Lewis said to me, 'We can't refuse this, you know. It's too good an offer for us.'

"And so we signed. I got miserabler and miserabler. And finally I said, 'I can't do it, Lewis, I can't do it.' So he said, 'What are we going to do?' And I said, 'Let's have another baby.' So a little while after, when I was sure, I wrote to Frohman and said, 'Alas, alas, I am in the family way and can't . . .' And he wrote back and said, 'O.K., go and have your baby and then come back. My offer holds good.' And I thought, 'What? Travel all that time and only do one play a year, when I like about three plays in three months? *And* be parted from my babies?' "

The Cassons were still wondering what to do about their careers when the miracle happened. In Salt Lake City Lewis had a letter from Miss Horniman, offering him the directorship of the Gaiety, as Iden Payne was leaving. Sybil Thorndike was also, of course, to be a member of the company. They were overjoyed, and wrote to Frohman that on account of John and the new child coming they felt that they must accept the Manchester offer.

The rest of the tour was extremely enjoyable. Indeed, the only drawbacks to the whole trip had been Sybil's unhappiness at being parted from her little son, and the dislike that both she and Lewis had for going on and on playing the same parts. They were both of them real repertory actors. But now that they knew that they would soon be back in England, they could enjoy themselves to the full. They loved the Frohman Company, and everywhere they met with a warm hospitality and free generosity that has been the essence of their love of America ever since. They had made delightful friends in New York, not only among theatre people but with artists, writers and musicians, and Sybil had had time to work at the piano, and both of them read a great deal—Sybil, in particular, pursuing her studies of Browning. And now, to end this rich chapter, she was able to share with Lewis her enthusiasm for California, the Rockies and British Columbia.

So with much excitement, but also with much mutual regret, Sybil and Lewis parted from their American friends and set sail for England, new work and family life.

"We came back after a year and a month, and of course John didn't know us. He was the most entrancing baby with golden curls. He was really beautiful! He was rather shy, and didn't like me very much. Mother had looked after him so wonderfully, and he had that nice little nurse called Alice, and when he'd been with me for a few minutes he'd say, 'Want Alice'. It was awful!"

The Cassons went to Manchester for Lewis to take up his new job, his first important production being *Twelfth Night*. This was generally acclaimed. "For pure mirthfulness and artistry," said the *Courier*, "it has never been surpassed." Sybil could not, of course, be in the play, but she made an important contribution by suggesting and helping to arrange parts of Beethoven sonatas as incidental music. She felt even then that she was being sacrilegious in turning such great music into dances and frolics—now she cannot tolerate the fashion of using classics as jazz.

They quickly found a pleasant little house near Heaton Park, engaged a cook-general and sent for their furniture and John and Alice. And here in January 1912, when John was two years and three months, Christopher was born. Eileen Thorndike, who had joined the Horniman Company in 1911, was able to be with Sybil at the time of the baby's birth, mercifully not quite such an ordeal as the first. A week later Lewis went off in charge of a contingent of the Gaiety Company with Miss Horniman for a

With the
car, 1928

Saint Joan, 1924

short season in Montreal, leaving Sybil with the children in Manchester. Although she greatly missed him, and was in general bored by domesticity and discontented when she was not working, she was happy to be with her babies.

The Gaiety season in Montreal was a great success. "We are doing a thing," Lewis Casson said in an interview for *Canada*, "which London could not do. There is no single manager in London at the present time who could take eleven plays,* representative of nearly every school of English drama, to the Dominions without months of preparation." The company was warmly invited to extend their visit to the States, but in spite of her desire to spread the gospel Miss Horniman decided against prolonging the tour. Lewis was greatly relieved, as this would have interfered further with his work as a producer, and his whole heart was now in this branch of theatre.

Russell Thorndike, who had been on a world tour with Matheson Lang, now also joined the Gaiety, so at last Sybil had once more the company of her brother, who had so closely shared the experiences of her childhood and early youth.

After six weeks Lewis returned to Manchester with the company, and produced many of the plays in the Gaiety's repertoire. Then in June came Sybil's first part since the birth of Christopher, in *Hindle Wakes* by Stanley Houghton, produced by Lewis. This was not presented in Manchester, but as a Sunday night performance for the Stage Society at the Aldwych Theatre.

The Incorporated Stage Society had been founded in 1899 by a small group of people, including Janet Achurch, Walter Crane and Grant Richards, to present plays of artistic merit by English and continental playwrights that were controversial and had not achieved a commercial production. The Society's reading and advisory committee was distinguished, including Arnold Dol-metsch, J. T. Grein and Mrs Bernard Shaw. Failing permanent premises the founders decided to present plays on Sunday nights in theatres, such as the Royalty, which were prepared to defy convention. The Stage Society was the vanguard for new

* Sir Lewis Casson commented that there cannot have been quite so many plays as this in a six weeks' tour.

drama. It launched Shaw with *You Can Never Tell*, the Society's first production. It also presented Tchekov to London with *The Cherry Orchard*.

Soon after the Stage Society performance, *Hindle Wakes* was put on in Miss Horniman's season at the Coronet, after which it was almost immediately transferred to the Playhouse for a West End run. The play, with its provocative poster, "Should Fanny marry Alan?", caused a great stir. The newspapers carried columns of correspondence, people preached inside and outside the pulpit about its immorality, London rushed to see it, and the Vice-Chancellor of Oxford University declared it out of bounds.

Edyth Goodall gave a remarkable performance as Fanny, the Lancashire mill-girl who for a lark goes off for the week-end with her employer's son, and then, when he unwillingly offers to marry her, turns him down. Sybil played Alan's fiancée, Beatrice, the daughter of a wealthy, self-made man, "a determined, straightforward girl of about twenty-three". She only appears in the last act, but it is a good scene and Sybil made the most of Beatrice, who insists that, in spite of Alan's and her real love for one another, he should sacrifice their happiness and marry Fanny.

Another important production of Lewis's this season was George Calderon's *Revolt*, in which Sybil had a sympathatic part as Renie Dalrymple. The chief interest of this play now, Lewis pointed out, is its prophetic presentation of the splitting of the atom. Shortly after this Sybil had a highly emotional part in Eden Phillpotts' play *The Shadow*, playing opposite the Cassons' old friend Jules Shaw. *The Shadow* is a strong and moving drama, with a good spice of humour, set in a village shop on Dartmoor, where Eden Phillpotts lived, and to which he was devoted.

He became a great friend of the Cassons. He had many qualities that appealed to them. Born in India, on Mount Abu, "The Hill of Wisdom", he was always influenced by the religion of the Jains and their aspiration toward purity in thought, word and deed. He was also versed in western philosophy—he was, in fact, what Sybil always reveres, an explorer. In addition to this he loved music and the theatre. His first ambition had been to go on the stage. After a little training and a few performances he came to the conclusion that he was no actor, but remained always an impassioned observer and developed into an excellent play-wright.

In his memoirs* he gives portraits of many of the leading figures in literature and the theatre whom he met in his "brief itinerary", among them Miss Horniman, whom he considers "should be better remembered and honoured for her generous devotion than appears to be the case".

"She was most fortunate in having Lewis Casson as her producer and Sybil Thorndike for leading lady . . . Not only had I the privilege of their combined talents when at Man-chester, but won the friendship of those brilliant young people. Though the dark skies and tremendous roar and bustle of that enormous city somewhat overwhelmed me, my welcome was better than sunshine, and with their triumphs yet to come, their impression upon the history of the theatre yet to be made, the Cassons had already created a sweet atmosphere around them . . .

"One memory clings to my mind from Manchester: the wondrous versatility of Sybil Thorndike. Even as a girl, for she was little more at that time, I marked her rare sense of humour in a comic part she was just then playing at night, and watched her rehearsing by day a stricken heroine with every apt and poignant emotion, mien and gesture, even to the expression on her face and the woe in her voice. Comedy and tragedy are alike to her and always were, for she has that protean gift to lose herself in any character, having grasped its intrinsic nature."

After *The Shadow* Sybil played the name part in the cockney classic *Jane Clegg* by St John Ervine, another role that affected her deeply. This time she was a tall dark woman, "living with her mother-in-law, her two children and her 'absolute rotter' of a commercial-traveller husband", who finally drives her past all possibility of love or forgiveness. The part of Jane Clegg needed

* Eden Phillpotts: *From the Angle of 88* (Hutchinson, 1951).

sterness and reserve, and Sybil, helped as always by Lewis, veiled her brightness and played the part well.

All these plays were repeated in a Horniman Season at the Court Theatre in the autumn of 1913, and now the critics began to prophesy a great future for Sybil.

And so their happy life in the theatre and at home in Manchester went on. The last play Lewis directed for Miss Horniman was *Julius Caesar*, an experimental and exciting production in which he himself played Brutus. He presented the full text, achieving unusual speed both in action and speech and, influenced by Gordon Craig's designs, used an apron stage, arches, pillars and steps, and revolutionary lighting from the front. The innovations of this brilliant son of Ellen Terry were bound to impress any producer as intelligent and adventurous as Casson. Practically all Craig's work was presented abroad, so Lewis had not actually seen any of his productions. But, besides starting the avant-garde theatre journal *The Mask* under a pseudonym, Gordon Craig had recently published his book on *The Art of the Theatre*, illustrated with his stage designs.

"To Craig, designing a production meant everything from scenery, costumes and props to lighting and movement . . . The imaginative quality of his designs will remain an almost spiritual stimulus to young artists in the theatre, and among his writings are passages that will always encourage them, for his ideas were big, he had great courage in pursuing them, and his mind raced years ahead of his time."*

Casson had the same approach as Craig to a production—it meant everything, with the addition in Casson's case of a tremendously strong feeling for the words of the play, and a preoccupation with the voices of the actors.

Most of the critics welcomed this somewhat revolutionary *Julius Caesar*—"C. E. Montague . . . indeed, greeted the production with something like a whoop of joy"†—but there were

---

* Edward Craig: *Gordon Craig* (Victor Gollancz, 1968).

† Rex Pogson: *Miss Horniman and the Gaiety Theatre* (Rockliff Publishing Corporation, 1952).

dissentients among the traditionalists, and chief of these was Miss Horniman herself. Gordon Craig's ideas were anathema to her, but although she had as usual attended the rehearsals she did not say a word of opprobrium until after the first performance, when she angrily complained to Casson that his production was "freakish". He was equally angry—apart from himself, any denigration of Gordon Craig made him furious—and to add to this contretemps the houses were less full than usual and the play lost money. In consequence, Miss Horniman cancelled the proposed production of *The Tempest* which Lewis had hoped to present in a similar manner, and late in 1913 he felt compelled to tender his resignation.

"So," to quote Sybil once more, "as I was in the family way again we thought we'd go back to London. Mother had a house. She was always buying houses and cottages. She ought to have been a business woman—and on the stage. She bought houses all over the shop. This one was in Bessborough Street, near Vauxhall Bridge—in Father's parish—and Mother had let the top floor off to an aunt of mine and we had the rest of the house."

Before they were properly settled in, however, Lewis had a new temporary appointment—as director of the first Glasgow Repertory, doing extremely interesting work, and with an excellent company which included Nicholas Hannen, Beatrice Smith and a number of other first-class actors—so he was only able to rush down on midnight trains to be with his family for brief week-ends.

While waiting for the baby Sybil learnt a number of new parts and practised Bach for hours each day, besides, of course, spending a great deal of time playing with her small sons. Christopher, she says, was always "a rather worried little boy", and she had to invent ways of keeping him happy.

On May 28th 1914 Mary was born—her parents both enchanted to find themselves with a daughter. Lewis's engagement in Glasgow had finally come to an end, so he was able to be with

Sybil and help her during the birth, which took place before the nurse arrived. When Sybil could move she and Lewis went down to Dymchurch on the coast in Kent, where John and Christopher had already been sent, with the faithful Alice in charge, to a cottage which Mrs Thorndike owned there. They found two exquisite little boys, golden all over from their fair hair to their toes. Russell, who was writing *Dr. Syn*, his novel about Romney Marsh which was to become famous, was living in the lifeboat house close by, so, when Lewis went back to London to do a number of productions, Sybil still had her brother's company. Lewis came down to Dymchurch whenever he could, and they all had a very good time bathing and teaching the little boys to swim, besides riding in Lewis's precious Ford "Hindle Wakes", which he was never tired of driving at top speed, or of "improving" with all kinds of innovations.

"So began the journey away from childhood and youth [wrote Richard Church in *The Voyage Home**], about which every individual has a unique story to tell, of fabulous adventure in a dew-glittering world, every detail outlined by a light which gives it an illusory permanence.

"People like to hear that story, repeated again and again . . . But who wants to hear of the gradual slowing-down and subsidence of early raptures, as the individual falls into step with the rest of the breadwinners, worthy but indistinct, for the remainder of his life? . . .

"The only persons to escape this hardening of the arteries of the spirit are those who remain young, naïve, innocent, while maturing physically and mentally. They are 'the movers and shakers of the world forever, it seems'. They are the only people whose middle and late careers continue to reflect the sunrise, that under-lighting glory of wonder and novelty which alone makes life worth while, and also the story about it."

What words could describe Sybil Thorndike and Lewis Casson more beautifully, or be more inspiring to the teller of the story?

* William Heinemann, 1964.

CHAPTER VII

THEATRE OF WAR

(*1914–1917*)

THE CASSONS WERE full of schemes for a season in London under their own management, if they could raise the funds. Then, one day towards the end of July 1914, Lewis came down to Dymchurch and said, "I'm afraid there's going to be a war". On August 2nd, two days before war was declared, they moved back to London.

Russell had already joined the Westminster Dragoons and so was called up, and when Frank, who was playing in *Mr Wu* with Matheson Lang, heard that the regiment was under orders for Egypt, determined not to miss such an exciting experience he went off without a word to the family, and joined his brother in this "posh" regiment under the command of Lord Howard de Walden. By good fortune the regiment's headquarters were in Vincent Square, Westminster, so Sybil was able to take the little boys round to gaze through the railings at their uncles at their drill, and the girls of the parish provided the soldiers with hot pies and coffee during the long night watches. But soon Lewis was driving Sybil and her father and the boys down to Russell's and Frank's port of sailing.

"Shortly after this—in mid-August—he came into the house with a set face and said, 'Put the children in the pram and come out with me'. So with Christopher and Mary in the pram and John trotting beside us, we went for a walk down the Vauxhall Bridge Road. 'I've got to be in this, you know,' Lewis said. 'It's the biggest thing that's happened in our lives—

one can't stand apart—it will be a war to finish war for ever. I do believe this, so now what about it?'

"Very soon I saw there was no choice, so we went round to the vicarage to tell Father and Mother, and they said, 'We'll see Sybil and the children are all right. You've got to do it,' and Father, a real soldier at heart, of a soldier family, wondered if he couldn't possibly enlist too. But Mother said, 'What nonsense, you're far too old!'"

And indeed Arthur Thorndike was well over age even for a chaplain—he was now in his sixties—while Lewis, who was thirty-nine, had to take a few years off his age in order to enlist in the Army Service Corps.

Sybil was not then, as she was later to become, a pacifist, although she did hate the idea of being at war with the country that had produced all the composers whose music she so much loved and with whose people she had had such warm friendships. But like everyone else she had to be in it, so she let John and little Christopher dress up as soldiers, and played *Tipperary* and the *British Grenadiers* on the piano, "with lumps in our throats and firm resolution in our hearts", as the troops kept marching past their windows over Vauxhall Bridge.

"Lewis was posted to St Albans, and a week after he had gone John went down with scarlet fever. I had quickly to wean Mary and send her and Christopher with Alice to the vicarage, and shut myself up with John for seven weeks. I slept in the room with him and we had carbolic sheets outside the door, and I took up the carpets and scrubbed the floor every morning. There was a dear woman who lived in the basement and cooked for us, which was lovely, but I did everything else. She and her children had all had scarlet fever, so she didn't mind, and she listened for John when I went out for a walk in the evening. John wasn't a bit ill, but there we had to be, shut up, you see, so we just had the most enormous games. I remember endlessly pretending to be a leopard. And I used to work at my Greek plays, John listening very carefully and hearing me my parts.

I also played the piano a lot and gave John his piano lessons, and of course he acted too—all our children acted from the time they could walk."

This is how John Casson later described those weeks to his Uncle Russell:

"Mummy used to get up very early and make a cup of tea, then put on what she called her party frock—a dreadful overall —her hair done up in a turban and rubber gloves which she used for scrubbing the floor over with carbolic, pushing me and the bed all over the room and pretending all sorts of absurd things. We used to get quite weak with giggles, and she read me tons of books, and we built glorious towns and villages with bricks, and Grandpapa used to come in every day, because he said priests and doctors never took infection. Mummy nearly killed me with laughing when she studied Medea. She would say one silly sentence for hours in different voices to get it right. There's one sentence now that I can never hear in *Medea* without bursting into a guffaw. 'But oh, not here the end is.' I used to wonder where the Indies had gone to and why she pronounced them Endies. When it got dark Mummy would go out for a walk while Grandpapa read to me, and she would come back with all sorts of tales about searchlights and the troops she'd seen, and I always hoped she'd see a Zeppelin; but that year there wasn't one."

"It was on my thirty-second birthday, October 24th 1914," Sybil said, "that John and I were set free, and four days later, on his fifth birthday, I took him for his first outing on the top of a horse bus and we went up round St Paul's Cathedral."

A few days later Sybil took the three children down to Dymchurch for a brief holiday, and there she got a letter from Ben Greet which settled her war-work for her.*

"There's a strange woman running a theatre in the Waterloo

* Sybil and Russell Thorndike: *Lilian Baylis* (Chapman Hall, 1938).

Road, you'd find her exciting, Syb, because you're as mad as she is. I'm doing some shows for her with Estelle Stead, so come and join us. *Comedy of Errors* week after next—you play Adriana; I've told them you'd be wonderful, though I don't think you'll really be very good. You always bounce too much —you'd be better as one of the Dromios, or our old pal Luce— still, you'll like Lilian Baylis, she's got ideals, and don't go telling her you've not played the part before because she says she wants the best and she's going to get it. God bless you, old Syb, your old friend B.G."

Ten days later Sybil moved the children back to London.

"Those two dear girls, Alice and Nellie—they were both little girls in my father's parish at Aylesford, and they used to say, 'When you are married, Miss Sybil, may we come and live with you?' And I always said, 'Yes', and now here they were, dear village girls, and they did everything. Oh, they were my dearest friends! I couldn't have lived through that war without them."

And so, one morning in October 1914, Sybil "careered off" to the Royal Victoria Coffee Music Hall, affectionately known as the Old Vic. Once highly disreputable, it had been taken over in the eighties by Emma Cons, one of a band of women doing social work at that time, with the aim of providing for "the work- ing and middle classes recreation such as the music hall affords, without the existing attendant moral and social disadvantages". In 1895 Miss Cons's niece, Lilian Baylis, came to help her aunt in the theatre, and three years later Miss Cons appointed her manager. She kept up her aunt's social work too, encouraging members of the company to go with her on her errands of mercy. Later Sybil was to be a faithful follower in this field. Elizabeth Casson, Lewis's sister, was another of Miss Cons's helpers, acting as a rent collector. She had previously done this work for Octavia Hill, the social reformer, who as far as possible collected the rents herself for the houses she sponsored for the poor, in order to have contact with the tenants.

Emma Cons had died in 1912, and soon afterwards the famous actress and teacher, Rosina Filippi, a distant relative of the Duse's "on the wrong side of the blanket", obtained permission to use the theatre for one night a week. In some desperation about making ends meet, Lilian Baylis allowed her to try the experiment of bringing Shakespeare to the people, with little idea that this was the beginning of one of the Old Vic's greatest claims to fame. This innovation was important to the Thorndikes in a more personal way, too, for in the last year of the war Russell married one of her twin daughters.

Rosina Filippi's season at the Old Vic did not last long—she and Lilian Baylis admired one another, but were perhaps both too domineering for a lasting partnership—and the next people to put on Shakespeare plays for Miss Baylis were Matheson Lang and his wife Hutin Britton. Now came West End scenery and costumes, which gave the audience a new vision of Shakespeare.

Before long the Matheson Langs left to fulfil other engagements, and their place was taken by Ben Greet.

Sybil wrote now to Russell and Frank, who were in Egypt:

"The morning I turned up for my first rehearsal at the Old Vic will always be a memorable one for me, because it was my first meeting with Lilian. Sitting on the dark, rather grubby stage—not depressing, no, not ever—the smell of sawdust was in the nostrils—the symbolic hoops of paper were there somewhere . . . sitting in the dark, I heard a voice, roughened—a bit cockney—warm, calling out, 'Bob, come here, you old devil, I won't have all this muck on my stage'. Symbolic again. Clear away the rubbish—she spent years clearing and making fresh. Then she spied me, and I was hailed in friendly fashion. Funny, I don't know what she said to me first, as I was a bit taken aback by the coming-on-sweep of her, but I remember, 'Well, you won't get much pay, but you like the work, don't you, and if your husband's in the army you'd better be doing decent work too—good for you *and* the children'. Then, 'Your father's a priest, isn't he? Church and stage—same thing—should be!' The sort of twist in the mouth that we all know so

well, and which everyone imitates when repeating her
characteristic and priceless remarks, this was the feature that
stuck in my mind—kind and sharp—humorous and scolding—
infinitely friendly—she never changed.

"Up to rehearsal room—now I knew where I was—daily
bread, rehearsal. I sneaked in and sat on a chair in a corner . . ."

Estelle Stead, daughter of W. T. Stead, the famous editor of
the *Review of Reviews*, had put money into the Old Vic, and
was now helping Lilian Baylis and playing leading parts. She
and Sybil became great friends. "Estelle Stead was one of the
most truly good people I have ever met. A darling woman."

"Then Ben Greet nabbed me and made me feel a fool, as
he always did, purposely, from the beginning to the end of our
loving friendship. 'Here's old Syb,' and then such remarks!
Andrew Leigh told me a few weeks later when we'd become
friends what a disappointment I was. B.G. had given them the
impression that I was a very strong Constance Collier-looking
leading woman. Oh dear! And I know I looked a sight."

Another young woman, who was to become a life-long friend
of Sybil's from the day of her arrival at the Old Vic, was the
actress Nora Nicholson, who had preceded her there by a few
weeks. Here is Nora Nicholson's description of that day:

"An autumn morning and some of us hanging about in the
stalls, discussing the new member of the cast, due to arrive at
any minute. The prospect of a newcomer was usually a source
of apprehension, particularly among those of us who had only
recently joined. I was desperately in love with the part of
Ariel, and just as desperately conscious that Ben Greet considered me skinny and far from an ideal soprano. Would the
newcomer be better covered and able to master *Where the
Bee Sucks* with the greatest of ease?

"And then she arrived: rather breathless, rather wind-
blown, and bringing with her a sense of good health, good

humour, and above all *goodness*. I felt this lovely quality of goodness at first sight, and I have felt it ever since. It has been a joy
each time I have been in a play with her—hard-working, happy
and full of fun, that's how it always is with Sybil."

"That first season when I was at the Old Vic was a pretty
hard time," Sybil says herself. "When I think of the Old Vic
now—the space and the comfort—I wonder how we got the
shows on at all. Four or five shows a week—at ten bob a show—
but that was a considerable help to my soldier's separation
allowance.

"Good troopers we had to be at the Old Vic, for Lilian was
a trooper and B.G. was a trooper. Did we mind washing out of
one basin—all us female actors? Five minutes before the curtain
went up 'Pretty Sweeting', the darling old dresser who managed
us all, brought round a tin basin, and that had to do us all for
the evening—no being fussy and wanting clean water . . .
Why be fussy about washing? There's more to actor's work
than luxury. The 'Peace and Plenty' meals of cocoa-butter-
tasting buns and coffee at the juicy eating-house at the back of
the pit seemed most delectable to us, although there were occasions when Lilian—no more comfort did she have than we—
shared a sumptuous steak, cooked on a gas ring in the prompt
corner, almost on the stage, with whichever actor she thought
looked most starved."

The company did a large number of Shakespeare plays, and
then, in January 1915, Lilian Baylis asked Sybil if she would like
to play Lady Macbeth with Fisher White as Macbeth. Naturally
she was thrilled, especially as Lilian Baylis was one with her in
seeing Lady Macbeth as an understandable human being, a
woman who loved her husband and was ambitious for him.

"I expect you feel that way too," Lilian Baylis said to Sybil,
"and if it wasn't that you go to Communion I daresay you'd
do all sorts of wicked things to help Lewis. I don't know why
you all make such a fuss about these great parts, I think they're
all just human beings."

Ben Greet did not agree with the views of Lilian Baylis and Sybil about Lady Macbeth. To him, she and Gertrude in Hamlet were fiends.

"Don't let me have any of this silly modern stuff," he said, "and don't let Lewis make you see things crooked—she's straightforward wicked!"

Sybil and Ben Greet had many arguments during rehearsals. Among other things he wanted her to wake during the sleepwalking scene, but this Sybil fought against, and after the third performance he gave in. "It was theatrically effective, her waking up, but it was wrong."

"Played Lady Macbeth last night," Sybil wrote to Russell. "Don't laugh. I was too appalling. The critics that I read all said I was unsuited to tragedy as my voice is too light and my features too small. That's rather depressing, isn't it? Never mind, something's got to be done about it, and I mean to jolly well swot until they do think me suitable. Tragedy is awfully difficult, I think, because it's so much larger than real life. I suppose real comedy is too, but one can enjoy quite small performances of comedy, but tragedy is either tragic, with a big T, or it's nothing. If it's pathetic, it's awful. I simply loathe pathos, Russ, it's so soft and weak. Tragedy has fight. I love Lady Macbeth, though my performance, so far, is nothing like her. I love people like that, all granity and iron, who fight on to the last inch, and even when something bigger than them smashes them, they still want to fight. I don't think they're very sympathetic people, unless of course they are funny like Richard the Third. They're inhuman to most of mankind. Unchristian too, I suppose. And yet I don't know, I'm beginning to think that there's something else in Christianity. Not what we've always thought. Something more like Hecuba and Prometheus and that gang. Perhaps it should be called Anti-Church. Tragedy isn't very churchy. Lewis goes to France week after next, so I'm thankful I'm doing tragedy, as it will relieve my feelings."

One night during the run of *Macbeth* a slight mishap occurred

—Fisher White, as Macbeth, had his head badly cut in the fight with Will Stack as Macduff. There is a tradition in the theatre that *Macbeth* is never produced without a disaster, and when, much later, Sybil and Lewis were doing a production with Bronson Albery, Henry Ainley playing Macbeth, such terrible things kept on happening that one night Lewis came into her dressing room and said, "Sybil, the Devil does work in this play—there is horror behind it—we must do something positive against it". And together they read aloud the 91st Psalm, which calmed and strengthened them.

During this production, however, far from anything disastrous happening to Sybil, Lewis came home on leave at the end of January before going to France, "and of course Lady Macbeth did it. Family way again." Each time, in spite of all her other enthusiasms, this event was a joy to Sybil.

She went on playing many Shakespeare parts until well into the spring, her parents coming to see each production. Performances of *Everyman* were given during Lent, vividly reminding Sybil, who played the name part, of the performance in Santa Barbara when the monks from the Spanish Mission laughed so heartily at the presentation of Death.

The Old Vic audiences were building up all the time. Children from schools were beginning to attend, and at several performances the gratifying notice "Standing Room Only" was seen outside the theatre, although this did not mean that the Old Vic was making a profit, as the prices charged were very low.

Presently it was time for Sybil to stop acting.

"So I take my three children and my unborn one and we go down to the cottage at Dymchurch, and there we lead a perfect existence except for the never-ceasing sound of the guns coming across the Channel; and Lilian wanted me back after the baby was born, and there were parts to study, and Lewis came home for his first few days' leave that August— and how thrilling to tell him face to face of all the happenings in our theatre. I wrote to him every day, and he wrote to me every day during the war, but face to face was better telling."

In the autumn, when they were back in London, came the first Zeppelin raid. Sybil took the excited children down to the cellar, John, now nearly six, begging nobody to speak so that he could hear the bombs, and Sybil herself watching from a window "the beautiful long ship passing over London—silver in the searchlight". When the all clear sounded her father came round to see how they were, himself overcome with wonder at the war in the air. He could not stay indoors when there was a raid on. "There was war in Heaven, Michael and his angels . . ." he would quote, and go out to watch.

Mother Dondon did not think it right for the children to be in London during the raids, so she took another cottage, a small one twenty miles away at Kingsdown in Kent, and there Sybil established the children with Alice and Nellie.

"They were wonderful. John was a great help to me always. I remember one day when Ann was on the way, at breakfast I put my head down in my hands and was groaning, and John looked up at me and said, 'Well, of course you don't feel well if you *will* go on believing in bad fairies.' "

Presently Sybil left her little family with her "two dear girls" and returned to wait for the new baby at the vicarage. Ann was born on November 6th, a little late.

"The morning after Lilian Baylis walked into my room. 'Well, when can you start *Hamlet*?' she demanded."

Before the month was out, Sybil was back at the Old Vic rehearsing Ophelia with Will Stack as Hamlet, Robert Atkins as the King and Beatrice Wilson as Gertrude.

Although it was exciting to be playing Ophelia and the other parts, this was "a very tiring and trying time". Not only were conditions at the Old Vic scarcely tolerable—"I dressed with Beatrice in a two-foot room, about twice the size of a telephone booth"—but rushing backwards and forwards to the vicarage to feed Ann and down to the cottage to see the other children on Sundays—"a five mile walk from the station, with no conveyance even if I could have afforded one"—was extremely exhausting. On top of this there was the endless anxiety about Lewis and her brothers. Lewis had leave in the spring of 1916, and then returned to France with a commission in the Royal Engineers.

Frank arrived home from Gallipoli, but the moment he had sufficiently recovered from dysentery and other disorders, he enlisted in the Air Force and was sent off again—though not before playing the part of Young Siward in *Macbeth* at the Old Vic—while Russell, wounded and with a dislocated spine, "bent double and looking like an old man", was invalided out of the army, and as soon as he was well enough to walk joined Sybil at the Old Vic. That summer they did a season at Stratford-upon-Avon, where Sybil played Perdita to Nancy Price's Hermione, and to solve a crisis caused by the overlapping of managements they took the part of Lady Macbeth on alternate nights. Thus yet another lasting friendship began.

"I find, looking back, that Lilian Baylis has given me some of my greatest friends. Through her and the Old Vic I found and still keep friendships most precious and lovely."

Father Andrew of the Order of the Divine Compassion, who was Lilian Baylis's spiritual adviser, compared her to St Teresa of Avila, one of Sybil Thorndike's "breakers of the mould", whom later she was to portray. "Her hatred of humbug and her direct approach to God were very reminiscent of the Spanish saint," he said, "though in all probability she had never read her life." The same might be said of Miss Baylis's approach to Shakespeare. It is doubtful if she had read many of the plays, and she seldom sat through a rehearsal or a whole performance, but somehow she "got" him.

There was a shortage of young men now in all the theatres, and the women had to play many men's parts.

"I frankly loved it. I've always been jealous of the men in Shakespeare—for every good woman's part there are ten good men's. In fact, except for Lewis and the children I would so much rather have been a man. For one thing, I prefer men's parts—Macbeth to Lady Macbeth, for instance. Now I had Prince Hal and Ferdinand—I enjoyed him awfully—and best of the lot the Fool of all fools in *Lear*. Oh, and the Chorus in *Henry V*—that was simply marvellous. I played Katharine at the same time, delicious doing that French girl trying to speak English. Naturally I enjoyed the women's parts too—Imogen, so gallant, and the comedy so lovely, getting a laugh each time on, 'I see a man's life is a tedious one . . .'

"And Rosalind—I played her better then than later when I tried experiments and made her too *gamine*. Julia in *The Two Gents* I enjoyed, and Viola—lovely girls, very much alike. I suppose Viola was my favourite. And Queen Margaret in *Richard III*, such wonderful tearing speeches, and then of course Ophelia. Portia too, but the audience never likes Portia very much, less than any of the other Shakespearean heroines.

"After I'd played the Fool in *Lear* I went and sat in a box with Lewis and Granville Barker, and he hadn't recognised me."

It was a chance observation of Lilian Baylis's at a rehearsal, that Sybil looked rather like Russell's shadow—he was playing Lear—that determined her to play the part this way.

"I made the Fool look like an egg—blank—no eyebrows, nothing but the shape of a face that could reflect Lear's moods."

On the first night of *King Lear* Waterloo Station was bombed. They carried on with the performance under the racket of gunfire and the dropping bombs, and just as Russell Thorndike reached the splendid speech beginning, "Blow winds, and crack your cheeks! rage, blow", there was a tremendous explosion and the whole theatre shook. Russell strode down-stage with Sybil at his heels, shook his fist at the roof and shouted, "Crack Nature's moulds, all GERMANS spill at once."* The applause of the

* "All germens spill at once . . ."

audience at the aptness of the misquotation almost drowned the sound of the guns.

Sybil's voice was now giving her trouble, which, because of the earlier crisis, somewhat alarmed her. From France Lewis wrote to Elsie Fogerty, begging her to go and see Sybil at the Old Vic, which she at once did. She found that Sybil was using her voice in a way that threatened its music, so that it was getting hard and ragged. She immediately went to work on it.

"It was just after I married Lewis that I first met Elsie Fogerty. Lewis had talked and argued voice and phrasing at me ever since I had met him a few months before, and he invariably finished the session by saying, 'Well, you'd better see Elsie Fogerty: she'll put all your troubles right'. I remember her meeting us at the station in London. She froze me by saying, 'You're a lucky girl to have married Lewis Casson—it's the best voice on the stage—the. purest production—and I hope you are worthy of it.' So inhuman, so objective, I felt—I wasn't married to a man but to a vocal production! However, something more human came to light as we drove off in a cab, and talked voice and politics all the way; she and Lewis differed widely about politics, which relieved me somewhat; but her personality did get hold of me in that cab—and never really left me.

"Several times in my career I have had a spot of vocal trouble, and gone at once to Elsie Fogerty to have it put right. She taught me how to work through a voice weakness—how to save it and increase its power while it was mending. She's the only teacher I've ever known who could make one's own quality develop. Her exercises have been the saving of many voices in the theatre. I have found that if one can spend a little while daily on her breathing and vocalising studies one can keep in trim through the hardest work. I have never ceased to be grateful for her vocal help, but more grateful still for the way she encouraged one to research personally into vocal problems—to seek for oneself, not merely accept a cure."

And 'Fogie', as many of Elsie Fogerty's devotees called her, said of the Cassons:

"Sybil came often, when time served, to work at a voice rather inclined to escape her control. She has never in all her life tried to do less than three things at once, always succeeding in at least two of them! As time went on, I realised more and and more that she and Lewis were the people we needed in the theatre—people for whom acting is a real career, a profession to be followed for its own great sake in bad times and in good; not a craze or a means of notoriety . . . I have still a lovely memory of the sound of Lewis's voice speaking the lines of the awakened Love in the first production of *Prunella*, back in 1905."*

Elsie Fogerty was another of the remarkable people who contributed greatly to the creation of twentieth century theatre, as much a pioneer in the realm of speech as Gordon Craig was in the realm of stage design. Like Sybil, she acted her way through childhood—she never played at any game but acting—but to help her family she sacrificed her desire for a stage career and took to teaching. She aimed at raising speech and drama to university level and making the theatre an honoured profession. She was also interested in anyone who had speech defects, such as a stammer—she was, in fact, one of the creators of speech therapy as we know it today.

She joined William Poel's Elizabethan Stage Society, sometimes acting for him, and always supporting him in the emphasis, speed and rhythm of speech which he insisted on in his Shakespeare productions. She developed a passion for Greek drama, and founded the Central School of Speech-Training and Dramatic Art, largely to provide Sir Frank Benson with well-trained actors for his Stratford company. Later she was to train many more of our leading actors, including Laurence Olivier and Peggy Ashcroft, who was one of her favourite students.

It would be difficult to imagine anybody whose tastes and talents would appeal more strongly to Lewis and Sybil, and she "remained an important influence always in the Casson-Thorndike careers. Of Sybil she said that she had never had a more perfect

* Marion Cole: *Fogie, The Life of Elsie Fogerty*, C.B.E. (Peter Davies, 1967).

pupil—'You only had to show her a thing to get it done'."*
Russell Thorndike adds:

"If Sybil's voice is praised it is because she still continues to
work at it like any young student. No one can afford to drop
the continual practice of his technique."†

Hamlet soon came on again, this time with Russell as Hamlet
and Sybil playing Gertrude, and, as Lewis was home on leave
for a few days, he was roped in for Fortinbras. The whole play
was given with a twenty-minute break for eating and relaxation.
Little John Casson was allowed to watch. Miss Baylis sat him on a
stair in the dress circle, and he refused to leave it during the
interval in case someone else should bag his place. So Miss Baylis
took him a "Peace and Plenty" bun and Ben Greet sent him a
packet of chocolate, both touched by such devotion.

"Lucky little boy," Sybil comments, "to be able at that age
to be so thrilled with *Hamlet* as to forget his meals. Lucky everyone who is able to be thrilled by *Hamlet* so as to forget themselves."

At Christmas time, with a little difficulty, the Thorndikes
persuaded Miss Baylis to let them put on a burlesque, *The
Sausage String's Romance* or *A New Cut Harlequinade*. Russell and
Geoffrey Wilkinson wrote the words and Sybil wrote the music
and played Columbine, and was able to clown to her heart's
content, a gift she has always had to the full.

In June 1917 Lewis was wounded at Arras, though mercifully
not very seriously—his brother Will had been killed in the Battle
of Loos—and after a short time in a French hospital he came home
and was awarded the Military Cross for gallantry under heavy
fire. He was now a major and, his chemical training having been
discovered, had been used in the preparation of gas missiles,
for which he had invented some mechanism. The memory of this
invention weighed on his mind, and contributed to his depression in the years after the war.

* Fogie.   † *Sybil Thorndike.*

He now began to work for Basil Dean, producing for the army camp theatres. It was by a merciful act of providence that he had come home then and was able to be near Sybil during the tragedies that occurred before the end of 1917, although he was not actually with her when the fateful news came on August 17th that Frank had been killed. He was just twenty-three. He had enjoyed every moment of his time in France, telling the family in his letters that flying was so exciting you couldn't care what happened to you. On his last leave, visiting the parish war memorial at St James the Less with Sybil and Russell, he had said, "I've been on every list in the parish—and sure as anything I'll be on that Roll of Honour—but if any of you starts being melancholy about me or wearing black I'll just haunt you all and make your lives a nightmare."

Try as they would, however, they could not but grieve for their beloved Frank.

"I adored him. He was twelve years younger than me, but he was my belonging, somehow. I taught him the piano—having terrible rows with him and pushing him off the piano stool because I loathed teaching so. He used to come to the Guildhall School of Music with me, and I played the 'cello with him and he was a little tiny boy and he was my great pal.

"Oh, the night they came and told me about Frank! Mother was in such a state, and Father said to me, 'Sybil, you will have to play the service tonight, Mother can't'. I wasn't an organist, but I did the whole service on the organ. And Father was too upset to preach."

Frank was buried in France, near Arras, but under his name on the family grave at Aylesford—"Frank Thorndike, Actor and Airman"—are inscribed the beautiful words said of Young Siward, after he was slain in fight with Macbeth, the part Frank had so recently played:

> He paid a soldier's debt:
> He only lived but till he was a man;

The which no sooner had his prowess confirmed
In the unshrinking station where he fought,
But like a man he died . . .
Why, then, God's soldier be he!

Arthur Thorndike bore his sorrow gallantly, insisting that it was a glorious thing to die for England. For Frank's memorial service the chancel was decorated as for a festival, and the music Canon Thorndike chose for it was triumphant. But his heart was broken. On Sunday, December 9th, he sang the vestry prayer before Evensong in magnificent voice and, as the choir came in with their amen, he fell down dead.

CHAPTER VIII

WEST END STORY
(1917–1920)

LEWIS WAS IN Cornwall, preparing to go back to France, when Canon Thorndike died, and he came home on compassionate leave. Ben Greet and Lilian Baylis both felt deep sympathy with the Thorndikes for the loss of their father, who was a well-known figure at the Old Vic, as excited by the plays as any of the young regulars. Sybil and Russell were asked if they would prefer their new Christmas revue to be postponed, but they were certain that both their father and Frank would have wanted the show to go on. One item was a skit on Ibsen's *Ghosts*, called *Spooks*, which Sybil and Russell performed in an invented language and made highly tragic and ridiculous. Hearing about it, C. B. Cochran sent his manager down to see the show, and the next day Cochran asked Sybil to come and see him.

"I was feeling very miserable, and I went up in the black coat and skirt I'd had for Father's funeral—we had to wear mourning in those days—looking like last week's governess, and the man who had seen the show was there with Cochran. He stared at me and said, 'Are you the girl who played in *Spooks* last night?' And I said, 'Yes, that was me.' Then Cochran said in a very kindly way, 'Oh well, I hope there will be something for you one day.' And that was that. A little later I was playing Lady Teazle, and Cochran himself was in front this time with Seymour Hicks. They came round afterwards and the next day Cochran, who was just beginning his London Pavilion productions, offered me a contract. I talked it over with Lilian Baylis, and she said she thought I'd better do it. 'You've had just on four years with us, dear, and done all the big parts, and now it's time for something in the West End.' [Sybil had in fact played every Shakespeare role she hankered after, except Hamlet.]

"So, in March 1918, I went to the Pavilion in support of Léon Morton, the French clown, who had come over with Delysia. He was a real little *gamin*. Vulgar wasn't the word for it. He was wonderful. I liked him tremendously. He couldn't speak any English, and every night he came on with a piece of fruit in a different part of his anatomy—to break me up. I don't think the audience saw, but you can imagine what fruits he could use. It was absolutely awful. I thought he was a love."

After six weeks Cochran asked her to go into his "fragment from France", *The Better 'Ole*, at the New Oxford Theatre in London, to play in *The Kiddies in the Ruins*, a war-time sketch adapted from the French of Paul Gsell and Francisque Poulbot.

"I really had the time of my life at the Oxford with Cochran. He put me in a dressing-room with the oddest collection of girls—six of us to a room. I didn't know about their kind of lives before. I think he did it on purpose to break me down—from the Old Vic and the vicarage. They were a lot of comics. I adored them, and so did Mother—she was quite unshockable. We had a wonderful dresser called May who was always reading love-stories. 'I can't change yer now, dear,' she'd say, ''cos I've just got to the exciting part. Ow, it's lovely. It's just where the Dook sedooces 'er. Ask one of the other girls to change you.' And I remember one day Gladys Ffolliott came in—she was the oldest in the room, a real bawdy old Irish woman and a very good actress. She used to bring three or four dogs into the dressing-room with her every night—with all us girls. And that night she came in and said, 'Girls, I've got a wonderful piece of tripe—I got it for 3/2d.' And she opened the packet and the smell almost knocked us out. 'Bad,

hell!' she said, and threw it out of the window. There was a
scream and an awful row outside—it had gone plonk on somebody's hat. Then there was a knock at the door and Gladys
said, 'Stick in with me, girls, stick in with me', and in came the
stage manager. 'They say a parcel of tripe was thrown out of the
window from this room,' he said. And we all said in voices of
astonishment, 'Tripe? From our window?' And May said,
'I don't know 'ow you 'ave the sauce to come and say that to
my young lidies in 'ere. Tripe? As if we'd demean ourselves!'

"It was during my time with Cochran that I first met Edith
Evans, although I had first seen her on the stage years before,
in a play by Gwen John. I had gone home then and said to Lewis,
'I've seen the most wonderful actress. She's not what ordinary
people call beautiful, but she's absolutely marvellous.'"

Sybil remembers being thrilled by Edith Evans coming to
see her at the Pavilion, and then walking back with her to the
little house in Westminster and talking for a long time. Dame
Edith does not remember this particular occasion, but then, as
she herself says, she lives so entirely in the present that she is not
one for memories. On the other hand she does recollect the
Cassons' little house and the children when they were small,
even to John riding his first bicycle, and one of the girls having
her first eiderdown for a birthday present.

"From the beginning," Dame Edith says, "Sybil has been a
great beauty, with that fine bony structure and those exquisite
features—the eyes perfectly set in that lovely forehead. And her
voice is magical with that wonderful diction. She's important
and has a very rich life. We couldn't be more different. I was
an only child, and now I have no relatives. Whenever I see her
I wish I were more like her."

"Edith is a really great actress," Sybil says. "We have played
a lot of the same parts and she has always been much better
than me."

Sybil continued to play Françoise Regnard in *The Kiddies
in the Ruins* until the armistice put an end to it. Lewis was not

yet back from France and life was rather hard, with little work, although she continued to enjoy her home life with her four young children, and she saw a great deal of her mother, who had moved into a small flat in Westminster.

Sybil likes to reminisce about her children when they were young, specially John.

" 'Do you know God, Aunt Elsie?' he asked Lewis's psychologist sister Elizabeth, and when she replied that she was trying to find out more about him he said, 'I know him quite well. I had tea with him the other day—and he got it all himself. And do you know what God's doing now?' 'I've no idea,' said Elsie. 'He's walking up and down doing his parts,' John informed her.

"Once he had to bring Mary to a matinée of *The Trojan Women* at the Old Vic. It was a disastrous afternoon—both the maids had had to go away on some emergency. I managed to park Ann, who was still tiny, and Christopher was all right because he was in the play, but I said to John, 'You've got to take Mary and sit in the front row and keep her quiet'—she was only about five. 'Give her sweets or anything, but keep her quiet.' When they came round afterwards I asked John if Mary had been quiet. 'Yes,' he said, 'but I don't think she understood *quite* all of it.' He was ten.

"Then there was the time when John and Christopher appeared with us in *Julius Caesar*. They were small boys of seven and five, and they walked in the procession as Brutus's and Portia's two sons. We were the last of the procession, and the boys were very slow coming off. Then there was a big round of applause, which had never happened there before. I asked John, 'Did you and Kiff do anything?' 'Oh,' said John, 'we just saw that poor man lying down, so we went to see him and we both felt very sorry.' I could imagine just what they did. You see, our children's whole life was the theatre, from the time they were tiny. Sitting in the wings and knowing that was discipline. As firm as any church discipline that ever was."

It was while she was understudying Madge Titheradge in *The Night Watch* that the next important development for Sybil occurred. Ellen Terry's daughter, Edith Craig, brought her *The Hostage*, the English version of Paul Claudel's *L'Otage*, which had been presented at the Théâtre de l'Œuvre just before the war.

In 1911 Edith Craig had founded the Pioneer Players, a society presenting plays on Sundays at such theatres as the Scala and the Strand. This society, in Shaw's opinion, "by singleness of artistic direction, and unflagging activity, did more for the theatrical vanguard than any of the other côterie theatres". Edith Craig had already presented *The Exchange* and *The Tidings Brought to Mary*, the first Claudel plays to appear in London. Claudel, although already in his fifties and famous in his own country, was scarcely known in England except by a small circle of followers, mostly Roman Catholic. Now Edith Craig, although she was not a Catholic, or indeed a churchwoman, was eager to produce *The Hostage*, which had been translated by Pierre Chavannes but drastically revised, like the earlier Claudel translations, by the woman writer and critic Christopher St John, who was an intimate friend of Ellen Terry and her daughter and closely associated with all the latter's theatre activities. Lewis had known Edy, as everyone from friends to stage-hands called Edith Craig, for many years, but it was not until the war that she first entered Sybil's life.

"It was at the Old Vic from 1914 that I began to know her. She would come and play for our special Shakespeare birthday shows with her mother, who gave us excerpts from the Shakespeare plays in which she had acted with Sir Henry Irving. I can see Edy now sitting in the wings, and always having to re-introduce us to Ellen Terry, who never really remembered any of us. Edy said she never recalled my name but always said, 'You know—that big girl', which slightly hurt my pride, because, as I wasn't tall, I knew it must have referred to my rather square bounciness, as was proved afterwards by Edy saying to me so frequently, 'Keep still—don't flounce and bounce.' My conscience was pricked then, for my darling old master, Ben Greet, said when he first saw me, 'Yes, your Phoebe is quite all right if you didn't bounce about so much!' Edy had an eye like—well, whatever has eyes sharpened extremely. She could pierce through a stage back-cloth, I think, and see where one was making a hash of something—or occasionally doing something not quite so bad; and in those Old Vic times she let fall many a hint which helped me in the years to come.

"It was during her Pioneer Theatre days that I came under her direction. The most memorable was her production of *The Hostage*. She cast me for the part of Sygne, the only woman in the play, and this proved to be one of my biggest spiritual experiences in the theatre. In Claudel's plays no stage tricks avail. One must cast aside the old ways and find new. I remember arriving for the first rehearsal at Edy's flat in Bedford Street, full of beans, loving the words of the play even when I didn't know what on earth they meant, but dashing at them in the forthright way one dashed at Shakespeare, hoping that verve and nerve would carry one through, then being laid completely low by Edy, who could 'scathe' as few people know how.

"But with her scathings and her mocking discouragements came a bigger thing—a sense of beauty hidden, waiting to be unfolded. One particular time I remember when she was showing me what she meant about a certain line. (Edy could always show you—she didn't just talk—just as Granville Barker used to be able to show an actor, not exactly how to do it, but with a significant suggestion.) She used her hand, in a pause, to convey the carrying on through, and her hand gave me suddenly a jump, realizing beauty. To me, it was like seeing the da Vinci hands for the first time, or a chord of Bach—putting me in a place where I was able to grasp and convey the meaning myself."*

Sybil Thorndike was intensely moved by *The Hostage*, a grave poetic drama set in a remote Cistercian Abbey while Napoleon was campaigning in Russia. Sygne de Coûfontaine was a perfect

* From Sybil Thorndike's contribution to *Edy, Recollections of Edith Craig*, edited by Eleanor Adlard (Frederick Muller, 1949).

part for her, a young woman of ancient lineage and profound piety, who marries a man in every way repulsive to her in order to save the life of the Pope, smuggled to her domain from his prison in Fontainebleau. Finally Sygne intercepts the bullet intended for her husband, because she considers death too good for him, and dies herself—in spite of the priest's entreaties and her own godliness, without forgiving her husband for the crimes he had committed.

Sybil devoted herself heart and soul to this part, feeling in it a deep religious significance and being careful not to play it as a "holybob".

"Edy once said to me, when I had felt it necessary to be particular reverential over a mention of God, 'Don't say God in that reverent, holy way, as if you were an atheist.' Goodness knows I'd been brought up in a godly, un-reverent vicarage atmosphere, but one always has to be on one's guard against the tendency of stage actors to put on a special holy face when speaking of spiritual matters, which gives away that they've no personal knowledge of what they're talking about! Edy came down like a ton of masonry on bogus religious speech."

The cast of *The Hostage* was a fine one, and Sybil was delighted to find herself playing once more with Milton Rosmer, who had been one of her old colleagues in the Ben Greet American Company.

Although there was some difference of opinion among the critics about the play—the *Sunday Times* writer, for instance, detested everything about it—there was, in general, high praise for the production, and particularly for Sybil's performance. Great things were now prophesied for her. J. C. Trewin spoke of her "compelling attack, the fierceness with which she thought, felt, communicated", and *The Times* declared, "We knew that Miss Sybil Thorndike was a very clever actress; we had never before seen her act with so much passion, so much sensitiveness, such a flow of agonising beauty."

Lewis was home in time to see his wife's first great success.

He came back from France just before the end of the war on his way to some important mission in America connected with the Royal Engineers. The armistice stopped this, and, still in uniform, he joined Robert Loraine to play Le Bret in *Cyrano de Bergerac*.

Tom Kealy, an energetic press and publicity man, had watched Sybil's career at the Old Vic with a growing belief in her gifts. Now he took a sheaf of her notices as Sygne to Leon M. Lion, with the suggestion that he should engage her to replace Ethel Irving, who was forced by ill-health to give up the lead in *The Chinese Puzzle*,★ which was playing at the New Theatre. Lion sent for the Cassons.

"I'm paying Ethel Irving sixty pounds a week," he said to Lewis. "As your wife is not well-known, I'll give her forty."

This was Sybil's first well-paid job, and she was always grateful to Leon M. Lion for thus establishing her status.

"An added boon was that my dresser, Billy, came to me then. She stayed with us for years. She was a marvellous character, and had a wise saw for everything. Mother and she were great pals. And after Billy there was Winnie, who was wonderful too, and also stayed with us for years."

Next Sybil was given the lead in *The Great Day*,† one of the last of the melodramas at Drury Lane. It was an honour in itself to play at the Lane, and a fine exercise in speaking and acting to that vast house. She found it a relief to let herself go and be larger than life, after the restraint needed in the part of Sygne.

In the autumn of 1919 Lewis was asked to do a matinée of Gilbert Murray's translation of *The Trojan Women* at the Alhambra to celebrate the founding of the League of Nations Union. This was a fortunate event, for since his return from France Lewis had been in a very bitter and irascible frame of mind. The horror, tragedy and utter folly of the war weighed on his mind, and he saw little hope for the future of mankind. The advent of *The Trojan Women* was therefore a double boon; the League of

★ By Leon M. Lion and Marion Bower.
† By Louis N. Parker and George R. Sims.

Nations gave him new hope for world peace, and provided him with a job that exactly suited him. He invited Bruce Winston, who had been with him in *Cyrano de Bergerac*, to do the sets and costumes, and their friend John Foulds to compose the music.

"*The Trojan Women* is such a cry against war," Sybil comments, "I felt that to play Hecuba was the most wonderful thing that could happen to me. I was just becoming a pacifist then—I think it was partly the influence of Maude Royden. Father, Mother and I used to go together to hear her preach—remarkable woman."

The Alhambra matinée of *The Trojan Women* Sybil remembers as a rather grand affair.

"The music was thrilling. I can hear now those twelve splendid trumpet chords which opened the performance. There were shouts at the end for 'Author!' louder than I have ever heard, and Gilbert Murray came up on to the stage. 'The author is not here,' he said. 'He has been dead for many centuries, but I am sure he will be gratified by your reception of his great tragedy.'"

After the success of that performance Lilian Baylis asked Lewis to put on some matinées of *The Trojan Women* at the Old Vic.

To quote J. C. Trewin once more:*

"So, on the afternoon of October 14 1919, Sybil Thorndike appeared as Hecuba. Tall Troy was down; Scamander ran red to the sea; nothing remained but the burning of the towers and the voyage to slavery. What's Hecuba to us? The Old Vic audience knew when Sybil Thorndike led the dirge, crying to Troy in its ultimate agony, making all feel how the play, and its assault on war, must have sounded in the ears of the Athenians, the names of Melos and of Syracuse fresh in their minds.

* J. C. Trewin: *Sybil Thorndike* (Rockliff Publishing Corporation, 1955).

Sybil Thorndike by Jacob Epstein in the Saint Joan
period

Ghosts, 1930

"Would you be wise, ye cities, fly from war,
Yet, if war comes, there is a crown in death
For her that striveth well and perisheth
Unstained.

"W. A. Darlington held that the most moving moments were when Hecuba stood silent, listening to the pitiful outbursts of Andromache. 'It is a real triumph of acting to achieve such a result by sheer unaided intensity of feeling.'"

Archibald Haddon, then critic for the *Daily Express*, said that Sybil Thorndike's Hecuba would rank in dignity and nobility with the acting of Geneviève Ward: to appear that night as the girl-heroine at Drury Lane was to be freakishly versatile. And Elsie Fogerty, as she listened to Hecuba, knew that all at last was well with the Thorndike voice: "I still remember the thrill of delight with which I heard her."

On one occasion, which Sybil likes to recall to show what this play meant to those audiences, an old woman who sold apples on a barrow in the Waterloo Road, and lived just behind the Cassons' little converted shop in Wood Street, Westminster, came up to her and said, "Well, dearie, me and me pals went to see your play, it was lovely, and we all 'ad a good cry and a nice walk home over the bridge and I got 'em some shrimps for tea. You see, them Trojans was just like us. We've lost our sons and 'usbands in this bleedin' war, 'aven't we? So no wonder we was all cryin'. That was a real play, that was, dearie."

"Gilbert Murray was delighted when I told him this," Sybil remembers. "He felt it was another score for Euripides."

Telling of the apple woman reminded her of another incident which occurred when she was living in the country. A neighbouring cottager, a dear old man, said to her most sincerely, "One of these days oi shall come up to London and see you goin' through your 'oops." "Lewis says I've been going through my hoops ever since."

After this further success, with the Old Vic packed out for these matinées, it was a question of how to proceed—of how Sybil was to scale the heights for which, as an actress, she was clearly destined, and which Lewis was determined she should reach; and how he himself should use his great gifts and considerable experience as a producer and an actor. It was suggested to the Cassons that they should try going into management themselves, but theatres were hard to find in this post-war period for anything other than light entertainment, and they were determined to go on with the great Greeks and other plays which they considered worthy of a serious public.

Charles Gulliver came to their rescue by allowing them to do a season of matinées at his music-hall, the Holborn Empire. These performances were such a success that Lord Howard de Walden, Sir Hugh Bell and one or two other enthusiasts provided money for a whole season at the Holborn Empire under a Casson-Bruce Winston management. This was the Cassons' first experience of management, and they at once decided that, although Sybil was likely to play most of the leading parts, she was to be treated in exactly the same way as any other member of the company, which included those excellent actors Nicholas Hannen and Beatrice Wilson, whose Andromache in particular was, according to Sybil, superb.

Early in 1920 they staged *The Trojan Women*, after which they asked Shaw's permission to revive *Candida*. Sybil had not met Shaw since those early days when she understudied the part, and she wrote to him now and said that she had done as he told her—married and had lots of children—and now might she please play Candida again? He warmly agreed, and came to help with the production, the Cassons once more finding him a fascinating companion and a brilliant actor.

Next came *The Medea*, a play that Sybil had long wanted to do, although she and Lewis both had doubts about her suitability for the part. Sybil Thorndike found understanding even for the vengeance of Medea, "her spirit wounded sore with love of Jason".

"I don't believe in complete evil. Evil is negative. If you dig down far enough into yourself you find evil, and then you exorcise it and go for the positive. You have to work harder. I think Medea was in a way justified. She had given up everything and done awful things to help Jason, and all she expected in return was his love. He rejected her and oppressed her, and she had the most terrible time.

Oh,
Of all things upon earth that bleed and grow,
A herb most bruised is woman.

"As I studied the part I thought a lot about the position of women in the world, the position of the under-dog—their endless struggle for freedom and fulfilment—and I came to see very clearly how oppression breeds hatred. How often I thought about this later when we were in South Africa and I saw the blacks pushed off the pavements and that sort of thing. I foresaw disaster then if they went on being treated in this way."

The Casson-Bruce Winston management also put on a couple of new plays, including *The Showroom* by Lady Bell. The last of them, however, appropriately called *Tom Trouble*, was a financial failure, and although Charles Gulliver was generous to his tenants, and Tom Kealy used all his powers with the press to aid them, in April it was agreed that the Holborn Empire experiment must end.

Domestic life continued full and happy, which does not imply dull, for Lewis's and Sybil's rows were frequent and violent, often ending, on her side, in passionate tears. They were both deeply concerned with their children—one journalist still remembers her shock when, going as a very young reporter to interview a leading lady, she found her enthusiastically bathing her little girls. And however busy the parents were, they found time to play games and to read aloud to the children. All four of them— John was now eleven and Ann five—went in turn to an excellent school just across Battersea Bridge, run by a Mrs Spencer, a remarkable woman with a great gift for teaching, and the mother of Penelope Spencer, the dancer. Bertrand Russell also sent his children to the Spencer School. The Casson children's upbringing was religious in a matter of fact way, the whole family attending a very high church, St Mary's, Graham Street. And holidays were mostly spent at Mrs Thorndike's cottages in Dymchurch.

John and Christopher moved on from Mrs Spencer's to King's College School at Wimbledon, where their cousins and close friends were—Tom and Owen, the sons of Lewis's sister Esther, who had married Arthur Reed, the authority on Thomas More. But one ambition prevailed with John and Christopher; they never wavered in their determination to go to sea.

"It never stopped. Could they go in a ship? So, as there seemed no prospect of getting into the Navy, in 1923, when John was twelve, we sent him to the Merchant Service training ship H.M.S. *Worcester*. He was absolutely thrilled. One day we took Christopher down to see him. The Captain said, 'This boy ought to come too,' and Christopher said, 'I want to, sir'. 'Well, go on, climb up that,' the Captain said, and in spite of my protestations he sent him up the rigging—over the futtocks— that awful thing you have to climb. Then he said, 'Certainly send the boy.' So the following year Christopher went to the *Worcester* too, but before long the Captain said his mathematics were so good, he ought to go into the Navy.

"So in 1925 Christopher moved to the Royal Naval College at Dartmouth—I remember him going, looking adorable in his full uniform. He had a wonderful first term, and then four years of misery began. We used to have three or four postcards a day from him, written like a lunatic—'I am in a haze, everything is misty, I don't know what is happening to me'. It wasn't the work that was upsetting him—I went to see his tutor and he said his work was first class. It was something inside himself. I don't know if it was being away from home—you see, in the *Worcester* he was with John. And then there was church—our church meant a lot to Christopher. I think he was a born religious, a born mystic, and he missed that very high church of ours. It was part of the children's lives, specially his and Ann's.

"After two hellish terms at Dartmouth I said to him, 'You must come away,' but he said, 'No, I'll stick it out. I'd be miserable anywhere away from all of you, but I'll stick it out.' And he did. He passed first class into the Navy. He was top at Dartmouth in science, and then he did his sea-going cadet's training.

In the middle of his midshipman's time we had a letter from the Captain saying, 'This boy has been to me with the most extraordinary story. He says he's only just realised that one day he might have to kill somebody, and he doesn't intend to do that.' He was a wonderful man, the Captain of the *Tiger*, and he said, 'If you don't want to ruin that boy's life you must take him away. We can't dismiss him, he is too good a young officer, but if he goes on longer it will be difficult for him to get out of the Navy. You ought to buy him out.' So we bought him out of the Navy, and he went straight into the theatre."

Meanwhile John continued for the time being in the Mercantile Marine.

"John is always happy wherever he is. He was born happy. In a way just like me. I'm naturally happy, and when anything goes wrong I somehow twist it so that I'm happy. And so does he. And my younger daughter's the same. The two middle ones have had to struggle with life far more, probably due to me, as I was going through rather a difficult time then myself, and temperamentally they are much more like Lewis, given to depressions. Of course Christopher, being a mystic, in that way is like my father, because Father was quite a mystic. But Lewis and I have had a close friendship with all four children, right through. We've been able to say anything to them, and they've worked in with us, and there has always been tremendous understanding between us all."

The girls pursued a normal education, in time moving on from Mrs Spencer's to the Francis Holland School, but when a child was needed in a Casson production they usually managed to smuggle themselves in. Ann, in fact, followed Christopher in playing Astynax to her mother's Hecuba at the Holborn Empire. As she grew older she became a promising young writer. She wrote a play, called *The Campbells are Coming*, which was produced at the Children's Theatre.

So, in the spring of 1920, the Cassons were once more without a management and without funds, but confident and eager for the next adventure. It came almost at once, and was an odd one. They were both offered parts in *The Mystery of the Yellow Room* at the St James's Theatre, which they enjoyed although the critics considered it rather feeble, and according to Russell Thorndike neither of them ever grasped the plot, which included a trial scene played by Sybil with great emotion, despite the fact that she never discovered who was being tried. Anyhow, it was great fun, and Father Olivier took his family, including the thirteen year old Larry, to see it.

This occasion was the first time Laurence Olivier became aware of Sybil as an actress, though he already knew the Casson family well, for the children had played together in Westminster. Larry was two years older than John Casson, and then there was Dickie Olivier and their sister Sybille, who was the oldest of all, and used to do a certain amount of looking after the little Casson children. When Canon Thorndike died Father Olivier was a great comfort to his widow. Shortly afterwards he moved to Letchworth, and Mrs Thorndike went to live there as his organist, and there Sybil and the children used to visit her. Mrs Olivier died when Larry was twelve, and he remembers the Casson children asking him why he was wearing a black band on his sleeve, and telling them it was because he was "very very sad". Larry, like the Casson children, was devoted to Russell Thorndike, who had a gift for making children happy. And his friendship with the whole family, particularly with Sybil, has continued ever since.

By now the Cassons had already recognised the young Olivier's unusual talent, particularly admiring the quality of his voice. They had seen him first as a child of nine, playing Brutus, and also as Maria, in *Twelfth Night*, produced by Father Geoffrey Heald, a priest with a remarkable knowledge of the stage, who taught at All Saints', Margaret Street, where Larry was attending the Choir School. Later, when he was fifteen, Father Heald produced him as Katharine in *The Taming of the Shrew*. This production was repeated in a special boys' performance at Stratford-upon-Avon, where other members of the profession, including Ellen Terry, recognised Laurence Olivier as a "born actor".

It was during the run of *The Mystery of the Yellow Room* that an event took place which was of great importance to the Cassons' lives and careers. Susan Holmes, a young woman who had been Cochran's secretary and was well versed in every aspect of theatre, became their secretary. She and Lewis had known one another before, and had been for long walks together when they were in Edinburgh. Now Susan was to become, not only the Cassons' secretary, but their beloved friend for more than forty years.

"The children adored her, and so did my mother. She was completely without vanity, and the greatest of her qualities was loyalty. She also had a fine sense of humour. She lived a bachelor life, but she was part of our family. In the theatre she could do everything—box office, front of the house—and she had more friends in the profession than anyone I've ever known."

Now Sybil appeared again for the Pioneer Players, this time in Christopher St John's translation of *Carnaval des Enfants* by Saint-Georges de Bouhélier.

"Edith Evans was in it too, playing a sort of governess. The leading part, which I had, should have been played by Ellen Terry—it was just like her. It was the first time I'd acted with Edith, and how exciting she was! But Edy Craig gave us such a lashing, we'd come away from rehearsals bruised beyond words—but with a feeling that there was something we *might* be able to achieve if we went down to the nethermost hell and then struggled back and up. Edy had that mysterious quality none of us can put a name to, but when we meet it in a producer we call it genius. I adored working for her. Marvellous woman, always breaking the mould and moving on to something fresh."

In the autumn of 1920 an entirely new project arose; José Levy came to the Cassons with an invitation to join his season of

Grand Guignol at the Little Theatre in the Adelphi, Lewis
Casson to produce and both of them to act. They accepted
enthusiastically, and Sybil insisted that Russell should join the
company.

"If you don't have him, you won't get me, because if you
want horrors he's got a mind like a ghost-story in the morgue."

CHAPTER IX

FROM HORROR· TO HEROISM

(*1920–1923*)

IT WAS COURAGEOUS of José Levy to bring Guignol to England. Although it was tremendously successful in Paris, he was the only person who thought that it could possibly please the London public. He took a long lease of the Little Theatre, and he and Lewis set to work. They were particularly well suited as partners, for Levy was bilingual so far as speaking French and English went, but was not proficient at writing English dialogue, while Casson knew French well and wrote excellent English. Talking of this enterprise half a century later, the Casssons said:

Lewis: I'm not a French scholar in any way, but I used to teach French at St Mark's College. I taught it for examinations— it may have been fairly learned, but it had nothing to do with this kind of writing. However, between us we managed the translations.

Sybil: I read French fairly easily and speak—well, I get along. I pronounce it better than I know it.

Lewis: Later we did some pretty original things with Ibsen's *Ghosts.* Archer's translation was the only one available in those days, and we found it rather stiff and difficult in places, so, not being able to read Norwegian, we took the French translation, which is far more flexible, and translated the difficult passages from this.

Casson and Levy chose their company with infinite care, both the technicians and the performers—the latter including Nicholas

Hannen, Athene Seyler, Dorothy Minto and George Bealby—for they all agreed that in this venture team-work was the essential factor. Nicholas Hannen and Athene Seyler, later to embark on a very happy marriage, were already old friends of the Cassons, for Hannen had been with Lewis in the Glasgow Repertory Company and then at the Holborn Empire, and Athene was a neighbour at Dymchurch.

"We used to drive down in Lewis's old car, Anxious Annie," Athene Seyler says, "and Sybil would nod off in the front seat. I can't remember a time when I didn't know her. Incidentally, she's my godmother."

"My great friendship with Athene has played a large part in my life," Sybil counters. "I knew her first when she was a brilliant student at R.A.D.A. We share a love of the Anglican Church, although we don't always agree. We love spicy arguments. If we're playing together we're awfully tiresome. We forget our entrances because we're arguing in the wings and have to be shoved on. Yes, Athene wasn't christened until she was grown-up, and Ingaret van der Post, Laurens' wife, and I were her godparents."

"Oh, the joy of launching the scheme!" Russell wrote of the Grand Guignol. "Never was there such an enthusiastic company. We took as much interest in the plays we were not in as the ones we were, and we all understudied each other. The lead in one play would gladly walk on in the next. We got to know each other so well that we could tell what each of us was thinking. The authors were brought into close touch with the players, and each play was given the most careful and original production, Lewis producing to create fear and panic rather than just sickening horror. Several complete sets were used in every performance [three or more plays made up each programme], but everything was done without hitch or fuss."

When Sybil first read the Guignol plays, although she thought them extremely clever they terrified her. *The Old Women* made her cower under the bedclothes, and tell Lewis that it was the most awful thing she had ever read. But when she acted in the plays fright vanished; "they did something for me, it was a kind of release". In spite of her robustness, Sybil has always had fears, and she frequently describes herself as a coward by nature. During the two years of Guignol the nightmares from which she has suffered all her life completely vanished, although unfortunately they recurred later; and even when she wasn't in the theatre she felt particularly calm and happy.

It was at about this time that their great friend George Booth declared that the Cassons could not go on living in such a poky little place as their Westminster house, and lent them his own house on Campden Hill, after which they moved to Carlyle Square. During the Guignol run Alice and Nellie, who had supported the family so faithfully for so long, left to be married. Sybil replaced them with a series of other maids. One of them, a Cornish girl whom she engaged on sight, turned out to be a special treasure.

It was at about this time too that Vi, the nursery governess, came into the Cassons' lives. She was a wonderful character, who shared all the children's activities and was adored by them. And there was Kenneth Ingram, the writer, whom they called "Flick" after the character in *The Rising Generation*. The Cassons met Ingram at their church, and he became a kind of Dutch uncle to the children, even on occasion taking some of them to Switzerland for a holiday. Russell, too, was a frequent and welcome visitor, always a source of fun. And Owen Reed, the Cassons' adoring nephew and cousin, came over constantly from Putney to share the jollity. This was altogether a very happy period for the whole family.

"It was wonderful to have so many extraordinary parts," Sybil says. "Acting all sorts of different kinds of people—specially in the big plays, the Greeks and Shakespeare—is a wonderful way of getting rid of things in yourself, awfulnesses and difficulties and fears. Even happinesses and boisterousnesses you get out of yourself and savour in a different form, a more symbolic form. In a way it's what the Church does for one, what the Sacraments do for you—you get things into a form. That interests me more than anything—form in every branch of art. When people try to make works of art without any form at all, just slopping it out as you do in life, it's no good. I think art must be symbolic, and theatre is a means of symbolising all sorts of things in your own life. It's no good making a to-do about things that have been wrong or unhappy—you've got to get them into a symbolic form, then you can get rid of them.

"Of course I've always discussed every play I've done with Lewis, even if he hasn't been directing it—gone down to the very roots of it with him—and he's sometimes helped me to find out things in my own nature. He wasn't as much affected personally by the Guignol plays as I was. For me playing terrible parts is really rather like a Confessional, only I find it more satisfying. I went to Confession in the Church regularly for years, then I had to give it up because it was making me niggling in myself—it wasn't symbolic enough for me. I can get things out of me much better in the theatre than I could in Confession. In the theatre you're left with a sort of clear slate, and when you play such a great variety of parts you find you belong to everybody, to people of every kind and age—to the ancient Greeks and the Israelites, to people in the past and in the future and people now. You're right outside your own body.

"I discussed this sense of release I got when I was in Guignol with a doctor once, and he quite understood, but thought it was rather hard luck on the audience to work all that off on them. I was able to tell him that it worked that way for the audience too, that I had had letters from people telling me how seeing those horrors objectified had in some way liberated them from their own terrors. I had one letter from a soldier saying that he had been haunted all his life by some sort of terrible fear, but that when he came out of the theatre after seeing *The Old Women*★ he felt 'somehow freed'."

Sybil realises, of course, that this was not the reaction of everyone who saw these plays. Some people were frankly terrified,

★ By André de Lord, adapted by Christopher Holland.

among them her own son John and his cousin Owen Reed. The boys went round to Lewis's dressing-room on one occasion, so upset that he told them to "drop it and run", and was so upset himself that he forgot his cue. And there were some, including Dion Boucicault of the Frohman days, who considered Grand Guignol sheer waste of energy and talent, and refused to visit the Little Theatre at all.

"When I think now of Grand Guignol [J. C. Trewin wrote*] there flickers to mind a note from Parson Woodforde's diary (June 6, 1792) on a neighbour 'entirely helpless owing to his falling out of a Cart when loaded with Thorns, every Nerve almost strained to a violent degree'. The Guignol was a cart loaded with thorns. True, its programme included fantasy and comedy; but London went to John Street for the *frisson*. Mad women in a lunatic asylum gouged out Sybil Thorndike's eyes with knitting-needles; she was a murdered *cocotte* stuffed into a trunk; as a war-widow she killed her scientist-brother, inventor of a bomb; she was neatly strangled; she did a little strangulation herself; with her lover she was crushed by a movable ceiling; her husband was tossed alive to the wolfhounds; and in *The Medium* she was encased in plaster. 'Just before I began playing this,' she said once with charm, 'I came across Fabre's very interesting book on spiders. In this he explained that spiders rested with their muscles taut. If this is so, I thought, then surely it might be possible for human beings to rest in a standing-up and rigid position.'"

Most of the critics were appreciative, and the audience continued to pour in. According to Russell:

"The much discussed 'lavatory' play [in which Sybil and Dolly Minto acted a pair of demi-mondaines in the cloakroom of a French restaurant] brought us a tremendous cheap advertisement. We were attacked by all the purity brigade, who, as Sewell Collins, the adapter, said, 'Rushed about whispering, "I hear it's simply outrageous. When shall we go?"' "

* *Sybil Thorndike.*

"The whole thing was absolute bliss," Sybil said, "although very hard work. We changed the bill about every ten weeks, and Lewis rehearsed us endlessly, inventing new things all the time for each play. We could have gone on for ever changing the bill if the audience hadn't demanded that each new play must be more terrifying than the one before, and we found it impossible to beat a masterpiece like *The Old Women*, which was the best of all. In addition to this, the Lord Chamberlain's office was becoming all the time more censorious on the grounds that it wasn't good for people to be too much frightened in a theatre."

During the strenuous run Sybil was given two days' leave to accept the invitation of the well-known American actor, James Hackett, to play Lady Macbeth with him in a special performance at the Paris Odéon, three different understudies playing her Guignol parts while she was away. The Paris *Macbeth* was a very grand affair, devised to foster goodwill between France, England and America, and to celebrate the peace terms. It had a cast drawn from the three countries. John Drinkwater, already a well-known poet, had the part of Banquo, Leslie Faber was Macduff, and Miles Malleson played the Porter. Firmin Gémier, the leading French actor, who had recently become *Directeur* of the Odéon, was determined to be in it too, so he had a small part as he only knew a few words of English. The play was directed by Louis Calvert. The theatre was packed, and it was altogether a most glamorous affair. James Hackett was given the *légion d'honneur*, and the company was received by Monsieur Herriot, the socialist deputy.

As soon as Edith Craig heard that Sybil was to play Lady Macbeth in Paris she said, "You must wear Mother's dresses. We won't have them cleaned, as they are now beautifully supple and will almost play the part by themselves."

"So I had those splendid dresses—the beetle-wing one in which Sargent painted his famous portrait of Ellen Terry, and the great cloak, and the sleep-walking blankets and everything.

And Edy was quite right. Those dresses brought something
of their own from greater performances, and fired me to act
all-out.

"I'm always very nervous on these big formal occasions, and
this was the first time I had played Lady Macbeth since the Old
Vic, but the instant I put on Ellen Terry's dress something
happened to me—not a tremble, not a quake. In the banquet
scene the splendid American star somehow lost himself—his
nerve went. So often in *Macbeth* people have accidents or dry
up, but the beetle-wing dress came to his aid. I wasn't a very
hefty girl then, but something pushed me on from behind, and
I seized that huge man—he really was enormous—and hurled
him across the stage, saying his words in his ear. "Oh, thank
you, my dear!' he said to me afterwards. 'I was lost and you
saved me.' 'Don't thank me,' I said, 'it was Ellen Terry's dress
that did it.'

"Edy was always against cleaning costumes. She said it took
the life out of them. And when a little later on I had a new dress
for *The Verge* she made me wear it for rehearsals so that it would
get dirty and become part of its wearer. And my *Medea* dress—
I never had that cleaned. My dresser said, 'But it's grimy,' and
I said, 'I don't care, it knows exactly what to do and it mustn't
be touched'. That grime was part of me when I played Medea.
It was a wonderful dress, red-purple, colours of flame, and it
had a long tail to it, hung from the arms. It was magical, I
only had to give it a little twist and it acted by itself."

Another and an entirely new experience for Sybil, during the
Guignol period, was making her first films—silent ones. The first
of them was *Moth and Rust*, in 1921.

"Of course I was interested in a new form of acting, but I
have never really enjoyed doing films, except *Edith Cavell*. I
find them frustrating. But they're very, very good for me, because they keep me quiet and make me underdo everything,
when I'm always apt to overdo everything. Being a real theatre
woman I'm always apt to make it all larger than life, and in a

film you must be infinitely smaller than life. The same on television. If you use larger than life technique you smash the camera. It was all a great surprise to me at first. Edith Evans has perfect film technique—and that's wonderful, considering how big she is on the stage.

"I did a series of short films then—tense moments from great plays—Lady Deadlock in *Bleak House*, and Jane Shore, the mistress of Edward IV, who was a lovely merry girl when she was young. I remember dying on the banks of the Thames with people in pleasure boats jeering at me as they passed, as I died with a cross plastered on my bosom, just as Jane Shore died, repentant, seeing the Lord. And I did Esmeralda★ with my goat. The goat was a perfect darling, and it behaved beautifully at all the rehearsals, but when it came to the shots and the lights it stood up on its hind legs and did its double business all over the floor. That's what goats do when they're frightened. We nearly killed ourselves laughing—it's a good thing we didn't do the same as the goat. Then I did old Mrs Garland in *Curiosity Shop* and a whole heap of other famous people—I can't remember them all—twelve altogether. But my first long important film was *Edith Cavell*: that was after I came back from Africa."

Besides these films and the Paris Lady Macbeth, during the Grand Guignol run Sybil took part in a number of special matinées, including playing Mother Sawyer in *The Witch of Edmonton*† at the Phoenix Theatre, "a creature," according to J. C. Trewin, "bent nearly double, croaking like a raven, hissing like a snake, hook-nosed, toothless". Edith Evans had a short part as a distraught woman, and according to Sybil and the critics she stole the show. Sybil was quite undismayed by her own part. "I got something out of the most depraved people, out of the most awful old women I've ever acted." Then there was *The Maid's Tragedy*, in the first act of which Sybil offered what James Agate called "enough bitter satirical largesse to defray the

★ Victor Hugo: *The Hunchback of Notre-Dame.*
† Dekker, Ford and Rowley.

comic expenditure of half the fashionable actresses in London throughout the whole year".

In the summer of 1922, when the Guignol season was at last coming to an end, Lady Wyndham was much impressed by Sybil's performance as Katharine of Aragon at a charity matinée, and offered to back the Cassons in their own management. This was a most exciting development, and after much discussion they decided to open at the New Theatre, which they have loved ever since, with St John Ervine's *Jane Clegg*, one of the great successes of their repertory days. They followed this with Lady Bell's version of Henri Bataille's play *Scandal*, "a fine play in the best French tradition". This was a particularly pleasurable production from a family point of view, as Russell's mother-in-law, Rosina Filippi, and his wife Rosemary were included in the cast, as was Leslie Faber, who used to say to Sybil, "Relax, relax, for goodness' sake!" "A thing I've had to go on learning all my life," Sybil comments.

As soon as *Scandal* was safely launched, the Cassons character-istically decided to put on a series of matinées, including *The Medea*; and now Sybil was able to play a part she had long set her heart on—Beatrice in Shelley's *The Cenci*. She greatly admired this play. What an enormous amount she has succeeded in reading, and, with her phenomenal gift, in remembering, all through her endlessly active life! And how completely she manifests Shelley's own preface:

"This story of *The Cenci* is indeed eminently fearful and monstrous; anything like a dry exhibiton of it on the stage would be insupportable. The person who would treat such a subject must increase the ideal, and diminish the actual horror of the events, so that the pleasure which arises from the poetry which exists in these tempestuous sufferings and crimes may mitigate the pain of the moral deformity from which they spring. There must also be nothing attempted to make the exhibition subservient to what is vulgarly termed a moral purpose. The highest moral purpose aimed at in the highest species of the drama is the teaching the human heart, through its sympathies and antipathies, the knowledge of itself; in proportion to the possession of which knowledge, every human being is wise, just, sincere, tolerant and kind."

Take Beatrice's appearance too, based by Shelley on the portrait at the Colonna Palace, painted by Guido during her imprisonment.

"The moulding of her face is exquisitely delicate; the eyebrows are distinct and arched; the lips have that permanent meaning of imagination and sensibility which suffering has not repressed and which it seems as if death scarcely could extinguish . . . Beatrice Cenci appears to have been one of those rare persons in whom energy and gentleness dwell together without destroying one another: her nature was simple and profound."

The Cenci, with its theme of incest and murder, had had one private performance years before, and then been banned for theatre productions. Now, exactly one hundred years after Shelley's death, this ban had lapsed, although the Cassons did in fact obtain the Lord Chamberlain's approval before staging the play. It was an outstanding success. The critics acclaimed Sybil's performance, although Agate, while "admiring her conveyance of moral grandeur", commented on what he called the hardness of her acting. "I should as soon think of being sorry for a marble statue as of being sorry for Sybil." Which is, of course, the price paid for grandeur. There is a tinge of patronage in "being sorry" for anybody, which Sybil's stature defies. And so does the stature of tragedy itself.

"Lewis did a strange, unrealistic, symbolic production," Sybil says, "and the part of Cenci was played magnificently by Robert Farquharson, that extraordinary actor—such an unusual personality with a highly individual voice. As Cenci he was the personification of evil—you really felt you were in the presence of the devil himself. Such a sweet person, too, and a great friend of ours—I'd played with him in a number of Sunday shows. Beatrice Wilson, whose work Lewis had always admired so much, played Lucretia, and it really was a wonderful production. Lewis knew the tune of every line; every syllable was pronounced musically, but none of it was elocuted. And the murder was performed with stark realism, very much like the *Macbeth* scenes. The whole thing really was most impressive, and the first performance was a great event—all the poets and famous literary people came to it."

Scandal ran for three months, the matinées of *The Medea* and *The Cenci* paying for its losses. At last, in December, the Cassons were free to go away for two weeks' holiday, the first they had had since before the war, and their first visit to Italy, "the greatest treat," Sybil says, "that I had ever had".

"Robert Farquharson, who knew Italy well, told us we must go to Rapallo first. We used to start very early every morning and walk till sun-down—up the little hills where we could see the Ligurian Alps. The hills were so high that the sun used to go down behind them quite early. Oh, I loved it all so much—the hamlets up in the hills, and the little churches. We knew just enough Italian to say a few words to the villagers.

"It was in Rapallo that we met Gordon Craig, a most stimulating experience. We took him for a long drive—that was the only day we didn't walk. We had decided to do *Macbeth* next and we planned to do it with him, and we all talked endlessly about how the production was to be."

On their return the Cassons found no suitable theatre for *Macbeth*, a great disappointment both to them and to Gordon Craig. Consequently they went into partnership with Lady Wyndham's son, Bronson Albery, and put on at the Criterion that lightest of comedies, *Advertising April, The Girl who made the Sunshine Jealous*, by the two drama critics, Herbert Farjeon and Horace Horsnell, an "airy persiflage" in which Sybil wore the most outrageous of costumes and played the part of a film star (the very last thing she has ever wanted to be). James Agate's reactions to her work are particularly interesting. He had known her as a promising repertory actor in Manchester, tending to play everything too much; now he was anxiously watching her rise to fame, but he did not, like some of her admirers, reproach her with skipping from tragedy to melodrama to light comedy. On the contrary he said, "Let her who is already a great actress be wise in her time and generation. Let her look not upon masterpieces only."

All her life Sybil has obeyed this injunction, but never more startlingly than when she followed her performance of Beatrice in *The Cenci* with *Advertising April*. She enjoyed the play and so did the audience, including Gilbert Murray, and after five months the Cassons took it on a provincial tour with a number of their other successes. This was a further treat for Sybil. She had not toured the provinces for years, and she loves to move about, not only from part to part but from place to place. At heart she is a strolling player.

Now came *Cymbeline*, first at Birmingham and then in London. She delighted to play Imogen once more, but the critics were not altogether sympathetic to her performance, or to Lewis's experiment in a new method of Shakespearean production. This was not one of the Albery-Casson management's financial successes, but it was immediately followed by *The Lie*, that small masterpiece of drawing-room drama by the veteran playwright Henry Arthur Jones, with an excellent cast including Mary Merrall and O. B. Clarence. The author had written the play in Provence during the winter before the war, while he was trying to discover the villa in which Rachel, the famous French tragedienne, had died.

"My searchings were in vain [he wrote in his dedication of *The Lie* to Sybil]. What does that matter? Rachel is dead, but you are alive.

"I have had many roaring receptions of applause from English first-nighters, but none of them has approached the thundering welcome they gave me when, under the shelter of your wing, myself moved by the inflaming sweep of your acting, I stood beside you to acknowledge the prolonged acclamations that greeted us on the 13th October, 1923.

"How lucky I was, after six years' absence from the London theatre, to return to it in such company as yours! What words of gratitude will fitly express my debt to you? What words of praise can I choose to describe the patient tenderness of your quiet early scenes, swelling into stronger but still reserved and self-contained emotion, startled at last into this poignant and terrific fury of your great tragic abandonment? Take all the dictionaries, and pick out of them all their superlatives of eulogy, and I will multiply them again and again."

But even while enjoying the part of Elinor Shale, grievously wronged by her own sister, in a play that was good theatre and filled the house every night, Sybil's eyes were fixed on the horizon, for there a vision was appearing of a figure who inspired her—Joan of Arc.

PART II

"Sybil Thorndike once conferred upon me one grain of eternal youth: it is this: that whenever I think of her I'm transported to the back of the gallery in the New Theatre, 1924. I am fifteen years old and standing at the back of that gallery watching, far below on the stage, the marvel of her St. Joan. The beauty and vigour, the simplicity and humour and command of her performance pierced the great distance between the stage and theatre roof with such precision that it recreates itself for me still: and recreates also my fifteen-year-old self and all the details of that afternoon forty-two years ago.

"So it is with Sybil in all her ways: she penetrates distance, and makes a strong living link between generations widely separated. She helps us to know that differences of time and place, of youth and age, need be scarcely discernible within the act of living. Her youth is with her still, playing its light across the generations, reaching the very young as it reached that boy in the gallery, and redeeming the time for those who are growing old. She plays the character of human life as we should all like to play it, with warmth, and gaiety and concern and eagerness. And we love her and thank her and bless the day that she was born."

—CHRISTOPHER FRY, on the occasion of
Sybil Thorndike's 83rd birthday

CHAPTER X

SAINT JOAN

(1923–1924)

WHEN HE WROTE *Saint Joan*, George Bernard Shaw was in his late sixties. He had written a great number of very successful plays since the early days of *Widowers' Houses* and *Candida*, but during the war he had fallen slightly out of favour, partly owing to an article of his in the *New Statesman*, "Common Sense about the War", which the Germans had been quick to exploit. Shortly after the war he had written the brilliant *Heartbreak House*, which was produced at the Court Theatre in 1921 with Edith Evans playing Lady Utterword. After this he set to work on the Metabiological Pentateuch, *Back to Methuselah*, in which he again examined the causes of the failure of our civilisation, and then translated *Jitta's Atonement*, a play by his Austrian translator, intended by Trebitsch as tragedy but turned into comedy by Shaw.

Late in 1922 he went to see *The Cenci*, and on his return from the theatre said to his wife, "I've found my Joan". For some time now Mrs Shaw had been urging him to write a play about Joan of Arc; now, not only had he found his Joan, but he was struck by a certain affinity between the trial of Beatrice in *The Cenci* and the trial of Joan. In 1923 he set to work on the play. Not a word about the project, however, did he say to the Cassons. Meanwhile, as Sybil was so eager to play Joan, she and Lewis had asked their dear friend, the poet Laurence Binyon, if he would write a play about Joan for them. "We actually commissioned it. He was such a beautiful writer. We had great talks about it."

Then suddenly they saw in a newspaper that Shaw was writing

a *Saint Joan*, and in consternation asked one another what they
were to do. There was only one answer. Lewis wrote to Shaw
saying that Sybil had always wanted to play Joan, and that
Laurence Binyon was writing a play for them. Shaw replied at
once—on a postcard, as usual—something to the effect of, "Nonsense! Of course Sybil plays my *Saint Joan*. Let so-and-so do the
other one. I warned off Masefield and Drinkwater, but I forgot
Binyon." The actual postcard was unfortunately destroyed, with
so much of the Cassons' precious correspondence, during the
blitz. Very apologetically, Sybil and Lewis put the problem to
Laurence Binyon, and he gracefully withdrew, saying with
characteristic generosity, "Shaw will write it much better than I
could." The Cassons then had one meeting with Shaw during
which he told them a little about how he visualised the play,
after which he said, "We won't talk any more about it." They
did not hear another word from him until they met him one day
in the House of Commons, where a number of writers and actors
had gone to present a petition.

"Something to do with our contracts, I think. Anyway, we
met Shaw and he said, 'This is the easiest play I've ever written.
All the words were there for me', which was a bit of an exag-
geration, because the opening is wildly original and he invented
a lot more of the men's dialogue too. But nearly all the things
he made me say were in the Records as what had actually been
said by Joan. Shaw said to me on this occasion, 'Have you read
the histories?' 'All of them,' I answered proudly, and Shaw said,
'Forget them. I'll tell you what to think.' "

They did not hear from Shaw again for some time, and then
he suddenly invited them down to Ayot St Lawrence with
Bronson Albery. One morning, in the winter of 1923, they sat
down in his country house with Mrs Shaw and Cherry-Garrard,
who had been with Scott on his polar expedition and was a great
friend of the Shaws, and Shaw began to read *Saint Joan*.

"We simply could not believe our ears. It seemed to me the

most wonderful first scene that I had ever heard. Very daring, very startling. 'No eggs! No eggs! Thousand thunders, man, what do you mean by no eggs?' It was extraordinary—and then the way he developed the mystery in that first scene. So daring and true, with that girl who was exactly as I had imagined her. When that first scene came to an end Lewis and I didn't say a word to one another. We both just felt, 'Oh, wonderful!' We could tell that Bronson Albery had certain doubts about it, but we had none.

"Shaw read divinely. Like an actor, but much bigger size than most actors. Yes, a big-size actor. I felt, 'This is too good, it can't go on and be the real Saint Joan I've always wanted.' But it did, and I got more and more excited. And then at the end of the Loire scene, where the wind changes so dramatically, Shaw said, 'Well, that's all flapdoodle. Now the real play starts', and went into the tent scene with Warwick, Cauchon and de Stogumber, the Chaplain—one of the best scenes, I think, in all theatrical literature. He got the whole argument of the play into this scene, and one could see why he had wanted so passionately to write it. He made it clear that Joan did for France then what we hope somebody may yet do for the world. All the little warring factions in France she linked together. She made the nation. Shaw called her the first Nationalist and, although she was a devout Catholic, 'one of the first Protestant martyrs'. He also brought out the fact that she was a born general—she actually invented a new way of using artillery.

"As the play progressed Lewis and I were more and more thrilled. The trial—I'd read the Records of it, and Joan's lines were word for word what she said. Except for the last big outburst, which was sheer poetry and pure Shaw. His two great speeches—the loneliness of God, at the end of the cathedral scene, and the great cry against imprisonment in the trial scene, those are the ones, and when people say Shaw wasn't a poet they should just read those speeches and consider whether they could have been written by anyone except a poet.

"When it came to the Epilogue Lewis and I were in tears. Bronson Albery wasn't too keen on it—hardly anybody was.

They said it was redundant, when the trial scene ended so
marvellously—'You have heard the last of her'. 'The last of
her? Hm, I wonder.' People said that was the right finish, but
Shaw said, 'No, that's not the finish. Now we've got to see what
the modern world says. If she came back now it would be
exactly the same.' "

And Sybil adds, "Had she lived today I should have followed
her without question."

Shaw also points out in the Preface that without the Epilogue
the audience would not know that Joan had been canonised.

"Hearing that first reading was the most amazing experience.
None of us had read the Preface then—in fact, it hadn't yet
been written—but even without it I felt something of what
Shaw wanted so desperately to say in *Saint Joan*. There's that
passage in the Preface where he says he has no use at all for a
Church which has no place for free-thinkers, which doesn't
in fact encourage free-thinking when it's really free. Although
he speaks in the Preface of his 'family habit' being Protestant,
Shaw didn't go to any church. But, in spite of anything he may
have said himself, he had a deep understanding of Catholicism,
very deep. Think of his friendship with Dame Laurentia, the
Benedictine nun. They had so much in common, including
music and also somehow faith. Once he brought her two stones
from the Holy Land. 'Who knows whose feet have trodden
on these?' he said. He directed that one of the stones should be
thrown on the path that the nuns trod every day. No one would
know which stone it was. The other was to be put in a reliquary.
'You must put our names on it,' Dame Laurentia said. 'Why?'
said Shaw. 'You know, I know and God knows.' I suppose it
was the Irish in him that made him get the Catholic view so
marvellously—with his own free-thinking on top of it. And this
Lewis and I appreciated, as we have always been very close to
Roman Catholicism ourselves, although we are Anglicans.

"Can one subscribe to the Church and remain a free-thinker?
That is one of Shaw's cries, and isn't it what we are all trying to

find in all governments? Discipline and freedom combined. Saint Joan was a true Catholic and a true Protestant in one, two opposing qualities making a balance, and she was also a free-thinker. So we burnt her. We are more civilised now—or are we?"

Many months elapsed between this inspiring first reading and the staging of the play in England, for the Cassons were still engaged with *The Lie*, and Shaw had promised his next play to the New York Theatre Guild, which had already presented the world première of *Heartbreak House* and *Back to Methuselah*. So *Saint Joan* had its first performance at the Garrick Theatre in New York in December 1923, with Winifred Lenihan in the name part. The play was on the whole favourably received.

To keep Sybil from being too impatient in these weeks of waiting for *Saint Joan*, there was not only *The Lie*, but also matinées of *Gruach*, Gordon Bottomley's verse play about the wild young Lady Gruach on the eve of her wedding with Macbeth, a part which suited Sybil well. This play was directed by Basil Dean for the Playbox.

"It was interesting working with him. I remember him saying, 'Don't when you get emotional go up on tiptoe'. I've always had a tendency to do that, probably not an unusual reaction for an actor. I always want to get higher. I have to make myself stay flat."

Then, in February 1924, while *Back to Methuselah* was running at the Court, Shaw asked the Cassons to take off *The Lie* and set to work on *Saint Joan*. He was to co-produce with Lewis, and he had already agreed that the latter's faithful colleagues, Charles Ricketts and John Foulds, should be engaged, so they were hard at work on the costumes, scenery and music. Shaw had told Casson that he wanted good Shakespearean actors, people who could speak "bigly—in the Shakespearean manner", and Casson had accordingly, in consultation with Shaw, engaged a fine cast.

"I shall never forget those rehearsals. First we all sat round and once again Shaw read the play to us, oh, marvellous! He had cut it quite a lot before he felt it was ready for production. We were bowled over, and the company, who hadn't heard it before, found it wonderful and perfectly extraordinary. Well, so it is. Shaw was breaking a mould all right. Nowadays we've got used to knocking everybody off their perches, but when this was written Saint Joan was still that dear little girl with skirts and a holy-bob face. And this was the real Joan— the tough revolutionary. It was the beginning, not of debunking, but of getting away from that saintly looking-up-to-heaven-all-the-time idea of saints. Lewis too felt that the play was saying something about sainthood that had never been said before. The Catholic Church had tried to turn Joan into a little sweetie, but Shaw wouldn't have any sentimentality. Joan was a tough, she could be violent, as when she chased the immoral women out of her army and broke her sword over the back of one of them—that's in the Records. I used to remind myself what Maude Royden had said about Joan earlier: 'She went down her road like a thunderbolt.' She was also a mystic, like Shaw, although perhaps Shaw was more a visionary than a mystic. Joan's voices predominated, but surely they were inside herself. When she's told they're all imagination, doesn't she say, 'That is how the messages of God come to us'? Shaw himself was a perfect Saint Joan.'"

People tend to think of Joan as a peasant, but she wasn't one. Robert actually says in the first scene that she is a *bourgeoise*. Although she helped on her father's farm, he owned his land and employed men to work for him, and Joan was furious when she was called "a farmer lass". Her mother was a very pious woman, who when she was pregnant with Joan went on pilgrimage to pray for another son—she already had three—who would save France. When the child came it was a girl with all the attributes of a boy. It is said that Joan never even had monthly periods. When she was quite small she already wanted to run away to be a soldier, and was only stopped by her father's and elder brothers' threats to drown her in the Meuse if she tried any such thing.

"Of course this boyishness appealed to me, because I've always wished I'd been born a boy—what I felt when I first met Lewis was so true. 'I wish I were a boy so I could have that man as a pal.' Lewis understood this, and something of that feeling remained always in our relationship. That didn't stop me loving having babies—I adore babies. So did Joan.

"Remember how she said to Dunois that she wished he was one of the village babies so that she could nurse him for a while. And when he retorted, 'You are a bit of a woman after all', she said, 'No, not a bit. I am a soldier and nothing else. Soldiers always nurse children when they get a chance.' I love playing a woman who has a touch of masculinity, Beatrice in *The Cenci* has this. I can't be sheer femininity. Feminine wiles I can't manage at all—and I don't want to.

"Well, then we went into rehearsal. Oh, I shall never forget those rehearsals! Shaw was so inspiring, always a better actor than any of us. He took the morning rehearsals and Lewis took the afternoon ones and undid, Shaw said, everything he had done in the morning. But according to Lewis he was interpreting Shaw to us rabble. And actually he did have to translate some of Shaw's intonations into English for us. But besides this Lewis had got Shaw's tunes—the tune of every line. I remember Shaw telling me to say the words 'Dear-child-of-God' and 'Be-brave-go-on' just like the chimes. Shaw had such a sense of rhythm that any player with an instinct for music had only to hear the lines with a musician's ear to learn them with a minimum of effort. But this didn't mean anything falsely musical, any more than Shaw's Shakespearean speech meant ham—no, not ham in the least, just bigly spoken and not elocuted. Of course I had to speak in a dialect, because Shaw said he wasn't going to have one of those ladylike Joans. He made me invent a dialect, a sort of Lancashire cum the West cum this and that—what Nigel Playfair used to call Lumpshire. I even used a bit of my Cornish maid's odd speech. In fact, I used something of her country-girl nature too.

"I simply lived in that part. I have never had anything in the theatre which has given me as much as *Saint Joan* did. Something more than just theatre. It confirmed my faith, it confirmed something in my life that I've always known intuitively from my father's saintliness and my mother's ridiculousness, and all the things I had to say were things I wanted to say. That was marvellous, and Shaw said to me over and over again, 'Yes, you've got it—just what I wanted. I don't have to tell you anything, you know it.' But he did tell me, lots. And I loved him—almost as much as I loved Gilbert Murray. One thing he said to us in rehearsal reminded me of what Edy Craig had said when she was producing *The Hostage*. 'Don't talk about God in holy voices, as if you are atheists.' And he liked us to be rather motionless, to stand about rather still, a thing he seldom did himself.

"It was a splendid company. Ernest Thesiger's Dauphin was wonderful. He spoke it beautifully, and he got a catty side into him that was frightfully good. When we did our scene together, oh, how we laughed! We laughed our heads off. Of course he was too elegant for that untidy, rather dirty little Dauphin. Ernest couldn't ever bear to put on anything dirty, and he never got anything he wore dirty either. I don't believe in that six months' run he ever had to have his dress cleaned, although all our other Dauphins had to have theirs cleaned every few weeks, they got so filthy. Teddy Swete's* Lord Warwick was marvellous too. He was the real aristocrat and the real cynic without any romance or any true religion—just using religion as a political force. He was wonderfully funny—Shaw had drawn him so brilliantly in that tent scene—what a feat of imagination that scene is! And Lewis was splendid as the old chaplain, de Stogumber—it was one of his best parts. Then there was Eugene Leahy playing Cauchon—he was a devout Catholic and understood the part perfectly—and Milton Rosmer did Bluebeard with such a flourish and such viciousness. And the Inquisitor was O. B. Clarence, who had been with us in *The Lie*. He did that seven-minute speech magnificently, never rais-

---

* E. Lyall Swete.

The Corn is Green, 1937

Treasure Hunt, 1949

*The Foolish
Gentlewoman,* 1949

ing his voice. Our old friend Bruce Winston was an excellent
La Trémouille, and Jack Hawkins, then a small boy, was
delicious as Dunois' page."

Three years later, in his autobiography, *Practically True,*[*]
Ernest Thesiger wrote:

"*Saint Joan* naturally brought me into close contact with Sybil
Thorndike, most lovable of enthusiasts, and her equally delightful husband. No one but a very simple and charming woman
could have survived the exaggerated publicity from which
Miss Thorndike has had to suffer, and no one with less of an
iron constitution could have achieved so much by sheer hard
work. Holidays from work, rest from indefatigable kindnesses,
are unknown to Sybil, but I was glad to note, in watching her
Queen Katharine in a recent revival of *Henry VIII*, that repose
was not an entire stranger to her."

And earlier in his book Ernest Thesiger observed:

"Seeing such brilliant artists as Irene Vanbrugh, Sybil Thorndike or Marie Tempest from the stalls, I should never have
thought that they had anything to learn, but when I worked
with them I was amazed to find how much they owed to their
husbands."

It is also interesting, in view of Sybil's statement that Shaw
was a better actor than any member of the *Saint Joan* cast, to
note Ernest Thesiger's remark:

"Of all the authors in whose plays I have acted, I found
Bernard Shaw to be the most helpful—chiefly because he knows
that he can write and doesn't think he can act."

Shaw was so much impressed by Ernest Thesiger's first reading of the part of the Dauphin that he told him to go home and

* Heinemann, 1927.

F

stay in bed until the first night. "You already know as much about the part as I do."

As for Sybil herself, after the wide variety of roles in which she had acted, giving herself fully to every one of them, delving down into her nature to find her link with it—this time she had no delving to do. Joan was there for her, and she was there for Shaw: she felt herself utterly fulfilled. Joan was not, Shaw says, "A melodramatic heroine . . . , but a genius and a saint, about as completely the opposite of a melodramatic heroine as it is possible for a human being to be."

The genius in terms of soldiering and politics was easy enough for Sybil to assume, and so was the spontaneous, sexless comradeship with men; and if she is no saint—which in Shaw's definition only means one eligible for canonisation—religion was, and is, as inherent in her as in Joan of Arc. She may not "hear voices", but she has always lived very close to God. She is not entirely orthodox so far as dogma goes, but praying is as natural to her as breathing, and by and large she takes her instructions from God, using her Prayer Book and her Bible as daily guides— a little Bible given her by a friend in 1904, when she first went on the stage, and from which she has never been parted except for one short period thirty-odd years ago, when it was being rebound.

"I often wish I'd been trained properly in prayer and meditation. My own way is clumsy, but perhaps it works—I hope so. Lewis and I loved and always used the Confirmation Prayer— 'Defend, O Lord, this thy child with thy heavenly grace . . .' —and also the Collect for the twenty-first Sunday after Trinity, 'Grant, we beseech thee, merciful Lord, to thy faithful people pardon and peace, that they may be cleansed from all their sins, and serve thee with a quiet mind.' We both loved the Book of Wisdom, too, and the ninety-first Psalm, 'For he shall give his angels charge over thee, to keep thee in all thy ways . . . Because he hath set his love upon me, therefore will I deliver him: I will set him on high, because he hath known my name.' During the war, after we heard that our son John had been shot down

over Trondheim and was missing, we used to say this psalm
every day—it made us feel that wherever he was he must be all
right. Then there were the Gospels, which also meant an awful
lot to us, specially St John. Our shared religious upbringing and
outlook were a great source of strength to us."

Sybil was no longer a girl when she played Saint Joan, but one
must remember that Joan was nineteen when she died—quite
a mature age in those days—so there was no need to represent
her as an adolescent. And Sybil was, as always, extremely young
for her age. "I'm only about seventy now," she observes in her
eighty-ninth year.

In the Preface, speaking of the statue in Orleans, Shaw says,
"It is a wonderful face, but quite neutral from the point of view
of the operatic fancier", and on Joan's first appearance in the
play he describes her as having, "Eyes very wide apart and bulging as they very often do in very imaginative people, a long well-
shaped nose with wide nostrils, a short upper lip, resolute but
full-lipped mouth, and handsome fighting chin."

Surely Shaw was thinking of Sybil when he wrote this description, for her beautiful limpid blue eyes "bulge", if one cares to
put it so unpoetically, when she is living in her vivid imagination.

"And so we came to the dress rehearsal. Charles Ricketts'
scenery and costumes were fantastic and wonderful, and John
Foulds had written the most lovely music. He took the Saint
Joan theme from a peasant tune, actually from Lorraine. We
used that real French music on all our tours, but, alas, it was
destroyed in the blitz. It was an inspiration, that music—
there was a splendid use of trumpets, too, as in *The Trojan
Women*. Well, it will never be heard again.

"My mother played the organ off-stage for the cathedral
scene—a Positive Organ, such as Lewis's father had invented.
We all thought the dress rehearsal was pretty exciting, but
Shaw was horrified. 'You've spoilt my play,' he said, 'dressing
yourselves all up like this. Why don't we do it just as it was in
rehearsal? Sybil in her old jersey and the rest of you just as you

were. You looked much better than all dressed up with that stuff on your faces.' He really was in despair, but we promised him that we would rehearse in our costumes and get rid of the dressed-up look. 'It won't be a costume play by the time we've done with it.' "

Many authors experience this shock at the dress rehearsal of their plays. The last rehearsal has been so perfect, every word, every expression, every movement realised, and now suddenly everything seems changed, words and personalities muffled by their trimmings. But it was Shaw himself who had chosen Sybil's costumes. He describes Joan's splendid armour, and says in the cathedral scene that she is "beautifully dressed, but still in male attire". It was by his direction that Sybil had real armour, which was extremely heavy to wear; he would not have any of the silver string concoctions that are so often used. He demanded "real chain armour which clatters as she walks". He and Ricketts had worked closely together on all the designs, and Bruce Winston had lent a hand too. Ricketts had a definite influence on Shaw in the visual aspect of the play, although he did not entirely agree with his conception of Joan. Ricketts would have preferred a more romantic figure.

"Ricketts was awfully funny with Shaw. He had a tiny little voice, and it got tinier and higher as he talked. 'You're so ignorant, Shaw,' he would say as we were all discussing the staging of *Saint Joan*. 'Your wife knows much more than you do.'

"We had something of the old theatre in that production— of the large-scaleness of the old theatre—plus something of the new. The first night was very, very thrilling. It's one of the only first nights when I haven't been paralytic with nerves, and I was exalted—that's the only word for it. Shock! You could feel the shock to the public from the moment the curtain rose. At the end of the trial scene the applause was tremendous, but after the Epilogue it was very doubtful."

Shaw and his wife were present at the first performance, given at the New Theatre on March 26th, 1924, but before the final curtain they stole away, so that it could be truthfully announced that the author was not in the house.

As anticipated, the notices were moderate; the simplicity of the play was on the whole welcomed—such a surprising change from the complexity of *Back to Methuselah*—and the Shavianisms and the Epilogue were generally deplored. Several of the critics did, however, declare that this was Shaw's best play, and all of them agreed that he was splendidly served by his cast. Not only did Sybil's radiant sincerity compel admiration, but Lewis was warmly acclaimed both for his brilliant portrayal of the English chaplain and for the "wisdom" and fineness of his production.

Granville Barker was one of the people who did like the Epilogue, and who found the "Platonic dialogue touch" in the argument between the three men in the tent scene, which the Cassons so much admired, the best in the play. Sybil used to change quickly each night so as to listen to this. Granville Barker thought that Shaw had made Joan too "glib" for a peasant girl, but added, in his letter to the author, "Her last speech, though, in that church scene is magnificent—and Miss T. did it magnificently."

"When we read the notices that morning Lewis said, 'Well, we are good for six weeks on Shaw's name', and when we went up to the theatre a few hours later we couldn't get near the box office. And we played for six months choc-a-bloc.

"I saw Shaw a couple of days later in Leicester Square, looking like a dark angel with the sleeves of his coat flapping. I chased after him—he always moved at a great rate.

" 'We're a success,' he said. 'What shall we do now?'

" 'A play about Elizabeth and Richard III—both together,' I said.

" 'Very well.' He laughed. 'And you and Ernest Thesiger can play both parts turn and turn about.' "

Some months earlier, to Sybil's particular pleasure, because of her warm association with the city, the University of Manchester conferred on her the honorary degree of Doctor of Laws.

"It was great fun. Lewis and I rushed up. I got my degree in the company of John Masefield and Dr Lang, the Archbishop of York. He refused to wear his hat, as he said it would make him look ridiculous."

To quote from the *Daily Mail*:*

"Dare I breathe a comparison with Signora Duse herself?" said Professor Alexander . . . as Miss Thorndike stood; an almost fragile figure in a scarlet robe . . . "Miss Thorndike . . . is dear to our hearts in this city since she first came among us in the great days of the Gaiety."

And the Professor then commented on her good fortune in learning "an exact and sincere method of acting" from Mr Granville Barker and her gifted husband Lewis Casson.

The Archbishop, expressing the thanks of the new graduates to the university, most charmingly said, "How admirable . . . would it have been if thanks had been expressed by a poem composed by Dr Masefield and recited by Dr Thorndike."†

This was an appropriate time for Professor Alexander to mention Duse in connection with Sybil. During the previous year, the year before Duse died, when after her long absence from the stage Cochran brought the great Italian actress once more to London, Sybil saw her for the first time in Ibsen's *Lady from the Sea* and *Ghosts*.

"I was *bouleversée*. I didn't know the language, but every word was distinct, and there she was, old and frail, without any make-up, with the sea in her veins, and there was Oswald's haunted mother. Superb.

"The Professor should not have even thought of comparing me with Duse. I've always been so much rougher, much more experimental, absolutely different."

As an actress, maybe, but, in spite of the utter difference of their

---

* November 12th, 1923.   † *The Manchester Guardian*, November 12th, 1923.

work and their lives, it is easy for thoughts of one of them to merge with thoughts of the other. Sybil shares Duse's concern for human suffering, her thirst for knowledge, her interest in everything, her love of the writings of saints and mystics, her seeking, serving and worship of God. Eva Le Gallienne speaks in one breath of Duse and Teresa of Avila, the saint Sybil loves so well and was so glad to portray. Both she and Duse shared Teresa's violence. "Mystics—far less saints—are rarely made of amiable stuff. There must first be an ego to destroy if one is to set about destroying it."* And both actresses believed *"il faut s'oublier"*.

One important thing that happened to Sybil during the run of *Saint Joan* was the birth of her interest in the Kingsley Hall Settlement, founded in Bow by Muriel Lester and her sister Doris. The Lesters were admirable and delightful women who, shocked by the slums they often passed through, had persuaded their father to give them the money that they would ultimately have inherited, in order to start this educational settlement in that desperately poor district of London's East End. The sisters lived in the settlement, allowing themselves very little money for their personal use, and they used to take groups of their members to see *Saint Joan* before they ever met Sybil.

Here is an extract from Muriel Lester's autobiography:†

"The heat of that summer I shall always remember, because I spent so many evenings in close contact with the theatre roof. Many parties were made up at Kingsley Hall. We would travel west together, stand an hour or more outside the gallery door, pay our one and threepence, climb up to the heights, and take our places on the benches. Such narrow benches! And so ill constructed that even those with short legs couldn't sit straight! Our knees had to point all the same way, to the right or to the left . . . I saw the play seven times that summer. Finally I wrote to Sybil Thorndike, feeling that she would want to know what *Saint Joan* meant to working people. I told her

---

* Eva Le Gallienne: *The Mystic in the Theatre, Eleanora Duse* (Bodley Head, 1966).

† *It Occurred to Me* (Harper, New York, 1937).

how, at the end of the first court scene, a girl thrust her elbow into Mary Jane's ribs and in the midst of all the applause exclaimed, 'Coo, Miss, when she says, "Who is for God and for Joan?" don't it make yer want to jump down on to the stage and stand beside her, and shout out, "I'm with yer!"'

"Sybil Thorndike and the Kingsley Hall people have been in love with each other ever since. She apparently finds Bow a nice place to stay in. Whatever theatre she plays at, she gives the stage door porter instructions to let anyone up to her dressing-room who comes from Kingsley Hall. We are very lucky."

"Almost all Bow saw *Saint Joan* in the end," Sybil says, "and the Lester sisters became our dear friends. We loved the Settlement—it was a sort of continuation of parish activities, which I'd always enjoyed because I love meeting people of different kinds and learning about their lives. And another strong link was that all Kingsley Hall leaders have been pacifists."

"Charity", than which no word is more beautiful, has come to have a somewhat dreary connotation, but nobody could contemplate the life of Sybil Thorndike without using it. Charity belongs to her in its dictionary definition—"Christian love of fellow men"—and she practises it with joy and compassion, and entirely without condescesnion. As someone once observed, "Sybil has no airs, only graces." Her charities are not "extras", they are woven into the fabric of her nature, just as other kinds of journeys are, all as essential to her living as are religion, music and the theatre, part of her being, heart and soul.

Gandhi, refusing luxurious official hospitality for the Round Table Conference in London, lived at Kingsley Hall and maintained his inflexible discipline. Celebrities who wanted to see him would seek him out walking at five in the morning on the banks of a dirty canal. It was there that Lewis met him, while Sybil was on tour. Never meeting Gandhi has been one of the great disappointments of her life. And at the Settlement they both came to know Raj Kumari Amrit Kaur, whom years later they would see in India. Sybil was immensely impressed by her beauty both of person and of speech—not only by what she said, but by her beautiful English. She had been educated in England, and Sybil always maintains that when Indians speak English well it is the best in the world.

"There was also Mr Keir, the High Commissioner, whom we saw again thirty years later in Bombay. He used a spinning-wheel—it was absolutely fascinating. Once, on Gandhi's birthday, Lewis and I went down to the Settlement very early in the morning. There were about twenty of us of many different nationalities. We all sat silent and still and Mr Keir spun. It was here too that we met George Lansbury, the Labour M.P., who was such an influence in my life."

Sybil has continued to this day to visit Kingsley Hall, now at Dagenham under the direction of Sydney Russell, who says of her:

"Caring is the secret of Sybil, always caring, irrespective of merit. And courtesy innate—the same to a duchess as to a dustman—not the slightest hint of change. Everyone feels of worth with her. She's always asking about my 'naughty boys', and her message always is, 'Show them you care'. Also she drives one on. She can be very emphatic if one shows any sign of giving way under the strain. 'Of course you must go on. The work must be done. Caring.' "

Saint Joan, still filling the house, had to be taken off because Matheson Lang was coming into the theatre with a new play, but it was revived before long very successfully at the Regent Theatre, Euston Road, and later at the Lyceum—"lovely to be playing in the theatre that Irving and Ellen Terry acted in"— and also in Paris, where they had a most enthusiastic reception, particularly by the Pitoëffs, who later played *Saint Joan* themselves and brought the French version to London. Many actresses have played Joan since, but the play has never ceased to belong to the Cassons. "To Saint Sybil Thorndike from

Saint Bernard Shaw" runs the inscription in the copy of *Saint Joan* which is one of her dearest treasures, for this play had a profound and lasting effect upon her life and her attitude to theatre.

Twenty-one years later her daughter Ann would play the part, and almost at the same time, during the Second World War, John Casson was to produce *Saint Joan* in his prison camp in Germany.

And can any one of us ever forget Joan's words that close the play?

"O God Who madest this beautiful earth, when will it be ready to receive Thy Saints? How long, O Lord, how long?"*

* In the printed version the line runs: "O God that madest", etc., but Sybil Thorndike, with Shaw's agreement, used the word "Who".

CHAPTER XI

OVER THE HORIZON
(1925–1928)

IT WAS DURING the six months' run of *Saint Joan* at the Regent, in the spring of 1925, that Edith Craig brought the Cassons *The Verge* by the American writer Susan Glaspell, an exact contemporary of Sybil's, who, with her husband George Cram Cook, had been one of the founders of the famous Provincetown Players in New York.

"Edy said, 'Here's a lunatic play. I don't understand it and I don't suppose you will. But it's wonderful and we must do it.'

"In fact I understood every word, and so did Lewis, and we agreed that we must do it. Here was another mould-breaker. In a way *The Verge* led towards what I was to find in the writings of Teilhard de Chardin. It was the first time I had come across the theory of the growth of the individual, the scientific concept which explains how certain unidentified creatures spring into another form of existence, and how it's always small, sensitive forms of life that make this leap, not heavily armoured things like dinosaurs which became extinct. Later I read about this theory in Gerald Heard's *The Source of Civilisation*, but the germ of it was there in *The Verge*, and I was thrilled by the whole idea. What Claire, the young woman whom I played, was trying to do with plants symbolised what she wanted to do in herself as a human being—feel out and get through into another state, as great spirits have been able to do, as surely Christ Himself did."

During this time the Cassons were also working for Edith Craig and her Pioneer Players at the Regent Theatre for a few special matinées of *Hippolytus*. At one of these Sybil had a dangerous accident. Nicholas Hannen was playing Hippolytus and Sybil Phaedra, "And as I rushed off to commit suicide—'Die, but how die?'—I very nearly did". She fell full force off the rostrum, but in spite of bruises and stiffness went straight on with her life of unending activity. This accident, for which she had no orthodox treatment, although a healer came to her dressing-room and made it possible to continue working, may well have been the cause of later troubles.

In her description of the first set for *The Verge*, Susan Glaspell writes:

"The curtain is drawn upon darkness and wind. It opens a moment later on the greenhouse in the sunshine of a snowy morning. The snow piled outside is at times blown through the air. The frost has made patterns on the glass as if—as Plato would have it—the patterns inherent in abstract nature and behind all life had to come out, not only in the creative heat within, but in the creative cold on the other side of the glass. And the wind makes patterns of sound around the glass house . . . This is not a greenhouse where plants are being displayed, nor the usual workshop for the growing of them, but a place for experiment with plants, a laboratory."

And this is what henceforth the theatre was to be for Sybil— a laboratory for research and experiment in human nature and the possible breakthrough, over the horizon. The words "over the horizon", which so aptly describe Sybil's philosophy, come from a sculptor. "The artist," he wrote, "is the sower who casts about his original thought, woven out of his intuition and imagination; when the conditions are right, germination takes place. The artist is the sower who at the harvest time is over the horizon—on his way to sow new ground."* Sybil Thorndike is a sower. She had many lines as Claire that were after her own heart—forty-odd

* Leon Underwood: *Art for Heaven's Sake* (1934).

years later she remembers them still. "We need not be held in forms moulded for us. There is outness and otherness . . . Plants do it. The big leap, it's called . . ."

Lewis played the part of Tom, the man who understands what Claire is trying to do and with whom she shares a deep and rare love. In one scene she describes her little son who died as a child. "He was movement—and wonder. In his short life were many flights." She is glad that he did not live. "Wonder would die—and he'd laugh at soaring. Though I liked his voice. So I wish you'd stay near me, for I like your voice too."

It always moved Sybil to say these words to Lewis, whose voice she had loved from the first time she heard it.

The critics on the whole praised the play, but Hugh Walpole was scandalised. He wrote urgently to Sybil, "I beg you not to go on with this play. It is destructive." She answered vehemently that it was quite the most constructive play she had ever been in.

Next came a little play called *The Round Table*, described by the author, Lennox Robinson, as a comic tragedy. It had just enough other-worldliness—the round table symbolising "the stupid going-round-the-mulberry-bush" of domestic life, which the heroine at the last moment rejects—to appeal to Sybil, but it is a slight work, and did not greatly please either the critics or the audience.

On, then, with *The Lie* again, *The Medea*, a tour of *Saint Joan* and various minor productions. Emlyn Williams has these memories of the Cassons' Oxford visit when he was an undergraduate:

"In June [1925], in Peckwater, I walked on at a flying open-air matinée of *Medea* given by Sybil Thorndike and Lewis Casson during their London run of *The Lie* at Wyndhams . . . The setting was the library façade and pillars; the performance must have been impressive, and perhaps more than that when Miss Thorndike flung open the great first-floor window, distractedly picked up her recumbent daughter Ann and seemed about to throw her at a startled front row of dons. Changing afterwards inside, I admired the professional bustle with which the Cassons packed before the dash for the London train; as they streaked across to Canterbury Gate, the youngest middle-aged couple I had ever seen—'Lewis darling, the thermos!'—and into a waiting taxi, I stood looking after them, a dog that had been left behind."*

And from this production Sybil specially remembers the Welsh boy, carrying a spear, who was to mean so much to her fifteen years later, when she created Miss Moffat in his play *The Corn is Green*. And she describes how the long tail of her wonderful flame-coloured *Medea* dress was blown by the wind right up a column, "so that it became a pillar of fire".

At the end of the year came her performance as Queen Katharine to Norman V. Norman's Henry VIII, a lavish production by the Albery–Casson management, rather daringly presented at the Empire, well-known as a music hall, with Charles Ricketts once more responsible for the visual side and dressing Sybil regally in ermine and velvet. Laurence Olivier played the first Serving Man and was also assistant stage manager.

"I was a marvellous A.S.M.," he says, "stopping people talking, protecting my saint and heroine. I ought to have stayed an A.S.M. all my life."

The following year *The Cenci* was revived, Olivier playing the Count's servant. He had only a few lines to say, but once again the Cassons recognised that he was that rare thing, an actor born with technique.

Life in Carlyle Square meanwhile continued full, lively and reasonably tempestuous. The little girls did a great deal of music with their mother, a side of their education in which their grandmother, who was living nearby in Oakley Street, also took part. Later, Ann and Mary had lessons in French and arithmetic from "Peggy"—Margaret Webster—"An extraordinary notion of Lewis's," she says, "which resulted in my learning far more than I taught".† She was a great admirer of the Cassons, playing

* Emlyn Williams: *George* (Hamish Hamilton, 1961).

† Margaret Webster: *The Same Only Different* (Victor Gollancz, London, 1969).

various parts for them then, and shortly becoming a very good actress and a highly competent director. On tour she understudied Sybil as Saint Joan.

John Casson, now sixteen years old, was about to go into the Royal Navy—to use his own words, "the hard way". Christopher had left the *Worcester* for the Royal Naval College the year before, and John, "slightly hipped by this", was more determined than ever to fulfil his own ambition to become an admiral. So in 1926 he too left the *Worcester* and joined the training ship *Erebus*. At about this time Christopher remembers his great pleasure when his parents came down to give a recital of prose and poetry at Dartmouth.

"The Headmaster, Mr Kempson, whose daughter Rachel married Michael Redgrave, warned us not to do anything patriotic, as the boys would hate it. All the same we gave them *Henry the Fifth*."

In March 1926 *Saint Joan* was again produced at the Lyceum with Harold Scott as the Dauphin and Russell Thorndike as Bluebeard, but the run was interrupted by the general strike, when most theatres had to close because of the total lack of transport. The Cassons were entirely on the side of the strikers, and Lewis enjoyed driving the trade union organisers in his car. They were both now very active members of the Labour Party and spoke at many meetings, numbering among their friends the Pankhursts, Margaret Bondfield, George Lansbury and many other leading socialists.

Just after this Ben Greet and the Cassons organised a special matinée of *Hamlet* at the Lyceum in support of the Sadler's Wells Fund, Russell playing Hamlet, Sybil Gertrude and Fay Compton Ophelia. Although Russell was not in a good state— he had suffered terribly from his war wounds, and the after-effects were hard to overcome—he did well as Hamlet, and adored playing with "those two glorious actresses", his sister and Fay Compton.

"A most extraordinary thing happened at the beginning of

that *Hamlet*," Sybil remembers. "The dress rehearsal was a shocker—really dreadful—the musicians, the trumpeters particularly, were mucking about, and Lewis came into my dressing-room and said, 'We'll never get this show on. I've had to take over from B.G. because he can't do it.' So he took over the production completely and he said to me, 'Look at the psalms. For goodness sake look at the psalms for today', and the first psalm I read was, 'The Lord shall rehearse it . . . The singers also and the trumpeters shall he rehearse; all my fresh springs shall be in thee.' Wasn't that wonderful? What day is that psalm for? The 17th. Then it must have been the 17th December. And today's the 17th too. What a nice coincidence that this should be the psalm for today. Well, that afternoon we gave an electric performance—Russell, Fay, me, Robert Atkins, Lewis and Lawrence Anderson, unforgettable as Brother Martin in *Saint Joan*.

It was during this same summer that the next play of note turned up for Sybil. This was Clemence Dane's *Granite*. "Clemmie the Dane", as the Cassons affectionately named her— her real name was Winifred Ashton—had known the Cassons since the publication of her fine novel *A Regiment of Women* and the production of her first plays *A Bill of Divorcement* and *Will Shakespeare*, both successes in 1921. Now they were to become very close friends. Clemence Dane had a genius for friendship. She was in every way a big woman, large in stature, heart and mind. She wrote, she painted, she was a sculptor, she cooked, she gave herself with boundless generosity to her numerous friends, and she was, perhaps, an actor *manqué*. She was very erudite and a tremendous talker, and she and Lewis used to have endless vehement arguments on all manner of subjects, to the great satisfaction of them both. Judith in *Granite* was another role in which Sybil was able to trace a counterpart in herself, and she found Clemence Dane most inspiring to work with.

"She was always delving down into essentials, and *Granite*

was tremendously interesting. It's a play of storm and sea, and I've always had a terror of the sea. I played Judith, oh, such a fierce character! Based on Emma Hamilton—Clemence Dane was mad about Nelson, and the play was founded on the Nelson tradition and set in those days, but on Lundy Island. There were three men in the play, and myself, and a girl who played the little maid who sang the song about Nelson and Emma Hamilton, by Martin Shaw, and had that telling line, 'The Devil always gives you your wish, and then when you're sorry he laughs'. Lewis played that awful nameless man who was really the Devil, and Clemence Dane said she never forgot his laugh. At the end, when I saw the man I loved—beautifully played by Beau Hannen*—pushed over the cliff by that Devil, Clemence Dane said I must give a terrible shriek, but I invented a very high whine. It really was awful, that whine, and it got tremendous notices. I think it's a frightfully good play, and so did Mrs Patrick Campbell, who came to see it several times.

"Another person who rather surprisingly came to see *Granite* was Rabindranath Tagore. Lewis and I had been friends of his for years, ever since I recited the poem Laurence Binyon wrote to welcome him to England. After that, whenever he came to England he sought us out and we had long talks which added to my passionate interest in India. One morning I went to his hotel at about eight o'clock, and he was there with a number of his fascinating Indian professors and talked to me about theatre. That night he came to see the play with his professors, and afterwards came on the stage and talked about what theatre should mean in the life of the people. It was wonderful, and the stage hands, who always dash away the moment the curtain comes down, all stayed and listened entranced. Afterwards I joined a dramatic society that was doing the plays of Kalidasa, who is the sort of Shakespeare of India. I remember having a bit of difficulty with my sari. We had darling Indian ladies to help us, and I asked the one who was dressing me for a safety pin, but she said my tummy

* Nicholas Hannen.

would keep it up. Well, my muscles weren't like Indian ones, and in the middle of my most impassioned speech I felt the whole thing slipping. I clutched myself round my tummy, and the next day one of the notices said, 'It was a most original way of showing emotion, but we felt something very true come from right down in her middle.' "

When *Granite* came off the Cassons, with their four children, went for a long holiday in France, travelling in Lewis's spanking new five-seater Armstrong Siddeley—he never lost his enthusiasm for cars. First came an eight-day visit to the châteaux of the Loire, especially those connected with Joan of Arc, such as Châteaudun, where there is a portrait of Dunois. Then they went on to Port Manech in Brittany, which was pure bliss. There was a long stretch of sand about a mile from the hotel, and Sybil used to swim that mile, while the others walked round on land.

She would not have been content unless she had been studying some role, so, as the Cassons were planning a big production of *Macbeth* shortly at the Prince's, with Henry Ainley as Macbeth and Lewis Casson as Banquo, she constantly declaimed her Lady Macbeth lines at the top of her voice, to the great astonishment of any natives who happened to be within hearing.

She was excited at the prospect of playing this part again, a role in which she felt that she had never yet achieved what she visualised. But this time the lavishness of Charles Ricketts' sets and costumes irked her; she felt that she could have done better in an Elizabethan setting and even in ordinary clothes. "I was trammelled by all the scenery and my dresses—even more gorgeous than Ellen Terry's. I had a dress like a wasp and a huge cloak." And although Henry Ainley's voice was magnificent, he was in a quite unstable condition. Early in the production, much against his will, he had to retire to hospital, leaving Macbeth to his understudy, Hubert Carter, a keen Shakespearean who had worked a lot with Tree and was an old friend and colleague of the Cassons.

The next play was *The Greater Love*, a study of revolutionaries in Czarist Russia by J. B. Fagan, which Sybil found very interesting, and which her small daughters revelled in, as did her secretary Susan Holmes. Fagan had actually written the play for Mary Grey, who was unable to do it, and Agate thought Sybil should have been more "scrumptious" in her portrayal of the character. However, she played it as she imagined Nadejda Ivanovna Pesloff, as a good revolutionary and a saviour of the people.

The Greater Love was not a success at the Princes Theatre, but proved very popular in the provinces. It was in this play that the young Charles Laughton first made a mark with his performance as a Russian General.

"Fagan couldn't see anything in him at rehearsals—he used to rehearse in a dirty old mackintosh and one couldn't hear a word he said. Fagan wanted to get rid of him, but Lewis said, 'No, there's something potentially right about his acting', and kept him on. In the end Charles was marvellous, frightfully funny—I don't think Fagan realised how funny that part was —and he fairly waltzed away with the notices."

In March of this year they presented *Angela* by Lady Bell, with Sybil in the name part. This play was chosen from among several others suggested to Queen Mary for a special matinée, which delighted Sybil, as Lady Bell was an important figure in her life.

"She was the wife of Sir Hugh Bell, the iron-master, and a very remarkable woman—they were the parents of Gertrude Bell of Arab fame. We had met her years before, in our Manchester days, when *The Way the Morning Goes*, the play that made her name, was produced. She had written to Lewis saying, 'There's a girl in your company I'd like for the lead. She's called Sybil Thorndike.' And Lewis wrote back, 'I'm glad you think she's good. I've just married her!' I wasn't able to do that play because of other engagements, but I sat with Sir Hugh and Lady Bell on the first night, and from that moment she and I were friends. Oh, I loved her! She was my mental guide, and made me work at my French and keep up my piano-playing. She was a very fine pianist herself, and we used to play together constantly on two pianos.

"She introduced me to that wonderful woman Elizabeth Robins, who with William Archer and J. T. Grein was responsible for bringing Ibsen to the English stage, and wrote such a number of fine books. I shall never forget the effect of Lisa Robins's eyes. Except for Duse, I have never seen such eyes.

"She was already an old woman then and I never saw her in any of her great roles, but as we became friends and talked about theatre she lifted me into another plane of being. And once, when she was staying in Northumberland, we visited her there. She came into the room looking like a little ghost with blazing eyes, but as we talked, age and illness dropped from her—and there was Hedda, there was Hilda Wangel, Rebecca West, all in a moment performed before us. We were overwhelmed and realised that this was true acting, this transforming of feeble flesh into spirit and fire; and it did not exhaust her but rather renewed her life.

"When I saw her for the last time, very, very frail, in her ninetieth year, I said to her, 'If it hadn't been for you, we might not have seen Ibsen—anyway not so soon'. She said, 'There is always someone to start a new chapter, and I am lucky to have taken part in that revolutionary chapter of the theatre.' I feel that in a way Lewis and I have shared in that luck."

In this same summer of 1926 the Cassons flew to Paris for performances of *Saint Joan* and *The Medea* for the International Festival at the enormous Théâtre des Champs-Elysées, organised by Firmin Gémier, whom Sybil had come to know when she played Lady Macbeth at the Odéon earlier, and who now became a friend. Russell Thorndike played Warwick in *Saint Joan*, Mary Casson was his page—her first speaking part, except in several of the plays acted by children of the stars, organised by J. B. Fagan, in which all the Casson children had appeared.

Sybil and Lewis now agreed to work for the Old Vic Company once more, for a nominal salary. The theatre was being restored, and while the builders were in, Nigel Playfair lent the company his theatre, The Lyric, Hammersmith, for a season of Shakespeare.

"It was a beautiful season," Lewis said, beaming with memories, "and Sybil and I had the leading parts."

The plays were staged simply in an Elizabethan manner, with the Cassons' old friend, Andrew Leigh, not only acting but directing, with Lewis's co-operation. The latter was therefore able to give his skill and energy to playing, and to remind the public what a fine actor he was. How much everyone enjoyed his robust Petruchio, vowing to woo Katharina were she "as old as Sibyl, and as curst and shrewd as Socrates' Xantippe or worse". He played Petruchio like a pirate sailor, Sybil says. Next came his moving Shylock to Sybil's witty Portia, and then they did *Much Ado About Nothing*, less successful than the other productions, perhaps because the best comedy scene was played in moonlight, which was far too dark. Now once more was heard the delicious line of Beatrice's that Ellen Terry made her own— "A star danced, and under that I was born", words which surely Sybil inherits. The gay Beatrice was always one of her favourite parts, and there are other lines that bring her character to mind: "There's little of the melancholy element in her . . . she hath often dreamed of unhappiness, and waked herself with laughing." The Cassons returned to these plays as to old friends, but always finding something new. "A play is quite different in each place you do it. We found this so clearly on our travels."

It was during this Hammersmith season that Herbert Wilcox invited Sybil to play Edith Cavell in the film—still a silent one— *Dawn*. Although she was not generally enthusiastic about playing in films, this time she did not hesitate, for she had a deep reverence for the heroic Edith Cavell, and admired Wilcox's work as a film director. She had Bernard Shaw's strong support in this new venture.

"Edith [he had written in the preface to *Saint Joan*], like Joan was an arch heretic: in the middle of the war she declared before the world that 'Patriotism is not enough'. She nursed enemies back to health and assisted their prisoners to escape, making it abundantly clear that she would help any fugitive or distressed person without asking whose side he was on."

And later on, when it came to the great controversy as to whether it were wise to present *Dawn*, in view of the offence to Germany, Shaw declared:

"That film, in rather a wonderful way, with the assistance of a great English actress, does bring home to the people that above all the regulations you can make, above all the laws you can make, above all the duties you owe to your country, above the laws of war, there is something higher than that, and that is the law of God."

"This was a really tremendous experience," Sybil says. "I used Edith Cavell's own *Thomas à Kempis*, lent me by one of her relatives, with the special passages marked on which she had meditated in her last hours. I lent this to Anna Neagle when she played the part. I can't describe what the end was like. I really felt I was going to be shot. I was shot in a field, and they played *For all the Saints*."

In her concentration on Edith Cavell, Sybil became so like her in expression and gesture that one young soldier, who had known and loved Nurse Cavell, fainted when he saw Sybil at the studios in the room which was so familiar to him. Others, too, found *Dawn* almost unbearably moving.

The Cassons' next venture was one of their rare failures—an elaborate production at the Strand of *Judith of Israel*, a play based on the Apocrypha.

"We lost about £8000 over that," Lewis Casson said, "and it served us right. We should never have done it."

"It was intended for Sarah Bernhardt, but it wasn't finished in time," Sybil added, "and again, I should have been more luscious. Lewis engaged all the down-and-out, out-of-work actors he could find for the crowd of starving people in the play, and at the dress rehearsal they all turned up in juvenile make-ups. Lewis was in a fury. 'Why the hell do you think I engaged you?' he stormed. 'Because you *looked* like those starving people.'"

When *Judith* closed, Sybil revived old memories by once more playing *Everyman* for Ben Greet, this time at the Rudolf Steiner Hall, very much a family affair as Lewis, Russell and Eileen Thorndike were all in the cast. Then came *The Making of an Immortal* by George Moore, in which Sybil played Queen Elizabeth and Charles Laughton Ben Jonson. Reviewing this play, Herbert Farjeon observed that Sybil in real life "is so full of enthusiasm that restraint on the stage comes to her as the relief experienced by many other actresses when they perform parts that are emotional". In fact no part is a relief to her; it is simply another exploration into human nature, herself forgotten. She went on from this to Leon M. Lion's production of *The Stranger in the House* at Wyndham's, but early in the run, in the spring of 1928, left with Lewis for their tour of South Africa. Bernard Shaw had sold the South African rights of *Saint Joan*, and he was anxious to fulfil his agreement there without further delay.

CHAPTER XII

NEW MEANING FOR MEDEA

(1928–1929)

RUSSELL WAS THE only member of the family who had been to South Africa, in the old days with Matheson Lang, and he had fired his sister with enthusiasm for the country—not a difficult thing to do, for Sybil lives not only in the characters she is playing, but also in the experiences of anybody of whom she is fond. She had long been looking forward to this new adventure, and had read a great deal in preparation for the tour, including Olive Schreiner's *The Story of an African Farm*. She continued her studies during the voyage with the excellent book on Johannesburg by Sarah Gertrude Millin, whom she was soon to meet.

The Cassons sailed from Southampton on April 29th, 1928, with their daughters Ann and Mary, now fourteen and thirteen years old, and a company carefully chosen for the South African repertoire: it included Carleton Hobbs, Walter Hudd and Colette O'Neill, who later married Miles Malleson. Planning their programmes in London, they had been advised that Shakespeare would not be wanted, but in fact *Macbeth* turned out to be in such demand that they had to cable home for the wardrobe.

It was a beautiful voyage, and after a brief stop in Madeira they sailed on to Cape Town, arriving in perfect autumn weather. During the three-day overland journey to Johannesburg the Cassons had with them Carrie Rothkugel, of the Johannesburg press, who had met the boat. She was a great help, not only in paving the way with excellent publicity, but in explaining Africa to the Cassons, to whom racial discrimination came as a horrifying shock, although apartheid at that time was far less

rigid than it is today. Carrie Rothkugel was friendly and kindly
towards the Africans, but she was shocked at the idea that they
should be treated as equals, and assured the Cassons that "the
natives must be kept in their place". Throughout the long
journey arguments raged, but none the less the Cassons succeeded
in keeping Carrie as a friend for life.

"I shall never forget our first breath of air in Johannesburg.
So high up, and so wonderfully pure. Soon after we reached
our hotel we met a most remarkable Indian, Mr Sastri,* a
high-caste Brahmin who was one of the founders of the
Servants of India Society and Agent of the Government of
India to South Africa, sent to help the immigrant Indians.
When he first arrived he had been made to stay at hotels for
Africans, because of the colour of his skin, although he was a
great scholar—he was lecturing at the Rand University—
but by now he had overcome this prejudice. In our hotel in
Johannesburg he was sitting at the next table to us, and we
became tremendous friends. He spoke the most beautiful
English, giving ordinary words a special meaning by his
pronunciation. He was a brilliant orator and had a great
influence on Lewis and me; he often took us to the Bantu
Centre, and through him we got to know many of the native
people, and liked them enormously.

"We opened with *The Lie*, which wasn't a very good choice,
as the audience was expecting something big—an all-white
audience, to our amazement and horror. But in the morning,
when we were rehearsing *Medea*, the cleaners, who were all
natives, gradually worked their way down to the orchestra
rails, and Lewis said to me, 'Just look at those men!' And
there they were, doing their sweeping and polishing to the
rhythm of the Chorus—with the most beautiful movements.

"One day, in one of the native clubs, we met a clergyman, an
African, who told me that he'd met me when I was reading to
students at King's College, London. 'There we were friends,'
he said, 'but here I mustn't walk on the same side of the street

* The Right Honourable V. S. Srimvasa Sastri.

as you, and I can't come to your plays.' So Lewis and I went to the management and said, 'We want the native people to come'. They protested, 'You can't mix them with the whites', and we said, 'Well, can't you shut the theatre to the whites?' They were horrified. 'No, no, we can't do that. It would be breaking our contract.' 'Then shut the dress circle to the whites,' I said, 'and let the natives come.' And they did—very broad-mindedly and kindly, they did. And oh, they were the most breath-taking audience I'd ever played to! You see, then, in my part as Medea, I was representing the Africans. I'd suddenly seen a new meaning to the play. Until now it had been for me a war cry for all oppressed people—now it was the blacks, as Medea, crying out against the civilised whites in the person of Jason, the Greek. And they felt it. You heard sort of deep-breathing sounds coming from the dress circle, and it was absolutely thrilling. It really was very broadminded of the management to let them come. When we went back to Africa later, things were far more difficult, although we had thought them bad enough then."

The company did their whole repertoire during that first eight-week season in Johannesburg—*The Lie, Saint Joan, Jane Clegg, The Medea, Macbeth*, with Lewis playing the Thane superbly, as well as most of the other leading male parts, besides directing every production. There was one new play, *The Silver Cord*, a domestic drama by Sidney Howard, first produced in London the year before with Lilian Braithwaite in the part now played by Sybil. Mrs Phelps, to quote one of the characters in the play, was "a type of self-centred, self-pitying, son-devouring tigress", and Sybil welcomed the part as a change from heroic roles. She still refused to be "catalogued". "Any human being is interesting to portray. That is what acting is about."

Saint Joan and *The Medea* were the most popular of their productions, and they even presented *The Medea* and *Jane Clegg* in a double bill, Sybil finding it fascinating to play those two deserted wives, the fierce, passionate Caucasian princess and the cold, restrained middle-class Englishwoman.

All the members of the company found their energy quite tremendous in the pure heights of Johannesburg, and when they were not in the theatre their time was filled with memorable experiences, which to this day Sybil relives with joy. One of their favourite adventures was going down to the gold-mines, where the workers, Sybil says, looked like Rodin sculptures. It was in the compounds here that they saw the Bantu and Zulu dances which excited them so tremendously.

"The dancing and the acting and the thrilling music on the Kaffir pianos and the drums—the wonderful different tones of these instruments, made by stretching skins over all kinds of tins and things, and the lovely laughing people—it was all so extraordinary and exciting. I don't think anywhere except India has had such an effect on my life and work as Africa— such vigour, and so ancient. We used to go to Mass, High Anglican Mass at St Cyprian's—a native church presided over by Wilfred Parker, later Bishop of Pretoria. We were the only white people there. We had Communion with them and everything, and their wild voices singing the *Agnus Dei* and the *Creed* were thrilling, like some extraordinary incantation. But what we enjoyed most of all were our excursions into the veldt—the vast space of it and the fresh smell of it.

"We used to go into the native kraals—all clean as a new pin and very sparsely furnished. That impressed us a lot, because one always has too much, and we felt this really was the way to furnish. The natives used to welcome us and give us some of their quite disgusting beer—at least, Lewis seemed to enjoy it, but I thought it was awful. Oh, I loved those visits! I remember once a woman came out of one of the kraals with a baby in her arms, and the baby's eyes grew double their size as she stared at Ann, who had a mop of very fair hair. She'd never seen a fair child like that, and we'd never seen anything like that little black baby's enormous eyes. We all of us simply roared with laughter.

"We made friends with many South Africans and found them delightful. One of the Dutch Afrikaners we particularly

liked was Judge Krause, the man who had handed over the keys
of Johannesburg to Lord Roberts. We used to go out into the
veldt with him and his English wife and stay for weekends—
the winter veldt with the early morning frosts turning the grass
to a lovely pinky beige."

Then there was the meeting with General Smuts, whom Sybil
described to Russell as "courtly and beautiful". He was at this
time closely connected with the League of Nations, and had
recently published *Holism and Evolution*, his book expounding
unity and continuity found in nature, and he was resolved to
reaffirm faith in the dignity and fundamental rights of human
beings.

"We went to see the General and his wife at their home in
Irene, near Pretoria, with Sarah Gertrude Millin, and Mrs
Smuts received us in an old dress and no stockings. I thought
she was the housekeeper. She was a brilliant woman and a
wonderful speaker, but she didn't care tuppence about appearances, and always carried an enormous umbrella. She refused to
be stylish even when the Prince of Wales visited their home.
The General asked her afterwards if she couldn't have given
the poor young man something a little more interesting to eat,
and she simply responded, 'Why? Wednesday is the day for
mutton hash'. All the flowers round the house were local
wild ones. General Smuts wouldn't allow any other kind to be
planted—he wanted the veldt to come right up to the door."

Soon the journeys started again.

"How we loved Durban! We used to go to the shows and
back again in rickshaws, Ann with Lewis and Mary with me,
racing each other through the streets. I learnt to surf in Durban.
It was wonderful, though one was always a bit scared of sharks.
I remember one day when all four of us were coming up out of
the water looking like the wrath of God, with our hair all over
the shop and smothered in sand, we were met by two very

smart Zulus, a man and a woman, exquisitely turned out, she hung over with wonderful beads and both of them beautifully groomed and walking like gods. At the sight of us they burst out laughing. They thought we looked the end—as we did. We thought they were magnificent, and we kept turning back and waving and shouting with laughter."

In Pretoria Sybil was delighted to meet her old friend Neville Talbot, whom she had dearly loved in her teens, and who was now the Bishop. Here, as in Johannesburg, they were fascinated by the liveliness of the church life. The Mirfield Fathers of the Anglican Community of the Resurrection, originating in Yorkshire, were largely responsible for this. The Cassons had known Father "Ted" Talbot, the Bishop's brother, who had been the head of this community in England, so they felt very much at home in the churches here, and those "violent vibrant native voices" were to them "live theatre".

And so up to Rhodesia. At Bulawayo there had been a drought for many months, but with the arrival of the company rain came down in torrents and they were treated as if they were gods. There were delicious swimming pools here, which they enjoyed with a retinue of dragon-flies. They made an expedition to the Victoria Falls, revelled in the cool of the Rain Forest, saw the Falls by daylight and by moonlight, and bathed in the Zambesi River, watched by families of baboons with faces like lions.

In Livingstone they played *The Lie* at the Bioscope. The back of the cinema was taken out and chairs were put right across the road to make room for the swarming audience. The pianola, which served as orchestra, had gone wrong, so Mary played the piano before the play and between the acts. But as the Governor was present it was imperative to have *God Save The King* at the end of the performance, so, as Mary did not know it, Sybil rushed down after her curtain calls and played it herself. Both the little girls were active members of the company, playing the two sons in *The Medea*, the two pages in *Saint Joan* and the children in *Jane Clegg*, while Ann was the little boy in *The Lie*. Mary also on many occasions stood in for her mother at rehearsals of *Saint Joan*, and Ann proved to be a most efficient secretary. The two girls had been allowed to leave school for this tour on condition that they continued their studies, which they did with considerable pleasure under the supervision of their parents. "We only learned *about* poetry at school," they explained, "instead of learning poetry."

On one occasion, when the Cassons were staying with Chris Botha, of the famous Botha family, and his wife Minna in the veldt outside Bloemfontein, they were invited to ride up a *kopje* —a mushroom-shaped hill. "Can you ride?" Sybil was asked, and though she had never ridden anything other than a donkey on the sands she replied at once, "Of course I can".

"I pretended I was Douglas Fairbanks, and I looked like him too. I rode all day and galloped a lot, holding on with both hands, and I wasn't sore at all."

Finally, after their long and highly successful tour they found themselves back in Cape Town, and were struck at once by the more liberal attitude to the natives that they found here, compared with the other places they had visited. They stayed right on the sea and swam to their hearts' content, "the water icy on one side of the peninsula as it surges in from the South Pole, and almost lukewarm on the other". They joined the Mountain Club, too, and did tremendous climbs.

"When we got to the top of Table Mountain, oh, my Lord, it was marvellous! And the leader said, 'We want you to come along to where they are building the cable railway and spit at it with us.' So we all went and solemnly spat, because we felt that nobody ought to get to the top of Table Mountain unless they'd climbed it. I've felt that about Snowdon and other mountains too. Nobody has any business to get to the top of a mountain unless they've climbed it. That goes for everything."

Early in the New Year of 1929 they sailed for home, "deepened and broadened by all our new experiences".

CHAPTER XIII

LAUREATE

(1929–1932)

THEY HAD SCARCELY set foot again in Carlyle Square before they started rehearsals for the production of *Major Barbara* at Wyndhams, delighted not only to be working for Bernard Shaw once more, but also to be in touch with Gilbert Murray, who had been closely associated with Shaw in the writing of this play. Adolphus Cusins, the Professor of Greek, is a portrait of Murray—he even recites lines from *The Bacchae* in Murray's translation—and in the original 1905 production Granville Barker, at Shaw's request, had made up to look as much like Murray as possible. The characters of Major Barbara and Lady Britomart were also designed by Shaw to bear a close resemblance to Lady Mary Murray and her mother, the Countess of Carlisle.

This aspect of *Major Barbara* charmed the Cassons. Moreover, not only was Lewis producing the play, but he was also playing Cusins, Murray's prototype, while the cast consisted largely of their friends; Michael Redgrave's mother, Margaret Scudamore, was Lady Britomart and Baliol Holloway her millionaire husband, Undershaft. Gordon Harker, who was particularly dear to Sybil because his brother had been in Gallipoli with Russell, played Bill Walker, while Harold Scott was Snobby Price.

Sybil found the part of Barbara, written so many years before *Saint Joan*, an excellent follow-up for her own work on the character of Joan. It strengthened her belief in the equality of human beings and confirmed her pacifism. She felt very much at home in the Salvation Army shelter scene.

The play, although it did not have a long run, was liked and admired, not least by members of the Salvation Army. Much later, in the excellent film of *Major Barbara*, directed by Gabriel Pascal, Shaw changed the part of Mrs Baines into the General for Sybil to play.

Major Barbara was followed by Clemence Dane's grim drama *Mariners*. Leon M. Lion directed it, so Lewis was able to devote all his energies to playing the part of the pathetic and saintly clergyman, Benjamin Cobb, married to the wreck of a once seductive barmaid, whom he cossets and protects from the disapproval of the neighbourhood. This was Sybil's part, and once again the Cassons found Clemence Dane inspiring to work with. Ann Casson played a child very successfully and Mary was one of the Ladies of the Choir.★ *Mariners* did not run long, the audience, Sybil opines, finding it too harrowing.

In June Sybil received her second Honorary Degree of Doctor of Laws, this time from the University of Edinburgh. Three months later the Honorary Freedom of the City of Rochester was conferred upon her, giving her, she was amused to find, all kinds of unexpected rights—not only free transport, but freedom, it really seemed, to behave just as she pleased anywhere within the city.

With all this recognition, "The trouble now was," as J. C. Trewin comments, "to find a new and worthy part. Not many dramatists matched a Thorndike . . . but there was surely no reason to flourish around as Madame de Beauvais in a little frisk called *Madame Plays Nap*,† even if it did allow Lewis Casson to look more like Napoleon than any other artist had done." Sybil, however, took it less seriously.

"He simply *was* Napoleon," she says. "He played him both young and old, a superb performance. And mine was a sort of *Madame Sans-Gêne* part, great fun. It may not have made

★ Although Mary acted well—she was, for instance, a great success as Wendy with Jean Forbes-Robertson in *Peter Pan*—she was not, like Ann, a dedicated actress, and later, after much discussion with her father, who was very sympathetic about her problem, left the stage altogether.

† By Brenda Girvin and Monica Cosens.

Waters of the Moon, 1951

At the Taj
Mahal, 1955

much mark in London, but later, in Australia and New Zealand, it was the most popular of all our plays. As a matter of fact, we had already done one play by those two women for a matinée way back in 1919—*Dr James Barry*, it was called. They were charming and quite scholarly. The play was about that extraordinary, well-known doctor in one of the African wars, who lived and practised medicine as a man, here in London too. It was not until her death that it was discovered that Dr Barry was a woman. It was a fascinating part to play—I began as a quite young woman who then decided to become a man and live as one."

In 1930, however, there was no shortage of parts worthy of Sybil. After taking the lead in Benn Levy's first play, *The Devil*, noted for one of Diana Wynyard's early appearances, and performing *Phèdre* in French at the Arts Theatre in the company of Celia Johnson, who spoke beautiful French, Sybil Thorndike appeared at the Everyman Theatre in Hampstead in Georg Kaiser's *The Fire in the Opera House*, in which Emlyn Williams had one of his early successes. This was followed at the same theatre by Ibsen's *Ghosts*, a play which Sybil has always particularly admired, finding it emotionally akin to Greek drama. Mrs Alving ranks with Joan, Medea and Hecuba as one of the parts she loves best —roles that touch her profoundly.

Meanwhile came another important experience—playing Emilia to Paul Robeson's Othello, Peggy Ashcroft's Desdemona, Ralph Richardson's Roderigo and Maurice Browne's Iago, at the Savoy.

"It was very interesting working with Paul. He was such a dear person—and how he worked! He was potentially a fine actor, but he hadn't the technique of acting, so he had to do everything *really*. He poured with sweat with the effort of it all. He was very courteous, and so was his wife Essie. And modest, too. In our big scene together I used to have to go on saying, 'This is *your* scene. Take the stage.' "

The play was produced by Ellen Van Volkenberg, the American director, who was Maurice Browne's manager and had at one time been his wife. She was a real pioneer, and one of Mrs Elmhirst's partners in the founding of the Art Centre at Dartington:

". . . An enchanting person with the finest ideals of the theatre. She became a great friend, and it was to her that one went when confused about theatre principles. But she hadn't quite the bigness needed for *Othello*. It was done Elizabethan, and I don't think Paul Robeson's costume was right for him. Negroes tend to bend their knees as they walk, and his dress demanded straight knees. In his white robe at the end he looked superb, and Peggy was so lovely and so gallant. I wish we had voices in the theatre like his now—deep, vibrant, masculine notes. We really seem to lack bass speaking voices today. The Russians have the best ones—low but never dull. Our big emotional actors all tend to be tenor."

In 1929 an event of great importance to the theatre had occurred, in which the Cassons were both concerned—the forming of British Actors' Equity. The first banding together of British actors had taken place before the turn of the century in a voluntary organisation known as the Actors' Association, to which the Cassons had always belonged. This aimed at improving the welfare of actors, at the same time stressing the latters' obligations to their managers and their public. The achievements of the Association were, however, inevitably limited; at the beginning it was not a union, and therefore did not have the protection of trade union laws, and, when later it was reformed as a union, it was not strong enough to deal effectively with dishonest managers.

Margaret Webster, who was chairman of the editorial board which produced British Equity's first magazine, gives a vivid description of its birth.*

"In 1924 the more unscrupulous among the managers seized

* *The Same Only Different.*

upon the situation to form a rival organisation called the Stage Guild. It was not a union, Heaven forbid. On the contrary. It was a kind of get-together friendship club. Each element in the theatre, actors, and managers had a separate section, but all were neatly tied up in a parcel so that nobody could take action against anybody else. . . . Conditions in the theatre became rapidly more chaotic than ever . . .

"It became vitally necessary to form a new actors' union. Bearing in mind the record and example of the American actors' counterpart, it was decided to adopt the name of British Actors' Equity . . . Many of the discussions took place [in the Websters' flat] in Bedford Street. . . . The dining-room became even more difficult to eat in than it had been during May's* wartime campaigns; it was generally occupied by anything from four to forty actors . . . When Equity finally acquired premises of its own, it took along the big mahogany table around which its founding committees sat. Suitably inscribed, this table still adorns its Council Room."

Equity differs from other trade unions in one very special way. It was not started by the actors who were being exploited by unscrupulous managements, but by eminent members of the profession in order to protect their less well-established colleagues.

The Cassons, who were members of the first elected committee, threw themselves heart and soul into Equity, and did a great deal of what was sometimes irksome committee work. Lewis became the second president, a post he held until 1945, when he was succeeded by Beatrix Lehmann.

In the spring of 1931 came the communication from the Lord Chamberlain's Office informing Sybil that, subject to her agreement, she was to be created a Dame of the Order of the British Empire in the forthcoming Birthday Honours.

She was taken completely by surprise, and convinced that she would never have received this honour had there not been a Labour Government in power, and that Bernard Shaw must

---

* Dame May Whitty, Margaret Webster's mother.

have had something to do with it. However that may be, she and all her family—particularly, of course, Lewis, who had contributed so greatly to her rise in fame—were enchanted by the news, and had hard work to keep it to themselves until it became public, on the first night of *Marriage by Purchase*★ at the Embassy Theatre in May, where Sybil was playing with Donald Wolfit. Congratulations poured in, and perhaps Sybil fully realised for the first time how much she was loved both inside and outside the profession.

When in June the day came for what she endearingly calls "my knighthood", she was rehearsing Madame Duval in the film *A Gentleman of Paris*, and they gave her the morning off.

"Lewis and I went together. I had a lovely dress, and they were tremendously courteous at Buckingham Palace. King George was so kind and asked me if I was acting in anything at the moment. And when I got back to the film studio everyone cheered."

Early in the following year *The Knight of the Burning Pestle* was revived at the Old Vic, with Sybil as the Citizen's Wife in this burlesque of knight errantry and comedy of errors.

"It was tremendous fun. When I said, 'I'm a stranger here; I was ne'er at one of these plays before', the audience simply roared with laughter. And I used to eat an orange and throw the pips into the first row until this was stopped as being too vulgar. I played it in Lancashire dialect, and Gordon Bottomley said this sounded close to the original. Ralph Richardson was so lovely as Ralph. He really is my favourite actor."

"I was much in awe," Ralph Richardson recalls. "Dame Sybil was the first great star I had played with. Five minutes before the curtain went up I wondered if I dared pay court and wish her well. I went to the door of her dressing-room, but I was afraid to knock in case she was communing with herself before that big part. Then I heard a buzz of talk inside, and

★ English version by Jocelyn Clive.

tapped. 'Come in, Ralph dear,' Sybil said. 'Won't you have a bun? There isn't really time for introductions.' She was feeding half-a-dozen schoolgirls with buns a few moments before the performance.

"I had seen her in every one of the Grand Guignol plays and as Saint Joan, and I used to talk endlessly to my mother about her. In those days—before my first marriage—I had no one else to talk to. My mother never went to the theatre, and as I went on and on about Sybil Thorndike a particular glazed expression would come over my mother's face. Since then I have often observed this expression, and learnt that I must avoid expressing too much enthusiasm to someone who cannot appreciate it. I'm afraid I bored my mother to death, but I don't regret it, because this was something I could not keep in—and motherhood has its penalties.

"What made Sybil's Saint Joan so wonderful was her understanding of physical pain. She got this through her sense of the macabre, and her profound study of torture for the Grand Guignol. As Joan she knew absolutely what to expect when she learnt that she was to be burned, and in spite of this she kept her faith—her saintliness. It was magnificent.

"Sybil sees sermons in stones and good in everything. She even saw good in my Othello,* which was an incredible piece of observation. It helped me to maintain pride in my fall. I often discuss this—in the spirit—with my friend Cardinal Wolsey, and he tells me how lucky I am to have known Sybil.

"She can make an actor act. Any actor. I've seen her do it. She could act with a tailor's dummy and bring it to life. Anything she touches comes to life—just as it does with Chaplin.

"In my contacts with Lewis I always remember my sheer cheek and his sheer courtesy. And of course his voice. He was an organ-maker, and he kept that splendid organ for himself.

"Although Sybil's well-known warmth of heart is true indeed, she has a stiletto—a stiletto for fools, whom she does not suffer gladly. But she keeps it carefully concealed, as stilettos should always be.

* 1938.

"My best time with her was in *Peer Gynt*, when she played my old mother. She has 'a certain alacrity in dying', to paraphrase Falstaff. She dies so splendidly that she will live for ever."

A very sad event cast a shadow over the sparkle of *The Knight of the Burning Pestle* before the end of the run—the death of Eileen Thorndike's sailor husband, Commander Maurice Ewbank, to whom not only Eileen but the whole family was devoted.

A film of *Hindle Wakes* followed, and a performance as Julie Renaudin in *The Dark Saint* by François de Curel—the story of a nun who leaves her convent. The whole cast consisted of women, Eileen Thorndike being one of them, and Catherine Lacey another, giving a beautiful performance. This play, also, was produced by Ellen Van Volkenburg, a work entirely suited to her gifts.

At about this time the Cassons moved into Mrs Thorndike's house in Oakley Street. It was a wrench to leave Carlyle Square; they loved the house and would have bought it earlier if they had had the means, but now it was proving too small when all the children were at home and Mother Don Don was coming frequently for visits.

Soon afterwards, having made careful arrangements for Mrs Thorndike's comfort in Oakley Street, Sybil and Lewis, with Christopher and Ann, set off on an extensive tour, beginning in Egypt and Palestine and covering both Australia and New Zealand.

CHAPTER XIV

DOWN UNDER

(1932–1933)

FOR SOME TIME now Bernard Shaw had been telling the
Cassons that Australia wanted *Saint Joan* and that, unless they
would soon take it there on tour, he would be forced to let
another company do it. "Shall I come to tea with you?" he
asked Sybil. "Or will you come to me? I don't drink tea." She
went to see him, and assured him that she wanted nothing so
much as to play Saint Joan in Australia, and that she and Lewis
were greatly interested in cultural relations with the Commonwealth.

Then came the question—how was the tour to be financed?
The answer was provided by three Russian Jewish musicians,
brothers, known as the Cherniavsky Bureau, who were already
friends of the Cassons'. With a promise of co-operation from
the Australian management J. C. Williamson and Tait, they
offered to help Lewis to finance a tour of some of their more
popular plays, and he accepted, deciding to precede this tour with
a visit to Egypt and Palestine under his own management,
helped by the British Council.

John Casson was now at the R.A.F. Station in Fife, training as a
pilot, and Mary was on tour as Wendy in *Peter Pan*; but Ann,
who had not long before made a great success as Daisy Ashford
in the all-children production of *The Young Visiters*, was able to
go on the first part of the tour, and Christopher was entirely
free for this adventure. After leaving the Navy in 1930 he had
joined Elsie Fogerty's School and had then gone to America
with Ben Greet, who released him for the Casson tour, to act

and to work as an assistant stage-manager. The stage manager for Egypt and Palestine was the Cassons' friend Matthew Forsyth, whose widow, Marjorie, is still Sybil's right hand. Bruce Winston, without whom no Casson company was complete, went with them, besides—to mention only a few of the company —Michael Martin Harvey and his wife, Norman Shelley, Zillah Carter and Atholl Fleming.

They sailed from Tilbury on March 26th, 1932. On the voyage Sybil and Christopher studied Ouspensky, whose doctrine, Sybil maintains, has always been a help to her.

"I met him when I got back, and he said to me in his voice from the depths of the earth [here she imitated Ouspensky's voice] 'I will tell you a little parable. You go out in the morning with your basket on your arm and buy your vegetables, a poor little thing down here buying your vegetables. And then you go up-up-up and you are there far above, looking down at that poor little thing buying your vegetables.' I have never forgotten that."

The boat called at Marseilles, where the Cassons and Bruce Winston took a car to Avignon.

"Lewis and Bruce insisted on testing the Palais des Papes for echoes. They made an awful show of themselves. I was frightfully ashamed of them, but I couldn't make them stop."

At Port Said they gave several of their plays, including two additions to their repertoire, *The Painted Veil*,★ which Lewis had produced with Gladys Cooper at the Playhouse, and which now became a favourite play of Sybil's, and the rather mild domestic comedy *Milestones*.† Two weeks in Cairo followed. They played at the Opera House, a lovely theatre, built purely of matchwood, so that the fire regulations were stringent and one lighted cigarette could have put an end to a performance. They

★ By Somerset Maugham.
† By Arnold Bennett and Edward Knoblock.

were slightly taken aback on the first night by being greeted with a prolonged hissing, but they soon discovered that this was the Arab form of applause.

As usual, they went on as many expeditions as possible, and were entranced by the beauty of the desert. The highspot was a visit to the Pyramids at night on camels. "How seasick they make you feel! But the Sphinx by moonlight is something one could never forget."

There were also interesting people to meet. Sybil spent hours conversing with the High Commissioner, Sir Percy Loraine, sitting on a property box with him and discussing the Sermon on the Mount. There was the Egyptian explorer, Hassanein Pasha, by whom Lewis and Sybil were equally fascinated, and King Fuad, who came to a performance. The company was warned not to look at the royal box, from which the strangest sounds emanated, for he had been shot in the throat, which caused him to speak—in French—in the most peculiar voice, and to produce a startling cough. The Arabs were delighted to be given walk-on parts in *Captain Brassbound's Conversion*, the only snag being that, in spite of Matthew Forsyth's repeated commands to them to look terrifyingly ferocious, they invariably came on screaming with laughter. Apropos of laughter, Christopher Casson says that he has never in his life heard such prolonged laughter as when his father, as Captain Brassbound, came on smooth-headed and clean-shaven, having exchanged his rough clothing for a frock coat, spotless shirt, elegant boots and a glossy top hat, with Lady Cicely (Sybil) on his arm. Each night the laughter stopped the play for several minutes.

At Alexandria the Cassons stayed with Mr Abdy, a hospitable millionaire, and had another successful run of their plays, Sybil enjoying playing *Macbeth* without the elaboration of Ricketts' décor, although even on tour they faithfully followed his settings and costumes for *Saint Joan*.

On this tour Christopher had an opportunity to study intensively his mother's approach to acting and his father's methods of direction. The great success of their Shaw productions, he says, in whatever part of the world they were playing, was mainly due to both his parents being such first-class Shavians, Lewis having an innate gift for dialectics and Sybil thoroughly enjoying them too. Thus, for them, in any Shaw play even if they were contending with the mediaevalism of Ricketts and the iconoclasm of Shaw, the argument was the salient feature.

About his mother's work Christopher says:

"In studying a part she sees it as a gradually emerging shape —a kind of plastic abstract shape—which disappears once the play is produced. It is as if the colours and patterns of ideas, conflicts, character, events, speeches and so on, evaporate eventually into life itself, existence itself, perhaps. Nothing is lost, but perhaps the final intuition is something like Mozart's ability to conceive a symphony with all its complications in one point of a moment, and then in performance the timeless vision is carried throughout the temporal enactment. It is perhaps like the mystic's progress from meditation—the lyrical sequence of pictures and precise thoughts—to contemplation, where inspiration or intuition has full sway. Gabriel Marcel's distinction between Problem and Mystery is much the same. A play is a problem, and a problem to be solved; but it is a mystery too, and a mystery can never be solved. But if the problem angle is avoided, the mystery when it comes can turn everything topsy-turvy, and the creativeness be lost or dissipated in some way."

These words of her son's could not, Sybil says, more truly and beautifully describe the philosophy and practice of acting that she has tried to evolve over the years. And one finds, as one studies her life that, however full it has been, every place, every person, every mental and spiritual experience has been savoured to the full and retained, just as music still claims her heart.

The company gave one performance of *Saint Joan* to countless welcoming airmen in a huge hangar at the R.A.F. Station in the desert at Ismailia, and then crossed into Palestine at El Quantara,

travelling all night, and waking early in the morning near Beer-
sheba to watch with astonishment the ploughing being done by
camels. "I shall never forget the smell of it all that first morning—
a new exotic smell."

The Cassons were immediately captivated by the atmosphere
of Jerusalem. They stayed in a beautiful Arab house belonging to
some old friends of Sybil's, and the company played for four
days at a cinema just outside the city, Sybil finding it very moving
to play *Saint Joan* so close to the heart of Christianity.

"Here too we did wonderful expeditions. The Jews and the
Arabs all seemed charming and friendly, although there were
constant fights as to which had the most right to the holy
places, and we saw a number of riots. The Deputy Governor
was an old friend of ours, and he asked us if we would like to
meet the Grand Mufti, but warned us not to get on to the
subject of religion with him. 'What! Not talk about religion
with the Grand Mufti! How silly!' I said, and of course I
did."

They explored the city, visiting the Wailing Wall and every
place of special interest, forgetting the commercialism that jarred,
as they became more conscious of the ancient atmosphere which
had endured throughout the centuries, and finding Palestine
altogether more beautiful than they had expected. They made
expeditions, too, to Bethlehem and Nazareth.

"On the way up to Nazareth I saw a beautiful little town,
just like a bowl upside down. 'Ka-n-na' they kept on telling
us, and I suddenly realised that this was Cana of Galilee."

Matthew Forsyth and Ann Casson now left the company to
return to London, and the others sailed on down the Suez Canal,
"seeing Mount Ararat and the Old Testament unrolled before us.
It was marvellous." They arrived in Colombo for Shakespeare's
birthday, were garlanded with jasmine and heard a Singhalese
clergyman give a fascinating rendering of passages from *Othello*.

Then they set sail again, with very few passengers, for a perfect voyage across the Indian Ocean, crossing the line with due ceremonies and overwhelmed each evening with the glory of the sunset. Great albatrosses circled around the silent ship, and when they drew near the Cocos Islands the inhabitants came out in boats and they threw down hampers of provisions to them.

It was May by the time they landed in Fremantle—autumn and growing rather chilly. Alec Cherniavsky and his wife were there to meet them. They settled down in Perth for several weeks to play their complete repertoire in His Majesty's Theatre, a good theatre with most appreciative audiences, used to playing in, and watching, first class amateur productions. Making her first speech in Australia, Sybil paid tribute to these amateurs: "A play you make yourself is of more value than six shows by visiting people."

Saint Joan, so eagerly awaited, was enthusiastically received, but everywhere *Madame Plays Nap* was also a favourite production.

"It was such a glorious trip. Every place we went to seemed better than the last. I remember how dazzlingly beautiful we found the flowering trees in Perth. And then there was the burning of the black-boy trees—short, stubby trees looking just like Negro boys, that had to be cleared away to make room for vineyards. I helped fire them on a hillside—exciting and rather frightening. They went up like fireworks.

"And the awful soldier ants—we went a special expedition into the bush with Christopher Storrs, the Chaplain of the University, and a lot of students to see them. We dodged about among the ant-hills—fun but terrifying. These horrible creatures with huge heads jumped at you in a menacing way from ten feet off. Soldier ants are about the nastiest people I've ever met."

They crossed the Great Bight in terrible storms to get to Adelaide—

"So beautifully built, all laid out in green belts between

slices of buildings. I remember going for a walk with Lewis and seeing a notice on a gate 'Cows only'. How clever of them to read, we thought, and laughed our heads off."

Here they met the brother-in-law of Sybil's "pram-day friend" of Rochester days, Kitty Jelf. This was Julian Bickersteth, the head of the University, later to be Archdeacon of Canterbury. They also met the well-known painter, Hans Heyson—Sybil has regretted ever since not having bought one of his pictures. "I ought to have. I even bought a picture *like* one of his later on. But we hadn't any spare cash then."

And so on to Melbourne—

"This lovely city, closer somehow to England than any of the other places, its graciousness reflected in the kindliness of its people. I was enthralled by it then, and have been on every one of my visits since. The green everywhere and the wonderful parks and gardens were unbelievably lovely, and Lewis and I discovered a wonderful church—our own kind, high Anglican. One of the priests was Chinese, but you wouldn't have known it except when he was saying Mass—then it became pure Chinese."

The theatre was an old one and excellent for sound, and again they settled down to play their repertoire, when suddenly Sybil's voice began to fail and she was afraid that the old trouble would recur.

"I had treatment, and I manœuvred somehow or other in the shows, with a false voice. I don't know how I could have got through except for Elsie Fogerty's exercises. And the moment we could get away Lewis and I went up into the hills behind Melbourne to stay with friends. We went up in a bus in a real blizzard with some people who had never seen snow before. I kept absolute silence except for those few voice exercises each morning, and Lewis and I had four days of complete bliss, trudging in deep snow. It was fantastic

up there, chipmunks and kangaroos running about in the
snow, and the most extraordinary birds—the whippoor-
will, the lyre birds and the kookaburra, known as the laughing jackass."

Late August found the company in Sydney, opening at the
Theatre Royal with *Saint Joan*, played to a highly distinguished
audience.

The *Sydney Morning Herald*,* having warmly praised Sybil's
Saint Joan, paid an interesting tribute to Lewis's Cauchon, the
part that he had now chosen to play.

"Beneath a close fitting green hood, his face had the hard
lines of a gloomy mask. He gained his effects by a persistent
reserve and stillness, so that where emphasis was necessary, the
merest fraction of extra weight in the voice seemed fraught
with significance and menace. It is a deep rich voice, whose use
might be an object lesson to everyone associated with the
local stage."

A perceptive comment on his style of acting. He had a fiery
temperament, but he had never needed, in the way that his wife
had, to subdue innate exuberance.

It was in Sydney that Christopher—who had graduated during
the tour from being, as he was in Jerusalem, for want of other
machinery, "The Bank of the Loire" in *Saint Joan*, making the
wind change direction and turn the flag, to playing the Inquisitor
—had the most important theatrical experience of his life,
"ruthlessly produced" by his father as Oswald to his mother's
Mrs Alving, with Lewis himself once more playing Pastor
Manders. Bruce Winston's set was simple, and altogether
Casson's production of *Ghosts* had the simplicity of Greek
tragedy. Instead of the usual interpretation of Oswald as a
painter, Christopher played him as a sculptor, an innovation of
Lewis's. The purpose was to present Oswald as a stronger, more
solid figure than he usually is, and consequently make the final
tragedy greater.

* August 22nd, 1932.

Christopher finds much in Ibsen's philosophy to match that of his mother.

"It is a positive attitude to life," he says. "Ibsen did not accept the darkness. Neither does my mother. The unopened bottle of champagne symbolises light and joy bottled up. The open bottle is Oswald's life as an artist, which might have worked out, had the whole truth been told. At the end Mrs Alving accepts absolute truth—and will not kill. My mother and father shared this deep belief in a life force."

In Sydney Sybil, though acclaimed as an actress, gave a certain amount of offence in her speeches by favouring married women as teachers, and by referring to Soviet Russia as an experiment of interest, worth watching. One paper referred to her as "under the thrall of the master-minds of Russia". A few explanations, however, made it clear that, while radical, she was not Communist; and although Mr Stevens, the Premier of New South Wales, disapproved of the Cassons' politics, he none the less invited them to an amicable luncheon.

"It was the women there," Sybil says, "who were the most forward-looking in politics. They got the vote before we did. We found the Jewish people wonderful theatregoers. One of their charming customs is to give one trees instead of flowers. We have trees planted in several places in Israel. The last one a kind friend gave me was here in Kensington, in memory of Lewis.

"We got to Brisbane just when the jacaranda trees were at their best—so lovely, all the side walks studded with amethysts. There were emus in the zoo there with the most elegant walk. They made a fascinating sound from their innermost innards that I tried hard to copy. We also went up north to the beaches. There were camels on the beaches—it was all quite fantastic."

After a further brief visit to Melbourne (during which Robert Helpmann, who was dancing there—this was before he ever came to England—saw a number of their shows), the company was given a splendid send-off at Sydney, and then they sailed for New Zealand.

"We had thought Sydney Harbour the tops, but when we saw Wellington Harbour, although of course it has nothing of Sydney's impressive size, we found it—with its high, wooded cliffs, reflected in lake after lake, gulf after gulf—quite magical.

"New Zealand is a heaven on earth. The only horrible things were the abattoirs, with the decoy sheep which led the victims up to execution. Beastly. It confirmed my belief that we ought all to be vegetarians.

"We went to no end of smaller places, Wanganui, Hastings, Dannevirke. One of the top things of the tour was a long weekend up at the Petoka property in the earthquake district, where we stayed with Hugh Cross and his wife, who was a Terry and had given up the stage to marry him. He had a huge sheep-farm and she worked like a slave.

"Rotarua, the centre of the geyser country, was amazing—great spouts of boiling water thrown high up in the air—and a lake that looked like boiling, bubbling porridge. People didn't need any fires. They baked their bread in the ground. Wherever you stuck your stick in there was smoke. You were living on a volcano—beyond words extraordinary. We bathed in the hot springs. Altogether this was a very strange experience.

"The Maori people were gentle and laughing, with lovely manners, and their dances are beautiful. We met a marvellous Maori woman, Rani Guide Rangi, who had known kings and queens and leaders of all sorts. We also met the sister of Lewis's greatest friend Jules Shaw. She had married the painter Christopher Perkins, who painted my favourite portrait of Lewis.

"Altogether we had a royal time. Then we crossed by night to the South Island. More beauty unimaginable—the towering Alps and the beaches with their black sand and blue water. Edmund Hillary told us later that the finest ice-training he had had anywhere was in the New Zealand Alps.

"The lakes were spectacular, and we played in all kinds of magical places like Oamaru and Timaru, and went right down south to the last city in civilisation—Invercargill [where Sybil played *Saint Joan* for the last time]. So many Scottish names here, and everyone speaking the Scottish tongue."

For Christmas the Cassons were back in Wellington, and telephoned their greetings—at what seemed then colossal expense—back to their family in Oakley Street, all feeling terribly homesick. Mrs Thorndike was not very well, but she sent them jolly messages and was persuaded to get on the line and say "Hullo" to Sybil—the last time, in fact, that Sybil was ever to hear her mother's voice.

Then they started on the voyage home, the rest of the company having already left. They came by way of the new southerly route, and were three weeks without sight of land.

"Going through the Panama Canal was a wonderful experience. We took eight hours, and it was thrilling watching the great locks fill up. Lewis and I thought about his grandfather, who had walked across where the Canal is now, carrying his boat."

Their next stop was at Curaçao, and it was after this that the sad telegrams began to arrive, the first to say that Sybil's mother was very ill, and the next to say that she had died.

"I was absolutely shattered. I hadn't realised she was so ill. She and I had had such fun together all my life. We had the same ludicrous sense of humour, and she made me laugh so much. She often irritated me beyond words, but she was such fun and so ambitious for us, and so lively. But she was never really happy after Father died. I was supposed to do all kinds of things for the ship's final festivities, but I was too sad, though I did do one Rosalind and Orlando scene with Lewis."

Two days before they landed they heard that Aunt Lucy, the

widow of Lewis's uncle Randal, had also died. She left Bron-y-garth to Lewis, whom she had loved, Sybil believed, more than anyone.

The next telegram was enlivening, heralding the future. It was from Bernard Shaw, inviting Sybil to play in the first production of *Village Wooing*, and she wired back gladly accepting. The fifth wire was very exciting indeed. "Look out for me at Plymouth, John."

John, who during his parents' absence had qualified as a pilot, had joined the Fleet Air Arm Squadron at Netheravon, and he now met the Cassons' ship in the channel. Up on the bridge with the captain, the Cassons saw his plane coming, looking like a tiny bird, and then he was over them, doing low-flying stunts.

" 'Don't do it, John!' I kept yelling, and the captain was worried too. John was at Waterloo Station to meet us, and be greeted with, 'How did you dare!', but oh, how glad we were to see him!

"Our dear secretary, Susan Holmes, had been on the quay to welcome us. And Ben Greet was there too. He started an argument at once. 'What ridiculous play are you going to do now? Why don't you stick to Shakespeare?' "

CHAPTER XV

THE MIDDLE YEARS

(1933–1939)

THEY WERE TREMENDOUSLY glad to be back. Much as they enjoyed and profited by their tours abroad, the Cassons were always homesick—sick with longing for home, and for any member of the family from whom they were parted. Family affection between members of the Casson and Thorndike families has always been unwavering. There is no sentimentality; they are all men and women of character, but their very differences of opinion strengthen the bonds between them. This was true always of Sybil and Lewis—both, according to their own account, "violent" characters.

"Lewis and I had raging arguments all the time. And I was jealous, too, of his occasional involvements with other women, although they generally became and remained good friends of mine. On the stage I don't know the meaning of the word jealousy. Whenever I see somebody better than myself I'm thrilled. I learn by it. But personally I'm possessive, so with Lewis I could be jealous. Of course I sometimes got slightly involved myself, but Lewis wasn't possessive. He rather approved of these incidents, thought they would make me understand human beings better. He was always freer-minded than I was. But I was mad at him and at myself on these occasions. I was too much a vicar's daughter, and still am. Infidelity depresses me terribly. But it wasn't really that with us. We were far too close. I suppose it was a sort of overflow of vitality."

With the ebullient Mother Don Don gone from their lives, the return to Oakley Street was inevitably sad; but it was home, well cared for by the faithful Vi, who had been the nursery governess for so many years, and her elder sister Nan, who had joined the household as cook.

It was now the turn of Sybil and Lewis to fly over John. In April of this year he sailed for the China Station in H.M. Aircraft Carrier *Eagle*. His parents hired a plane and, with Ann and Mary, flew round and round high over his ship, "I sobbing—I always sob on such occasions—the others very excited. I was envious, too. I always wanted to go to China."

Soon after they got back, in early April, John Van Druten and Auriol Lee brought Sybil his play *The Distaff Side*, which Auriol Lee was to direct, and she gladly accepted the part of Mrs Millward for the following September, Shaw agreeing to postpone *Village Wooing*. The prospect was in every way exciting, for both Van Druten, whose earlier play *Young Woodley* had brought him fame, and Auriol Lee, who not only produced his plays but sometimes collaborated in the writing of them, were old friends whose work Sybil admired.

As soon as they returned from Australia Lewis had gone into *Diplomacy*, a translation of a play by Sardou, produced at the Princes Theatre by Gerald du Maurier, who also played the leading part, while Christopher joined Donald Wolfit's *Hamlet* for Ben Greet. When their engagements ended all three went for a holiday at Bron-y-garth. They gave Lewis's nephew, Hugh Casson, his first job, making extensive alterations to the building. They all had a fine time climbing the mountains and Sybil went on with her Welsh, helped by the shopkeepers, who refused to serve her unless she asked for things in Welsh. Sarah Bailey, the housekeeper, had been at Bron-y-garth since she was a maid of fourteen, and Sybil had had a warm affection for her ever since the honeymoon days.

The Distaff Side opened in Edinburgh before moving to the Apollo in London. Sybil liked playing the part of Evie— "the first time I had played a real modern woman"—and being produced by Auriol Lee, who was always a most stimulating director.

Not only was Sybil now playing a middle-aged woman, but she was actually fifty herself. "There was no change in me," she says. "It was just a going-on. One remains the same person all one's life."

The Distaff Side had on the whole a favourable press, the actors more praised than the play, and most notices mentioning Sybil's new restraint and quietude. James Agate in the *Sunday Times*★ said that she made the character of Mrs Millward "glow like a day in late October", and commented:

"It is only fair that we should recognise as a property of this actress, and as a possession in her own right, that beauty of mind for which Messrs Euripides and Shaw have too often bagged the entire credit."

While *The Distaff Side* was still running and Lewis was acting in other productions, Sybil took the part of Mrs Siddons in the clever play of this title by Naomi Royde-Smith, produced for a matinée by Bruce Winston, who also played Mr Siddons, with Mary and Ann as the Siddons girls, Eric Portman in the lead as the painter Lawrence, and John Laurie playing John Kemble. Ernest Milton, who was married to Naomi Royde-Smith, helped with the production. It was a long part to learn for a single performance, but Sybil had remained a "quick study". She and Lewis had quite different methods of learning their lines.

"Lewis's way was most extraordinary, and I can't describe it. For each part he had a notebook which only the Lord God Almighty and he could understand. This was because his memory wasn't his strong point, but once the thing was there it never fled. I learn very quickly, but nowadays not so surely. I learn visually. I must see the words on the page—and I must only have one book, so that it always looks the same, otherwise I'm thrown."

The Distaff Side ran until March of the following year, when

★ September 10th, 1933.

Sybil went straight into *The Double Door** at the Globe Theatre, her first engagement with Hugh Beaumont—"Binkie".† In this terrifying melodrama she greatly enjoyed playing with Owen Nares and Christine Silver, "the born murderee", and also the experience of working with yet another producer—this time Henry Oscar. She missed Lewis both as co-player and director, but continued to study each of her parts with him.

The maniacal Victoria Van Bret, who dominates her Fifth Avenue family with crazy sadism, could not be more unlike the quiet, almost saintly Mrs Millward of *The Distaff Side*. Sybil welcomed the change and the chance to be violent again on the boards—to let off steam, as in the old Guignol days. Then, after a brief appearance in Dryden's *Aureng-Zebe*, at last came *Village Wooing*—one of Mrs Shaw's favourites among her husband's plays. It was put on at the Little Theatre under the management of Nancy Price.

"I learnt it hindside before in Cockney. 'Very clever and very bright,' said G.B.S. at the first rehearsal, 'but I didn't write it in Cockney. I wrote it in a much more beautiful English, without an accent—western, and I don't mean by that West End, which is a very poor form of English.' He had in fact been thinking of the speech of a postmistress in the west of England, so I had to learn it all over again to get it right for him.

"It was great fun doing *Village Wooing* at the Little with Arthur Wontner, but more fun still when I played it later with Lewis."

After this short run, in September 1934 Sybil sailed with Auriol Lee and Clifford Evans for the New York production of *The Distaff Side*.

"I was simply miserable leaving Lewis. It was awful. But we wrote to each other every single day, and he came over for

* By Elizabeth A. McFadden and Hermine Klepac.
† Of H. M. Tennent Ltd.

Christmas. And although I really was unhappy without him, I managed to have a wonderful time. I do love the Americans —their warmth and friendliness and endless hospitality. And I love their theatre, too. I used to go to every matinée when I was free.

"I had a marvellous time. I stayed at the Gotham Hotel, and Tallulah* had the room below me. She was a darling, and so generous, and she hadn't any inhibitions at all. Often when I came in at night I'd find a great bunch of roses in my room with a note telling me to come down to a party. Her parties used to go on all night—I could never stay to the end. Tallulah used to give some of the best performances of her life at these parties, excerpts from her parts, and keep us all in stitches. She was a real night girl. Quite often, as I was starting out for rehearsal at about ten in the morning, she'd come in and say, 'I'm just going to bed, darling—shan't stir until the show tonight.'

"There were the wonderful Lunts, too,† and Kit Cornell and Guthrie,‡ Kit such a lovely person—fascinating. Edith§ was playing the Nurse to her Juliet then, and it was during this time that her husband died. I remember going over to her hotel and spending that terrible day with her. New York was wrapped in fog, and the boat she was to have gone back to England in couldn't dock. It was tragic, and of course she couldn't go on playing, but she was enormously gallant. Later she talked about her marriage with such humility and deep feeling. We have always been very good friends, although we don't agree about a lot of things, and anyway, she's the greatest actress we've got. The only thing I regret is that she won't play Lady Macbeth—she doesn't really like to play evil, she doesn't think of it as a catharsis as I do. But although she's so accomplished she never lets technique get the better of her. Some actors do—they know how to do it all, and much too well.

---

* Tallulah Bankhead.   † Alfred Lunt and Lynn Fontanne.
‡ Katharine Cornell and her husband Guthrie McClintic.
§ Edith Evans and George Booth.

"To go back to America, I liked the critics there very much too. John Mason Brown, oh, and others—they were immensely helpful. So many delightful people come to mind as I look back on those days. There was Alfred Loomis, whose father, the great humorist, Charles Battel Loomis, had been so good to Russell and me in our young days in the States. And then there was that splendid van Loon—a very happy friendship, that. His books had always been a thrill to me, but his lectures were staggering, shocking everybody. I was inspired by them. He used to write to me and draw elephants all over the envelopes. Oh, yes, and there was Marc Connelly too. We used to meet in the lift nearly every day. I liked him so much, and his beautiful *Green Pastures*.

"And I knew that gorgeous actor Otis Skinner, the father of Cornelia, and Milly Natwick, quite a young woman, who played the part of the old mother in *The Distaff Side* beautifully. And there was that wildly generous and absolutely crazy woman who had my dressing-room done up for me. I can't tell you what it was like. I had a very plain little dressing-room—just what I like, and that's how they generally are in New York—but one evening when I went into the theatre the doorman gave me a very odd look and said, 'Have you seen your dressing-room?' And when I went in—my heaven! It was all chiffon and lace and bows and bottles of this and that —two of everything, couldn't have been more unlike me— and a great copy of Whistler's Mother and an almost life-size statue of the Virgin Mary. Unbelievable. Half New York came to see that dressing-room of mine. 'Whorehouse!' someone called it.

"Going to Harlem at night was a special thrill. Such marvellous shows—the Negro people are born actors.

"Another funny little thing I remember was somehow getting a poisoned toe and having to play in a slipper. The doctor rather scared me about it, but one day between the shows, when I was really in torture, the stage carpenter brought a piece of fresh pork and bound my foot up with it. When I told the doctor he was simply horrified, and said I might have got any kind of infection. But it did the trick—took the pain and everything away like magic."

Early in 1934 John Casson had become engaged in Hong Kong to Patricia Chester-Master, and when Sybil returned to England in April 1935 the young couple came out in a tender at Plymouth to meet her. This was an extremely important event in her life, and she was very nervous of meeting her future daughter-in-law, facing the ordeal more as vicar's daughter than as stage star. The encounter went off extremely well, however, mother and daughter-in-law-to-be each recognising the high quality of the other, and sharing their love of John and his love for them. In June John and Patricia were married at St Paul's, Knightsbridge, and two months later John sailed for Alexandria in H.M.S. *Glorious*, to be joined a little later by his wife. In the following year, while Lewis was in America, Mary married William Devlin, the actor.

In the same month as John's marriage, Sybil appeared in the first of a series of interesting parts. First came Blanche Oldham in *Grief Goes Over*,* once more directed by Auriol Lee, in which Owen Nares's son, Geoffrey, who was to die during the coming war, gave a tender performance as Sybil's young son. Next she was Lady Bucktrout in Robert Morley's *Short Story*, directed by Tyrone Guthrie with a superb cast, including Marie Tempest and her husband William Graham Browne, Margaret Rutherford, Ursula Jeans, Rex Harrison and Denys Blakelock, who took over from Rex Harrison when he left to go to America for his first great success in *Sweet Aloes*. Sybil has many vivid memories of Marie Tempest, whom her friends called "Mary".

"She was a quite extraordinary woman, very wonderful in lots of ways. I remember, for instance, our going to that mental home in Bristol together. You see, Lewis's sister Elsie, Dr Elizabeth Casson, was a pioneer in the world of psychiatry. She had been on the staff at Bethlehem (the old Bedlam), where she used to take me quite often when I was studying

* By Merton Hodge.

mental cases to help me in my Grand Guignol work. She then had an eminent position at Virginia Water and Lewis and I used to visit her there. I have always been closely connected with people whose minds are deranged, and in a kind of way been not so very far from it myself.

"Then Elsie started Dorset House in Bristol, a home for borderline cases, and one day Marie Tempest asked if she might go there with me. We went round talking to the inmates, and Elsie said, 'There's one person we can't get to speak at all, we can't get her to do anything!' And Mary sat at the end of her bed and smiled at her, and the woman looked at her for quite a long time. Then, 'You're Dorothy,' she said—she had remembered seeing Marie Tempest in that play, and from that moment she began to recover. Mary just being there had wakened something in her mind and she spoke for the first time. Wasn't it extraordinary? Mary was tremendously bucked, because she had never thought of herself as a healer—but this was real healing.

"She was such an odd mixture—she could be so frightfully difficult with people, and so wonderful. She was charming to me the night I bumped her on the nose with a pineapple. You see, at the end of the first scene of the play, which was just a bit of nonsense and awfully funny, I was waving a huge pineapple and it landed on Mary's nose just as, thank heaven, the curtain came down. I apologised profusely, but she just said, 'Oh, that doesn't matter, I was in the wrong place'. Which she was. I remember Tony Guthrie asking her to show Rex Harrison how to hold a telephone and do a lot of other things all at the same moment, which he couldn't manage—and how wonderfully she did it.

"On the other hand, she would get up to all sorts of tricks to stop other people getting laughs. In this play Ursula Jeans and I learnt to outwit her, and Mary thoroughly appreciated this. 'You're a clever actress, aren't you?' she said to me out of the corner of her mouth as we sat down together on the stage, and I answered, 'Yes, I am'. I remember her having a terrible row with Willy Browne in front of all the stage hands. He walked out and she said to me, 'Do you think he'll ever come back?' and I said, 'I shouldn't think so, if you treat him like that'.

"When he came back she apologised to him in front of everybody. She could be a bitch, but she was big. I loved her. And she loved Lewis. When during this run of ours he signed a contract to go to America in *Victoria Regina*,★ she said, 'Don't let him go. You never know.' I said, 'I'll risk it', but oh, I did hate those separations!'

Denys Blakelock had vivid memories of those days, the first time he had acted with Sybil or had a chance of real talk with her.

"You're a Roman, aren't you?" she asked me (as if I were something out of *Julius Caesar*). And when I replied in the affirmative she said, "Are you ardent?"†

Comparing her with Marie Tempest, he wrote:

"Mary spent every penny she earned on purple and fine linen and the good things of this world. Sybil, on the other hand, hates living in style; and as regards food she would not know whether she were eating peacocks' tongues or a hardboiled egg."

Lewis was away for several months playing Lord Melbourne to Helen Hayes's Victoria, and during this period he also headed a delegation to the Moscow Theatre Festival, sponsored by the British Drama League. Margaret Webster went with him, and they greatly enjoyed their sightseeing—not least the famous collection of pictures in the Hermitage.

Margaret Webster tells this story of their departure from Leningrad:

"We were immured in a huge kind of shed for a couple of hours, no food obtainable, and spasmodic protests met with

★ By Laurence Housman.
† Denys Blakelock: *Round the Next Corner* (Gollancz, 1967).

grunts by the military-looking guards on the doors leading to the docks—the boat was in. Towards midnight Lewis stood up —with panache—nobody could miss it. Picked up his coat and hand-luggage. 'We're going,' he said and marched straight to the doors with me on his heels. The rest all followed suit. Lewis didn't pause, just slammed the doors open, the guards too astonished to stop him. Outside he drew a huge Casson-breath and started to march towards the ship, singing the old imperial national anthem at the top of his voice, most of us joining in, with the bewildered Russian officials scurrying alongside. We expected wholesale arrests, but not a word. White-faced sailors directed us to our cabins—and we sailed."

All this was during the run of *Short Story*. Patricia had meanwhile returned from Alexandria to have her first baby in England.

"While I was waiting for news in Shrewsbury, where we were playing in a big cinema, I drove round and round the town with Denys Blakelock. I was distraught with anxiety, and he couldn't have been kinder. Then I heard that Anthony had been born."

As usual during a long run, Sybil appeared elsewhere, this time in a Sunday performance of *The Farm of Three Echoes** with May Whitty, Jessica Tandy and Russell Thorndike, and enjoyed playing a Boer farmer's wife. By the time Lewis returned in the summer of 1936 she was playing Mary Herries in *Kind Lady*, a play by Edward Chodorov based on a terrifying story by Hugh Walpole in which a woman lets into her house an apparently derelict man who then brings in his supposed wife and child and a whole gang of thugs, and takes complete possession of her life. Sybil Thorndike had read this in Toledo during her American tour and longed to play the part, though it frightened her so much that she put her head under the bedclothes as in the old Guignol days—but this time she had not got Lewis beside her.

* By Noel Langley.

In August the four Cassons—Sybil, Lewis, Christopher and Ann—went with Nora Nicholson and Nicholas Phipps on a tour of the British Isles.

"We did D. H. Lawrence's unfinished play *My Son, My Son* —we finished it ourselves, and I adored my part as the old mother, with Christopher as my impudent young miner son. A short while ago they did this play at the Royal Court, as *The Daughter-in-Law*, extremely well, though I liked our version better, except for the last act—theirs was brilliant. And I liked our interpretation of Noël's* *Hands Across the Sea* better than his own. His was cruel—we changed the emphasis, so although ours was cruel too it became a kind of tract, and I like tracts. I thoroughly enjoyed my part—a cruel bitch— and Ann was brilliant, a caricature of cruelty, aristocratic and so funny. People raved about her. She's a real comedian. I daresay we overacted frightfully, but I like overacting. Anyhow, in the provinces they enjoy more colour than you get in the natural conversational style of the West End. And so do I.

"There was Noël's *Fumed Oak* too, which was great fun, and *Village Wooing*—lovely to play that again, with Lewis now, but the highlight of the tour was *Hippolytus*, which we did for matinées. It was quite different this time, and Gilbert Murray said it was the most Greek of all Lewis's productions. We were all of us the Chorus, sitting in a row on either side of the stage, slanting towards the screens at the back, behind which we disappeared to reappear in our parts. We were very solicitous towards Ann, who was playing the tragic part of Phaedra. Christopher was Hippolytus, I was the nurse and the goddesses, and Lewis was the henchman with that splendid long speech. I can hear his voice still. It was a bravura speech, and most musical. Lewis always generously said that he could never have played it as he did if he hadn't heard Granville Barker. But much as I adored G.B. I don't think he could have been as good as Lewis, because although his voice was very flexible it had no bass notes in it."

* Noël Coward.

Sybil also made her first film for several years, playing Ellen, the old nurse, in *The Tudor Rose*. She enjoyed working with Nova Pilbeam, although she still didn't really like the medium of the screen for herself.

"On December 11th, the night of the Abdication, we were playing in Blackpool. The play was put on early so that we could hear the broadcast. When it was over we sat down and wept."

Soon after this Sybil and Lewis went to Malta to join John, Patricia and the nine-month-old Anthony for Christmas.

"How I love Malta! The goats and the lovely little fields. John flew over every morning and dipped his wings above our house. And then one day he said goodbye and went off in *Glorious* on exercises for several days. But that same evening he walked in again. The Governor of Malta had sent for him to come back and do conjuring tricks for his children's party, and the Captain gave him leave. How like the British Navy! John was a frightfully good conjuror, you know. Still is. A member of the Magic Circle.

"We had drinks in *Glorious* on Christmas Day—and it *was* glorious. We stayed in Malta until the New Year. I remember a splendid evening seeing the Marx brothers when we nearly fell out of the box with laughter. Lewis and I were busy a good bit of the time studying Miles Malleson's beautiful tragic play *Six Men of Dorset*,* which we were going to do shortly after our return to England."

This play tells the grim story of the "Tolpuddle Martyrs", the dialogue based on the diary of that splendid man George Loveless, the protagonist, and the letters of various other people concerned in the shocking travesty of justice which in 1834 caused these honest farm labourers to be deported to Australia in a convict

* By Miles Malleson and H. Brooks.

transport ship. Their conviction of the crime of "conspiracy" was based on the fact that, after the failure of their plea to the farmers for wages high enough to keep their families from starvation, they had formed an Agricultural Friendly Society for mutual succour—the forerunner of the trade unions.

Miles Malleson directed the play with much help from Casson, who played George Loveless with Sybil as his wife.

"We were all passionately concerned with the subject of the play. Nora Nicholson was in it too as the eldest child—we were most of us keen Socialists. After the morning rehearsals Miles used to come back to Oakley Street with us for lunch—we were ravenous, and Nan would have cooked the most enormous meal—so we went back to rehearsal half-asleep and full of suet pudding. How Miles adored those meals. He had shown the play to the Trade Union Congress, and as a result we were asked by them to take it on tour and they put up the money for it, with Ernie Bevin and Walter Citrine as its godfathers. They didn't lose their money, either. We went to all the big industrial towns, and we were packed out by trade unionists.

"I remember Nottingham specially. There was a big strike on, and we had a great meeting in a cinema and met all the miners. One of them talked to me about *Saint Joan*, and said he had read the book by Anatole France. I supposed he meant in a translation. 'Oh no,' he said, 'in the lingo. I was in the French mines then!' Pretty good, wasn't it? They were a wonderful lot, and tremendously intelligent.

"We weren't allowed to put the play on in the cinema—it was against the rules—so we did some of the best scenes in a field outside. The miners sat round in a circle—the first circular theatre in England! The play never came into London, through some idiotic misunderstandings with Miles's partner.

"A great change came into Lewis's and my life now. We moved from Oakley Street to Swan Court. I'd always wanted to live in Swan Court. I'd watched it being built, and thought it looked like a monastery—and I've always wanted to live in a monastery. I said, 'The children are all independent now, and I'm not going to keep this great house going any longer'. So we came over and this flat was vacant, and we took it and we've been here ever since, except while we were bombed out. Of course we still had Bron-y-garth then as our country home."

Yes, My Darling Daughter★ followed at the St James's, another complete change of class and kind for Sybil, in which she was glad to act with Leon Quartermaine. Besides all the variations of plots and parts, she still welcomed the experience of acting with so many different kinds of people, whose lives and natures always interested her, and thus further broadened her understanding of human character. During the run of *Yes, My Darling Daughter* she once again played Hecuba for a matinée and then went off, much to her annoyance, to play Mrs Conway in J. B. Priestley's *Time and the Conways* at the Ritz Theatre in New York. Not that she was other than delighted to be in a Priestley play—he was an old and valued friend—but she would never have agreed to go to New York had she not thought that Lewis would be there too, as planned.

"We were the most miserable company in the ship on Christmas Eve. We sang carols and cried buckets—I without Lewis, and half the others in some sort of matrimonial tangle. And the play wasn't a great success, though it was beautifully directed by Irene Hentschel, and Jessica Tandy was so good. It was too odd for New York, I think.

"However, it turned out to be a perfect mercy I was there, for during the run Christopher was taken ill in Boston, where he was playing in T. S. Eliot's *Murder in the Cathedral*. Henzie†️ rang me up, bless her heart, and told me that he was going into hospital at once to have his appendix out. I walked up and down my room for two hours saying, 'Our Father which art in Heaven' over and over again. Then at last Henzie rang again and said it was all over and that he was perfectly all right, and had gone

★ By Mark Reed.   † Henzie Raeburn, wife of E. Martin Browne.

under the anaesthetic singing. Just like Christopher, he's always singing. [So, incidentally, is his mother.] I changed my prayer to 'Glory be to the Father, Son and Holy Ghost'. Oh, was I relieved! And when my play shortly came off I was able to go to Boston to be with him. I broke my wrist during that run, too—still got a lump on it. Went to stay with charming friends and slipped on the ice—but I didn't miss a show, oh no!"

To quote once more from J. C. Trewin:

"In 1938 she came back to tragic splendour, Volumnia in *Coriolanus* at the Old Vic, a part she should have acted long before. Everybody had begged her to do it. Agate had; so had Herbert Farjeon . . . When Sybil Thorndike thrust at Volumnia at last, she had Laurence Olivier as her Coriolanus . . . The Old Vic première was lightning-streaked. Olivier ('There is a world elsewhere') rose like flame on marble. In the supplication Dame Sybil stood for eternal Rome. Earlier she had been something too cosily domestic, but at Volumnia's height—

This fellow had a Volscian to his mother;
His wife is in Corioli, and this child
Like him by chance.—Yet give us our dispatch:
I am husht until our city be a-fire,
And then I'll speak a little . . .—

the verse struck with a cutting edge of tempered bronze. Here was the classic tragedienne. Dame Sybil's voice had a defiant certainty; we knew that Rome was behind her. She spoke for the centuries."

"Of course it was wonderful playing with Larry," Sybil says. "He's such a splendid person, so gifted, but quite without conceit. His Coriolanus, directed by Lewis, was superb. One could feel his perplexity, his uncertainty as to whether he was doing the right thing. I always feel he's such a supreme comedian, but there was real tragedy in his performance. Tragedy

H

isn't easy. Of course, comedy isn't easy either, but it comes more naturally. Tragedy you have to drag out of yourself, and it hurts so frightfully that many actors dodge it. But Larry's Coriolanus was magnificent. He and Lewis worked all-out on it. I remember them having a breathing competition during the rehearsals. Lewis said, 'You've got to do this speech all in one breath', and Larry said, 'I bet you couldn't', but Lewis did. Larry has a longer breath than anybody I know. He could do the Matins exhortation 'Dearly Beloved Brethren' twice through in one breath. Lewis could do it in one and a half, and my father in one. All of which is pretty good. As children we used to listen fascinated in church to see if Father could get through the collect in one go.''

Then Emlyn Williams brought Sybil his play *The Corn is Green*. He had admired her greatly ever since that first encounter at Oxford, when he carried a spear in *The Medea*, and by now they were good friends. With her great love of Wales and the Welsh, *The Corn is Green* appealed strongly to Sybil. And so they went into production, and opened at the Duchess Theatre in September 1938, the author both directing and playing the fifteen-year-old pit boy, Morgan Evans, and Sybil in the very sympathetic part of Miss Moffat, the spirited teacher who recognises the boy's unusual talent.

"I shall never forget Sybil at the first reading," Emlyn Williams says. "She was absolutely superb, she didn't really ever need to put any more colour into the part at all, but, being Sybil, she wouldn't have considered she was earning her salary if she hadn't worked all-out at it. It was a lovely performance, and she was delightful both to direct and to act with."

"Miss Moffat was a portrait of Emlyn's own teacher, Miss Cook," Sybil adds, "a remarkable woman, whom I met during the rehearsals, which helped me very much with the character of Miss Moffat. She lent me Emlyn's old exercise books and told me he had been the ideal pupil. All the miner boys in the

play were real miner boys. The cast was nearly all Welsh,
except for me and Freddie Lloyd and Kathleen Harrison. She
was the real cockney among all the Welsh—frightfully funny—
it was the first time I ever played with her. Emlyn of course
was quite wonderful, and they all sang the lovely songs in
Welsh. [Here Sybil hummed bits of the Welsh songs.] The
play was a great success.

"Just as we opened, Lewis's *Henry V* with Ivor Novello
came on. This was perfectly splendid, a very elaborate production, rather on Tree lines. Ivor was astonishingly humble. He
went through the tune of every line with Lewis, and of course
being so musical he got it at once. I thought he was marvellous, though his adorers couldn't bear him doing anything
except a musical. And Dorothy Dickson was delicious as the
French Princess. It didn't run for long, because nobody
wanted to see anything connected with war. Munich had just
happened, and we had all danced on the stage with joy to think
that there was not going to be a war."

Shortly after this Lewis went to the Old Vic and produced and
played in a number of shows.

"He and I and John and Patricia went to Bron-y-garth for
Christmas. They had two children now—my grand-daughter
Penelope had been born in 1937, after they returned to England.
We had all been at her christening on board *H.M.S. Glasgow*.
Now John had joined *H.M.S. Vindictive*, based on Chatham.

"I didn't feel awfully well at Bron-y-garth, and on the
evening of Christmas Day I had to go back to London for the
matinée of *The Corn is Green* on Boxing Day. We were doing
two shows a day that week, and I felt very odd. I couldn't eat,
and I just kept going on a little brandy and milk. I didn't have
any pain—perhaps that was due to my Christian Science way
of thinking. It has always been a tremendous help to me. But
by the time the Friday matinée came I found it terribly difficult
to stay awake. I remember praying, 'O Lord, let me keep
awake to hear my cues'. Emlyn didn't notice anything, but

when I finally got to my dressing-room I said, 'Send for a doctor. He must give me something to keep me awake'. The doctor came and examined me, and looked very grave and said, 'You've got an appendix. I'm afraid it's burst. You must go into hospital at once.'

" 'I can't,' I said. 'I'll come on Sunday and you can do anything you like to me, but I must finish the week.'

" 'You won't be here by then if you don't come in now,' said the doctor.

" 'Send for Lewis,' I said furiously. 'He won't let me be carted off into hospital like this.'

"But he did. He came with me to the nursing home and then went off and fetched Ann, who was in *George and Margaret*, so they were both there during the operation.

"My dear friend Athene Seyler took the part over, and was marvellous in it. I was out of the bill for ten weeks. I had peritonitis. I had never been in a nursing home before, and I enjoyed every minute of it, except having to say goodbye to Lewis before I was up. He went off in January on a Mediterranean tour in charge of the Old Vic Company, with Esmé Church as joint director.

" 'Don't you worry about him,' Esmé said to me. 'I'll look after him. I'll be his second wife.' So I didn't worry. She was such a darling. I went to Bron-y-garth to convalesce, and then I came back to London to *The Corn is Green*, and stayed with May Whitty and Ben Webster in their Bedford Street flat. Apart from Lewis being away I was very happy with them. May was such a good Christian Scientist and we talked about it a lot. Just as Edith Evans and I do now. Although I have never seen any reason to join their church, having had a perfectly good one of my own all my life, their philosophy has always appealed to me, and it was through May Whitty that I had first learnt about it. She helped me very much to get well again now."

The Corn is Green continued all through the spring and summer. Lewis returned from the tour and went into *Pygmalion* at the

The Chalk Garden, 1957

Sybil watching Lewis at work

Haymarket as Colonel Pickering. Then, on the night of September 2nd, the Duchess Theatre was almost empty. Emlyn Williams said quietly to the audience, "Please come to the front, and we will play for you."

On the following morning, Sunday, September 3rd, 1939, war was declared and all theatres closed.

CHAPTER XVI

WAR ON THE ROAD

(1939–1944)

"WE WERE ALL at Mass when that first siren sounded for the alert just after the announcement that we were at war. Lewis had felt that war was inevitable, and nothing could be done about it. He would have joined up if he hadn't been too old, and he immediately went into the Chelsea fire services of the A.R.P.,* but I felt simply terrible about it. You see, over the years, since Christopher became a pacifist, I had gradually become such a convinced one myself.

"I had come to know Sybil Morrison, that staunch pacifist who went to prison for her views and whom I admire and love so much—the other Sybil, we call one another—and Myrtle Solomon, too, who became the editor of *The Pacifist*. I was and still am a sponsor of the Peace Pledge Union, and a member of various other pacifist organisations, and it felt like going back on my deepest beliefs to acquiesce in war. I went to see George Lansbury, the Labour M.P., who remained unshakeably pacifist and thought it would be better to be overrun by the Germans than to fight. But I couldn't go as far as this."

After three weeks the London theatres opened again, and Sybil returned to continue her role of Miss Moffatt. Emlyn Williams had disappeared, but was discovered in an odd corner of the Ministry of Information, decoding telegrams and looking for spies, and was brought back to go on with the leading part in his own play.

* Air Raid Precautions.

In May 1940 John Casson joined H.M.S. *Ark Royal* in command of a dive-bomber squadron, and said goodbye to his parents in the wings of the Duchess Theatre. Two months later, when this run had just ended and Lewis was playing Alonso to John Gielgud's Prospero at the Old Vic, a telegram arrived stating that he was missing, believed killed.

"I walked round and round the room in a daze, and then I went down to the Old Vic to catch Lewis before the matinée. He said, 'You must go straight down to Patricia'—she was at a farmhouse near Winchester with the three children—'and tell her to move at once to Bron-y-garth.' "

After Lewis died Gielgud described his gallantry on that awful day:

"Lewis . . . was Alonso, the King, whose son Ferdinand he thought to be drowned. One afternoon the word quickly went round the dressing-rooms that John Casson, Lewis's eldest son, was missing. Every line in the Alonso scenes seemed to refer directly to the agonising situation. We dared not meet each other's eyes or his. But Lewis never faltered, went on acting just as usual, betrayed no flicker of emotion—a little brusquer, perhaps, than usual, but strong and unshakeable as always."*

"Strong and unshakeable" indeed, but his family know how nearly this break (mercifully only a temporary one), in that magically close family circle, led to his collapse.

"Patricia was always convinced that John was alive," Sybil says. "She felt that she would have known if he had gone, and I had a very kind letter from Cedric Holland, the Captain of the *Ark Royal*, whom I had known since childhood. He did his best to reassure us. He said John had given him such a beaming smile and had waved as he took off, and he felt sure that he would come through. But it was a terrible time for us all."

* "Herne's Oak has Fallen", an article in *Plays and Players* (July 1969).

Nevertheless, life had to go on, and before long a new and important organisation came into being with which Sybil and Lewis were to have a close association—CEMA, the Council for the Encouragement of Music and the Arts. This outstanding body was eventually to become the Arts Council, which describes itself in an annual report* as "the post-war model of a body improvised in the winter of 1939 to prevent the black-out of the Arts". CEMA's formation owed a lot to the late Dr Thomas Jones, C.H., who was at that time secretary of the Pilgrim Trust. During his years with the Trust he had fostered many ventures to encourage the practice and appreciation of the arts, and had now become one of a small number of people deeply concerned with the position during the war of the non-combatant artist, using the word in its fullest sense. In the first war the artist had tended to have a poor deal, his potential contribution to national morale being largely ignored. Dr Thomas Jones and his colleagues were determined that this time things should be different, and thanks to their efforts the necessary financial support was obtained from the Pilgrim Trust and from the government, through the Board of Education. So, early in 1940, CEMA started to provide employment for artists and art of every kind, bringing entertainment to workers in mines and factories, and particularly to people evacuated from the cities who often lacked any occupation for their leisure, and later, when air-raids began, boosting morale in shelters and rest centres.

CEMA differed entirely from ENSA,† which had been founded in 1939 by Basil Dean to provide entertainment for the troops, an objective which he succeeded in carrying out with unfaltering efficiency. Sybil was co-president, with Lilian Braithwaite, of the Hospitals Entertainment Committee of ENSA.

CEMA began by helping to expand existing amateur organisations, but quickly moved into the professional field; and Mary Glasgow, than whom no wiser choice could have been made, was seconded from the Board of Education to be the secretary.

* *The First Ten Years.* Arts Council Report, 1955–56.
† Entertainments National Service Association.

Later, as general secretary of the Arts Council, her skill and energy further contributed to the Council's vast success.

In the summer of 1940 Lewis, who had recently joined Granville Barker in producing Gielgud's *Lear*, himself playing Kent, became CEMA's honorary director of professional drama. The first company to go out under this banner was the Pilgrim Players, directed by E. Martin Browne, the distinguished producer of T. S. Eliot's fine play *Murder in the Cathedral* and one of the pioneers of the Religious Drama Society. With his wife, Henzie Raeburn, he set off into the provinces to play in churches, schools and halls, the repertoire including *Murder in the Cathedral* and Bridie's *Tobias and the Angel*. The next to go was Lewis's company, with which he and Sybil toured South Wales under the aegis of the Old Vic, Casson having persuaded Tyrone Guthrie, then administrator of the Old Vic, that this theatre, dark now, and with little prospect of reopening in these days of growing menace, should throw in its lot with CEMA. In November 1940, thanks to Jo Hodgkinson, the advance manager, the Old Vic transferred its headquarters to Burnley in Lancashire, and thus ceased to be purely a London theatre. With the CEMA link its function as a national organisation began.

Sybil remembers the CEMA organisers asking Lewis what plays he proposed to take on his first tour.

"*Macbeth*," he said.

"Good Lord!" they exclaimed. "Poor miners!"

To which Lewis retorted, "I know my countrymen. They like drama."

"And he was right. That *Macbeth* was a triumph—the most interesting I've ever played in, the best I've ever seen. We did it with screens, and in the '45 Rebellion dress—kilts and tam-o-shantas—really more to our taste than the elaborate Ricketts sets and costumes. And we had choruses linking up the scenes and explaining the action—very effective.

"Just before we started rehearsals of *Macbeth* at the Old Vic for the tour, the glorious news came. Patricia, still at our home at Portmadoc, was told by the vicar that in Lord Haw-Haw's latest broadcast he had said that John Casson of Bron-y-garth, Wales, the son of Dame Sybil Thorndike, was a prisoner in Germany. Patricia telephoned to me. Lewis was out at a show with Leon M. Lion. They got back very late, and as they came in I shouted out, 'John's safe!' We both burst out crying, and so did Leon M. Lion. Then we drank everything in the house there was to drink. Next morning Lewis and I went to Holy Communion, and in the middle of the Creed he had a panic. 'What's the matter?' I whispered. 'I don't believe it's true,' he said, and sat down.

"That same morning I had to go to Drury Lane to see Lilian Braithwaite about the hospital entertainments, and Lewis went off to the Admiralty to find out if there was any information about John. He came in while I was talking to Seymour Hicks and said, 'It's true. He's safe'. Floods of tears again, of course."

So the Cassons—Lewis, Sybil and Ann—were able to start on the CEMA tour with lighter hearts, although they were now homeless. Indeed, they were among the first people in London to lose their home through the raids. Returning one night from a rehearsal they found that Swan Court had been bombed, and their flat was uninhabitable. A few days later Tyrone Guthrie announced that rehearsals would be finished in Wales. "Leaving Paddington at noon—if Paddington is still there."

During their first night at Newport there was a terrible raid, and the house of the people who were managing for them, and with whom the Cassons were to have stayed, was razed to the ground. The man and his wife were saved, but their two children were killed.

"It was a perfectly ghastly beginning to the tour, those two small children buried under the ruins. The parents were splendid people—they carried on—he was a wonderful manager. And she was simply heroic. The man who dropped the bomb was captured, and she visited him in hospital. What made her kindness to the German airman even more remarkable was that she

and her husband were Jewish. The poor man told her that he
had tried not to drop his bombs on any towns, but he'd had
to get rid of them. She was an angel, that woman. Incidentally,
she was a fine musician. Not long afterwards her husband died
—as a result of that awful shock."

The splendidly successful tour of *Macbeth* began, continuing
in local halls all through the South Wales valleys. The company
stayed in each place for one or two nights, and were met everywhere with warm hospitality and overwhelming enthusiasm.

"The miners' trade unions were our sponsors, and the miners
were the most glorious audiences. So alert. The poorer and
more deprived they were, the quicker-minded they appeared
to be.

"And they were such darlings! They always sang hymns at
the end of the play, and of course the Welsh national anthem
too, in their beautiful voices and beautiful language. All the
company learnt this so that we could sing it with them.
Naturally, being Welsh they were very religious, and many
of them were pacifists, simply hating war. All the boys had
gone by then. And there were raids every night, as we were
on the direct route to Liverpool.

"We had tremendous fun, too. There was the young boy
who asked as he watched us arriving, 'Which is the Dame?',
to be answered by a scornful friend, 'They're all Dames'.
And there was the dignitary of the church who introduced me
at a big gathering of educationalists as 'a famous member of
the oldest profession in the world'. There was a gasp. Nobody
dared smile, let alone laugh, and I've never heard the end of that
remark!"

At the beginning of the war the actress Freda Gaye★ was
working in repertory, and the Casson influence had filtered
strongly through to her. When she heard that they were to tour
in *Macbeth* she wrote at once to Tyrone Guthrie asking if she

★ Editor of *Who's Who in the Theatre* from 1958 to 1970.

might go with them. Her memories of this great adventure are
vivid.

"From the first performance in Newport it was clear that the
choice of play was right. We played not only to full houses, but
to audiences fairly ravenous for the play.

"The production had been devised not only for its adapt-
ability to a variety of stages, but also for the compactness and
simplicity in transport, since we should be travelling by bus
and van. I remember one occasion when the van with its
precious load was delayed, and the actors stood silently on the
bare stage watching the clock, nervously considering their
chances in duffle coats under three naked light bulbs before a
fully booked audience. Then the cry came, 'They've arrived!',
and everyone heaved a sigh of relief. All but one. 'You're
disappointed, aren't you, Lewis?' said Sybil. 'Yes,' replied
Lewis. 'I thought the actors would have to *act* for once!'

"Accommodation was one of the hazards of the tours.
Travel-weary actors descended from their vehicles to be met by
suspicious-looking landladies, and then the terrible question
had to be settled of who was to share rooms with whom, and
the fear of having to share a double bed. I remember one actor
announcing, 'I *will* not share my bed with another man', and
Lewis declaring, 'I *will* not take another company on tour unless they are all married couples'.

"But in fact it generally worked out all right. All the
company had to learn to be good companions whatever the
conditions, and also the extra art of being good guests. In this
we had the perfect example of the Cassons, who always showed
a genuine interest in the households they joined, and unfailing
courtesy even when their deeply held convictions were involved. I remember Sybil saying somewhere, very emphatic-
ally, 'I am *not* a servant of the public. I am a servant of the
theatre', but she remained always the perfect guest, and everyone adored her."

"On those tours," Sybil observes, "I found myself a Conservative when we were with Communists and a Communist

when we were with Conservatives, even if I did manage to behave with discretion."

After they had toured the west coast they went right up the middle of Wales.

"In the Rhondda valley," Sybil remembers, "I said to a vicar how wonderful it was for the miners that, though they had to do such awful work, they lived in such beautiful country. And the vicar replied, 'The lovely country air isn't much use to them when they get that terrible miners' disease—silicosis.' He really put me in my place. We often stayed with miners; they were wonderfully hospitable, and of course we were always warm, because whatever else there wasn't, there was plenty of coal.

"What a lot of parts I played in *Macbeth*! Lady Macbeth, one of the witches, the cream-faced loon, and the voice of little Macduff. It gave the scenes a dream-like quality. [In fact the press did not perceive that these parts were doubled.] I did little Macduff's voice off because the Welsh boys we picked up in the different places to do the part couldn't manage the words. They were extraordinary, these children. Politically conscious from the age of five, joining in our conversations, talking about the war. One little dumb boy who had never said a word suddenly observed in his strong Welsh accent, 'We made a great mistake after the first war'."

The unexpected financial success of that first tour—during which they visited thirty-seven places in ten weeks—led to a decision to continue with *Macbeth* in north Wales, where they found the audiences quieter but no less enthusiastic. By the end of March they had reached the Cassons' own town of Portmadoc, where they were in time to welcome the arrival of a new grandchild at Bron-y-garth, Mary's baby, Diana Devlin.

They were then playing at Blaenau Festiniog, the district of the Cassons' quarries, where many pictures from the National Gallery were now in safe-keeping, and they went on to Aberystwyth, where there were also pictures stored, and where later, at the university, Lewis received a doctorate.

The CEMA bulletin of April 1941 reported the Council's delight that the Cassons were prepared to continue with these tours, although this meant refusing engagements which would command larger salaries than the Old Vic could afford to pay and involve less fatiguing travel and less exacting conditions of work.

Sybil's sister Eileen and her daughter Donnie were at Bron-y-garth too, Eileen suffering from a severe nervous breakdown. Widowed early through the death of her husband, and with four children to bring up, Eileen had had a rather hard life. She was a very good actress, working often, like all the family, for Ben Greet—Charlotte Brontë was one of her most successful parts—and she played many times with Sybil, to the pleasure of them both. For many years now, until it closed at the outbreak of war, Eileen had been Principal of the Embassy School of Acting in North London. Now, at fifty, she had developed a form of melancholia which led to this breakdown. Sybil told her to settle down and live quietly at Bron-y-garth, leaving all the work to the young ones.

"Eileen said that this sounded a very dull way to live. 'Dull!' I said. 'Of course your life will be deadly dull unless you snap out of it.' Which she immediately did. The next morning she was up scrubbing the bathroom floor."

Eileen was soon leading a normal life again, and at the end of the war she resumed her theatre work, acting and teaching at the Central School of Speech and Drama and directing at the New Lindsey Theatre. She was an excellent teacher, and unlike many principals she did not discourage would-be actors. "Have a go at it," she would say. "You can always give it up if it doesn't come off, but if you don't have a go you'll regret it all your life."

Eileen's eldest daughter, Phyllis Mary, was a convinced pacifist, and when she refused to be drafted into war work Sybil went as a witness to her tribunal.

"It was uproarious," she says with glee. "I kept on inter-rupting, and the judges roared with laughter. 'Dame Sybil, you'd better be quiet,' they said. 'But my niece keeps on telling you untruths!' I replied. They asked her if she belonged to the Church of England, and she said 'No', and I shouted out, 'Oh, that's a lie!'

"We had a glorious time, and at last they said to Phyllis Mary, 'It's very evident you're not going to be a member of the forces, so we'll send you to a farm in Lincolnshire.' It was a crack farm with prize Friesian cattle—so she married her boss and had four brilliant children, each one born six months before each of Ann's."

Then Guthrie and Casson merged their two companies for a production of Shakespeare's rarely seen tragedy *King John*, Howard Wyndham and Bronson Albery undertaking to present the play, after a short tour, for two weeks at the New Theatre in London. Guthrie and Casson produced the play together, Guthrie giving free rein to his vivid and graphic imagination and Casson, as always, paying meticulous attention to the word. In June 1941 the new company piled into a bus for their tour through the Lake District to Scotland. Then they left for London.

King John was a spectacular production, with Ernest Milton in the title role, Sybil as Constance (a favourite part of Mrs Siddons), Esmé Church as Queen Elinor, Abraham Sofaer as Philip of France and Lewis as Cardinal Pandulph. Sybil was unrecognisable in her strange make-up—the actors all wore woollen wigs—"her face folded in sorrow," says Trewin, "who almost reconciled one to the wailing woman, so desperately snobbish in her grief."

During this fortnight one matinée of *The Medea* was presented, the last time that Sybil acted this memorable part in London. Of her performance Ivor Brown wrote:

"It is a tremendous role, containing both the woman wronged and the woman wronging. In the first aspect Dame Sybil has the russet majesty of a tremendous oak through which the

winds of tragedy are sighing; in the second she blazes like a
forest fire."

After a final performance of *King John* at Burnley, where
Tyrone Guthrie was established with the Old Vic in a fine
theatre, the two companies separated again, and the Cassons
took the road back to Wales, this time with *The Medea* and
Candida.

It was during this visit to Burnley that Sybil, fired with
enthusiasm by *The Medea*, began to learn ancient Greek—Lewis
buying her a lexicon. She has continued ever since to study the
language, particularly enjoying reading her New Testament in
Greek, which she does every day.

Once again Lewis's instinct in his choice of play was proved
absolutely right. The miners revelled in *The Medea*. "This is the
play for us," Sybil remembers one miner saying, "it kindles a
fire." And Freda Gaye recalls another one observing, "There's
no light pastry about this. It's good solid meat." The play was so
popular that the villagers would walk miles from one valley to
another to see it again. They had little Welsh boys in this play
too, and Kathleen Clark, "Clarkie", the popular manager of the
Old Vic, who had now joined the Casson management, remembers Sybil, about to mourn off-stage for her murdered children,
observing thoughtfully, "I mustn't wail too loud. They can't see
me, and they'll think it's a siren."

Candida, on the other hand, which Lewis had been strongly
advised to take on the tour, "as Euripides would be too difficult
for the miners", was an utter failure. The Welsh audiences either
did not understand the play at all or else found it tiresomely
frivolous, and before the end of the year it was dropped.

In January 1942, when they were playing at Tenby, the Cassons
first met Douglas Campbell, who was later to marry Ann.

"It was a most amusing encounter. He had been engaged by
Tyrone Guthrie to join our company and had hitch-hiked from
Glasgow. He hadn't had much stage experience at this time.
He came to see us in our bedroom at Tenby, and we became

involved in tremendous arguments. When he left Lewis said, 'That's an opinionated young man. But I like him and I'm glad he's with us.'

"He joined us in *Medea*, and we soon discovered that he'd been a pacifist all his life. His father had been a friend of Keir Hardie, and he had been brought up in the most idealistic way. His family weren't Christians—I mean, they weren't orthodox —but they lived in a truly Christian fashion. Tramps and beggars—nobody was ever turned away from their house, and Douglas hardly knew what it was to have a room to himself. He and Ann became good pals, but they were always falling in love with somebody else, and they didn't actually get engaged until after the war. Even then we were all very surprised—nobody thought of them as a pair, and when Ann telephoned to tell us the news, I shrieked 'Oh, no!' And Lewis said, 'That's exactly what Mother Don Don said about me. Don't be so beastly, Sybil! Say something nice.' So I changed my tone, and I soon changed my view too. And now they are acting very successfully together in the States and have four children."

Laurence Housman, who had been a friend of Lewis's ever since the latter played The Statue of Love in his *Prunella* during the Vedrenne-Barker régime, had recently suggested that Lewis might like to produce one of the Old Testament plays that Housman was then writing. They decided upon *Jacob's Ladder*. Sybil played Isaac's wife Rebekah in the first act, and Chorus Two, with Lewis as Chorus One, throughout the play, sitting one on each side of the stage, just within the proscenium. Ann played Rachel, and Freda Gaye "the tender-eyed" Leah, which for Housman meant so short-sighted as to be nearly blind. Actors and audience alike found the play both original and delightful.

Some time before Sybil had promised to take the lead in Russell's macabre play *The House of Jeffreys*, and Lewis thought that the time had now come to fulfil this engagement. In the summer of 1942, therefore, Chorus Two in *Jacob's Ladder* was taken over by Clemence Dane, and Sybil joined her brother at

Bron-y-garth to work on the script with him ("knowing the Bible hindside before was a great help with the quotes").

"I adored doing Georgina Jeffreys. I always wanted to play a missionary gone wrong. I had a gammy leg and was a real old tough, with a converted cannibal as my attendant who had really converted me to his savage rites. Robert Adams played this part, a negro with a magnificent voice rather like Paul Robeson's. I had a little portable harmonium Russell and I bought for ten shillings from a man in the street, and I sang 'Let God arise, let His enemies be scattered', and played with the gusto of Mother Don Don. It was like the old Grand Guignol days."

The play was produced by Henry Oscar and put on at the Playhouse. The press did not share Sybil's liking for the play, in which the spirit of Bloody Judge Jeffreys, glowering from a canvas on the wall, exerted such a terrifying influence.

During this time Basil Dean found himself needing a change from the bureaucratic job, which he did so admirably, of directing ENSA's activities.

"I became obsessed with the desire to use music and drama in some kind of positive assertion of the nation's belief in itself. Then an idea came to me . . . 'An Anthology in praise of Britain' ".*

He invited Eric Linklater to prepare the script and, although Linklater was unable to undertake the work, it was he who suggested the title—*Cathedral Steps*, since Basil Dean hoped to have the first performance in front of the west door of St. Paul's. Dean then went up north to see Clemence Dane, still acting in *Jacob's Ladder*.

"She embraced the idea with her usual enthusiasm [he wrote]. In a short while she sent me the script, which needed very

* Basil Dean: *The Theatre at War* (Harrap, 1956).

little alteration, save to restrain a certain predilection for Queen Boadicea that might have involved Sybil Thorndike in a chariot race round St. Paul's Churchyard.''*

Cathedral Steps was first performed on September 25th, 1942. It was a dazzling occasion. The traffic was diverted from Ludgate Hill, and as the great clock of St Paul's began to strike twelve, dense crowds of people converged on the cathedral. As the half-hour boomed the great west door opened, and the procession of some hundred civic dignitaries, all in their robes and chains of office, filed from the cathedral. The drums and trumpets sounded a fanfare, filling the air with the wings of fleeing pigeons. The organ resounded from within, the massed choirs sang *Fairest Isle, All Isles Excelling*, and the actors appeared.

First came the Fighting Men in scarlet, led by Eric Portman as Valour, and the Men and Women of Peace, in blue and white, led by Sybil Thorndike as Patience, wearing light blue and a chaplet of laurel and oak-leaves. Then, to the words of her great poets and the music of her great musicians, heroic moments of Britain's history were re-enacted.

On the following Sunday *Cathedral Steps* was repeated among the ruins of Coventry Cathedral to another great audience, but further performances proved impossible owing to the high cost.

Soon after this, while Lewis was playing in Steinbeck's *The Moon is Down*, Sybil paid a visit to Dublin to play for the Hilton Edwards-Micheál Mac Liammóir Gate partnership at the Gaiety Theatre, where they were now giving two seasons a year. Sybil and Lewis had been to Ireland briefly during the war to give poetry recitals, always making a joyful expedition to the zoo in memory of their first enchanted conversation. This time Sybil was to be both Mrs Alving in *Ghosts* and Lady Cicely in *Captain Brassbound's Conversion*, plays particularly chosen to give first-class examples of tragedy and comedy.

Although she was alone she very much enjoyed the visit. Dublin was a complete respite from the war—almost pastoral, with peat fires, scarcely any traffic, easy living and lighted-up

* *The Theatre at War.*

nights only occasionally disturbed by gunfire when any plane crossed the sky. Best of all, Christopher was there. He had gone to Dublin some time before to play in Micheál Mac Liammóir's company. During his stay he had become a Roman Catholic, joining as a Tertiary of the Third Order Dominicans, and in 1942 had married the Irish artist Kay O'Connell. He and Kay and their year-old daughter Glynis were living in a flat in Herbert Street, and it was a great joy to Sybil to be with her family. Christopher would have played Manders in *Ghosts* had he been free, but at the time he was acting in *The Cherry Orchard* for Lord Longford's Company. He did, however, manage to see both plays from the front, and still considers Mrs Alving to be perhaps his mother's greatest role, and her Lady Cicely, a part originally written for Ellen Terry, to be the perfect creation of this character.

Of Dame Sybil Thorndike Micheál Mac Liammóir had written:

"Essentially English she is yet nationless, essentially of her period she is timeless, a classic creature, golden and brave as a lioness, with a face to reflect every mood of human experience and a voice poured into her throat by the winds of heaven. 'Oh, but it took such a lot of work!' she cried when I said something about it. 'Lewis was often in despair about me.'

"No one could describe Sybil Thorndike: you might as well try to describe the Parthenon. She, like it, radiates a sense of power, of sanity and poise, a kind of golden reassurance. I think it would be impossible to be anything but oneself with her, to evade or invent or pretend: her complete understanding of one's reason for affectation or deception would make it all useless. 'But you're telling lies, my dear,' she would probably intone, laughing and shaking off the silly useless tinsel with a swift downward motion of her hand. 'You can do better things than that.' And one would not be embarrassed but superbly reassured. Essential truth is the secret of her acting. When, many years later, she came to Dublin to play Mrs Alving in *Ghosts*, this was the lesson she taught me: that to be completely and faithfully oneself is the image to be held constantly before the eyes; and how difficult it was, how difficult it still remains for me to learn to risk, to dare it all."*

As soon as she returned to England Sybil played Mrs Hardcastle in *She Stoops to Conquer* at the Theatre Royal in Bristol.

"It was lovely playing again in that old theatre which I'd known so many years before when it was just horse-boxes. It had all been re-done now, but it still had the old painted stars on the ceiling and was quite beautiful. Ivor Brown had written an ovation for the opening, and I recited it in my elaborate Mrs Hardcastle get-up. Queen Mary was there, and I went round to her box. She said how much she'd enjoyed the performance and that she considered the Theatre Royal her own theatre. Then she said, 'I hear you are doing another play. What is it called?' I said, '*Queen B. With a Dash*,† Ma'am.' 'How very amusing,' Queen Mary said. 'I shall come.' And I said, 'You won't like it, Ma'am, I'm awful in it.'

"Queen Mary did come to the first night and sent for me to her box and said, 'You're quite right, you're awful, but it's very funny!'"

Sybil's next part, in Enid Bagnold's *Lottie Dundass*, was different enough to satisfy even her taste for playing contrasting characters. Ann Todd was in the name part, and gave an excellent performance of the stage-struck young girl who murders the actress about to rob her of her chance to act. Mrs Dundass, Lottie's remarkable mother, was a very sympathetic part for Sybil. The play was imaginatively produced by Irene Hentschel at the Vaudeville, and a friendship began between Sybil and Enid Bagnold which was never to end. Later Sybil was to act in two other of the latter's plays.

In her autobiography,‡ Enid Bagnold describes how *Lottie Dundass* came to be written. She was suddenly asked to read the

* Micheál Mac Liammóir: *All for Hecuba* (Methuen, 1946).
† By Judith Guthrie.
‡ *Enid Bagnold's Autobiography* (William Heinemann, 1969).

prologue at the opening of a play at the Theatre Royal in Brighton because Lady Juliet Duff, who was to have read it, fell ill.

"To find myself on the boards behind footlights was such an ecstasy that I spent all night learning the words of the Prologue. Juliet, however, got up and came on the following night . . .

"'I could kill her!' I said in baulked fury to Maurice.*

"'Make a play of it.'

So I wrote *Lottie Dundass*."

After a run of several months in this play, Sybil took part in a special performance of a work by Gilbert Murray, to whom she had always remained devoted. She played Myrrhinê in the recently published translation of some of the fragments that remain of Menander's *Perikeiromenê*, welded into a comedy by Professor Murray, and at Bernard Shaw's suggestion given the odd title of *The Rape of the Locks*.

Clemence Dane, meanwhile, had been making a stage version of the *Alice* books, and Christmas 1943 found Sybil gleefully playing The White Queen at the Scala.

"It was gorgeous. I flew. The most lovely sensation— coming down from so high. I got a real feeling of flying which I always hope to get in aeroplanes, but never quite do."

The White Knight, in the person of Geoffrey Dunn, says that Sybil so much enjoyed her wire that not only was she suspended but rehearsals were too.

Early in 1944 Sybil went off alone to Scotland and the Orkney Islands to give recitals of dramatic poetry to the troops.

"It was delightful, except for having horribly sweet tea in every camp. I was specially pleased at going to Elgin, where my beloved grandfather had lived. I got up very early and walked through the snow to see where the family post office had been.

* Maurice Baring.

And that night I recited some of the lovely old poems my grandfather had read to me as a child."

When she returned to London she and Lewis were able to move back to their restored flat in Swan Court, and before long Ralph Richardson came to ask her to join him in establishing the Old Vic Company in London again after its years of exile— Lewis being occupied with a number of CEMA and ENSA tours with Ann. The theatre in the Waterloo Road was still in its wartime garb, having long been used as a shelter in which hundreds of people slept and had their meals, so in August 1944, with a distinguished repertoire, the Old Vic Company re-opened at the New Theatre. Bronson Albery had been appointed joint administrator, with Tyrone Guthrie, and the first production was the latter's memorable *Peer Gynt*.

CHAPTER XVII

THE CIRCLE JOINED

(1944–1945)

"DAME SYBIL'S AASE to Ralph Richardson's Peer Gynt was her meridian," wrote Trewin, and indeed Sybil had loved this play ever since Russell had played the part for Robert Atkins, nearly twenty years earlier, with John Gielgud, at the age of seventeen, making his first appearance among the trolls and peasants.

"Russell *was* Peer Gynt," Sybil says [and Gielgud remembers this too]. "He looked so like him, he didn't have to do anything to his face, and he fulfilled Aase's opening line in the play, 'Peer, you're lying', because Russell never has known the difference between truth and imagination. But Ralph Richardson was wonderful too, and it was a great joy to be acting with so many friends. Tony* was directing, and there were Joyce Redman and Maggie Leighton,† Maggie's technique so perfect that it tended to over-ride her feeling, whereas with some others of us feeling tended to over-ride technique, and then there were Beau‡ and Billee Williams§ and Larry —so ordinary, but so frightening as the Button Moulder. What a comedian he is! My part of Aase, the old mother, I simply adored. The Grieg music is so lovely too. I can't think why they don't always use it. After all, it was written for the play, and it is peasant music that sets the atmosphere. Reece Pemberton's imaginative decor also added greatly to this."

It was in every way a starry production, and the fame of this

---

* Tyrone Guthrie.   † Margaret Leighton.   ‡ Nicholas Hannen.
§ Harcourt Williams.

Old Vic season was growing all the time, with people queuing night and day, replacing one another in shifts as the only way to secure seats.

Some critics thought that Sybil overplayed the part, but as she found Aase "big, like Hecuba", for her it needed big acting, and surely from Ibsen's standpoint she was right. The scene in which Peer plays coachman at his old mother's bedside, galloping with her to the gates of heaven, is unforgettable. As Trewin says, "Aase's dying voice would have melted marble."

Next in the repertoire came Shaw's *Arms and the Man*, with Sybil reincarnated as Catherine Petkoff, "a woman over forty, imperiously energetic, with magnificent black hair and eyes, who might be a very splendid specimen of the wife of a mountain farmer, but is determined to be a Viennese lady [she is in fact Bulgarian], and to that end wears a fashionable tea-gown on all occasions." In this production Sybil particularly admired Olivier's performance as the young Sergius. Some of her critics continued to deplore her own leaps from one character to another; they had started this cry right back in the Grand Guignol days, saying that she had lost her own personality by playing so many parts alien to it. But she has never wanted to project her own personality on the stage. "I don't know what it is and I don't care. What I'm interested in is the personality of the characters I'm playing. That's what acting is and always has been to me."

So to *Richard III*. Sybil had played Queen Margaret to Russell's Richard at the Old Vic during the first war, so this production with Laurence Olivier, directed by John Burrell, awoke many memories, besides being a new and stimulating experience. Trewin wrote of "Olivier's Crookback moving down the ensanguined road to Bosworth Field", and of Sybil's Margaret, "specialist in cacodemons and bottled spiders, [who] poured the vitriol so generously that we regretted a cut that denied a second draught to us."

With her phenomenal energy, when Christmas approached, Sybil managed to slip over to the Palace Theatre in the mornings to play the White Queen again and eat fish and chips—"the best food ever"—from a newspaper in her dressing-room,

Margaret Rutherford taking over the part in the afternoons.

In the new year Tchekov's beautiful *Uncle Vanya* was added to the repertoire, again produced by John Burrell, with Ralph Richardson in the lead and Sybil playing Marina, the tender yet practical old nurse who succours each sorrowing member of the household with vodka or some other form of comfort, in the same way that she protects the straying chickens from the crows. It is a small, finely drawn part, which Sybil was to repeat very movingly in 1962 for the two opening seasons of the Chichester Festival Theatre, with Lewis playing Telyegin.

It is sad to remember that Marina has been Sybil's only Tchekov part. There are such perfect roles for her—Madame Ranevsky and Madame Arkadin, to mention only two characters in whom she and her audiences would have rejoiced. She regrets this omission, and also the fact that *Ghosts* and *Peer Gynt* have been her only Ibsen plays. "There just hasn't been time," she says. From the beginning plays have come to her, she has never gone out to look for them. Poetry has in a way been more her own discovery, ever since, during the youthful tours in America, she wrote to tell Russell that he must read Browning, Walt Whitman being one of her early discoveries, and Edna St Vincent Millay another in her later days.

Plays have come to her largely through Lewis, and by some strange chance he too missed out on Ibsen and Tchekov. Perhaps it never occurred to either of them that there would not somehow be time and room in this life for everything. Of course some things have had to be left out; but the fact that there are such rare signs of stress and strain in the richness of Sybil's life is a proof not only of her famous vitality but of the relationship which she has maintained with the whole orchestra of her existence. Music is the basis of her philosophy, and Johann Sebastian Bach her master to whom she still turns for the daily discipline, without which she feels that neither life nor art can fulfil its function. She draws this discipline also from poetry and from religion and, if Lewis has been the first violin in her orchestra, the conductor is God, and her life is a vast symphony based on musical and mystical precision.

Her generosity is a byword; she has helped endless individuals and charitable bodies, chiefly, in the early days, charities to help children and young people, but later embracing the aged too. She has recently opened a Thorndike Home for the aged at Southwark.*

On VE Day, May 8th, 1945, when the end of hostilities was announced, she was on tour with the Old Vic Company in Manchester and Lewis was in Cheltenham with Ann.

"When I heard the news I walked up and down Deansgate, wondering and wondering where John was. Then as I went into the theatre for the evening performance I was called to the telephone—and it was John. He had arrived from Germany that very day and was at Ashstead with Patricia and the children. Oh God, it was wonderful! Of course I couldn't stop crying after all these years of stress. Larry was simply angelic. He is a truly kind man. I can't tell you what a help he was to me when Lewis died."

As soon as their engagements permitted, Lewis and Sybil joined John and his family for a joyous family reunion. Mary was there too with her baby daughter Diana. Not long afterwards, to the great distress of her parents, her marriage to William Devlin came to an end, but her second marriage to Ian Haines, a schoolmaster, was to be a very happy one.

John had made the finest possible use of the years, treating prison as his university. He studied German and Russian, theology, semantics, philosophy and logic. After about two years at a small camp near Frankfurt he was moved to Stalagluft 3, the camp in Silesia famous for Operation Wooden Horse. Here the prisoners built a theatre, and John and several other prisoners were connected with it, notably Kenneth Mackintosh and Rupert Davies, then known as Pud, later known as Maigret. John took part in the production of a number of plays, including *I Have Been Here*

* 1970.

Before, *Arsenic and Old Lace*, *Macbeth*, with Kenneth Mackintosh, six foot two in height, as Lady Macbeth, and *Saint Joan*. His prowess as a conjuror was also a welcome asset to the camp's entertainment.

His freedom regained, John was uncertain what to do with it. His desire to stay in the Navy had never wavered, but, with five years, in which he would otherwise have had steady promotion, torn from his life by his imprisonment, this hope had died. So in the end he resigned, having proved himself in every way a splendid officer and been decorated for his outstanding services while a prisoner. Matthew Forsyth presently offered him a job as assistant stage manager at Glasgow Citizens' Theatre, and he immediately accepted—working, at the age of thirty-six, under a girl of twenty-five, and earning £7 a week. He was assistant to James Bridie, from whom, he says, he learnt an indescribable amount about human beings. He cannot speak too warmly of Bridie or the privilege of working with him.

John's parents were full of admiration over this decision. Sybil was simply thankful that he should be in something unconnected with war, but Lewis, who was apt to worry about finance, was not unnaturally in something of a panic about how he would manage to support a wife and three children on this meagre salary. But manage it he did, and soon rose to directing in this excellent theatre.

Only a couple of weeks after this family reunion Sybil, Ralph Richardson, Laurence Olivier and the Old Vic Company started on an ENSA tour of western Europe.

"We were all in uniform (rather fancied ourselves). We went straight to Antwerp where we were met by Graham Sebastian, the Consul General, who was our host here, giving parties for us in his lovely flat, which was a welcome change from the meagreness around. Then we went to Brussels—our headquarters for a time—with visits to Bruges and Ghent, playing in beautiful theatres. The theatres in Belgium were like royal palaces.

"In Brussels I met a very remarkable woman, Ninette Jeanty, who had just been released from a mental home

Saint Teresa, 1961

Lewis, 1969

Sybil and Lewis
at the piano

where she had feigned madness for two years because she had heard that the Germans would not kill the husband of someone insane. How she managed to keep it up I cannot imagine, but one day she broke down and came out with her story to the German doctor in charge. He was very kind, and through him she got her freedom, but in the meantime her husband had been shot by a sniper while being moved from one prison to another, and her son was living underground. Later she came to England to lecture on international relations and met Canon Raven, a Cambridge professor and a great pacifist, and married him and carried on with her work. We have been close friends ever since that first meeting in Brussels.

"Then came our nightmare journey into Germany. In Lüneburg we were met by the Army of Occupation, and were given orders never to speak to a German—not a single word, not even to say thank you when we were served with meals. In fact, to ignore the Germans completely. This seemed to us—specially to Billee Williams and me—a harsh, rude, un-Christian attitude, but when we demurred we were told we should be sent back to England if this rule was infringed.

"When we drove into Hamburg it seemed flat to the ground —with people peering out of holes. I went to my room in the seedy hotel where we were billeted and couldn't stop crying, it was so awful. And Billee told me afterwards it had been just the same for him. We found absolutely no antagonism towards us in Germany, and we bought music in Hamburg, so we were able to talk to the Germans.

"There were some buildings left standing in the centre of the town, the lovely theatre being one of them. Here we played to troops, and wonderful audiences they were. We played at Lübeck too, and finally came Belsen, where we did one matinée for the staff. This was an unforgettable horror. The outside looked so clean and tidy, but inside the stench was appalling— all the disinfectants couldn't drown it. The camp was still smouldering, and the children were still there. The sight of those little distorted creatures nearly paralysed us. They were being treated by a specialist brought over from Dublin and nursed by a Jewish peasant woman, who had seen her own husband and children killed. Some of the children were cured, we heard afterwards, and some mercifully died. We left completely sickened by the hideousness of it all."

The company then flew to Paris in an army plane, sitting on the floor in great discomfort, and arrived at their small hotel in the Place de l'Opéra Comique. It was a great delight to Sybil to be playing at the Comédie Française.

"It was the most luxurious theatre I'd ever been in—the dressing-rooms were like drawing-rooms. I had the marvellous room always given to the doyenne of the theatre. Paris itself was sad and shabby, and we saw girls turning over dustbins to find something to eat."

When the Old Vic Company had been in Paris for about a week Lewis and Ann arrived to present *Saint Joan* at the Marigny Theatre, Lewis directing and playing Warwick, but before their arrival Sybil had received a cryptic message from him: "Remember the name of our black Scottie? Well, that's what's come to me. But not a word."

Sybil puzzled for a while, and then remembered that their black Scottie had been called Knight, and so understood that this was Lewis's secret way of telling her that he was to be named in the Birthday Honours. His knighthood was a profound joy to her.

"It was wonderful their coming to Paris, and I dashed along after my performance and just managed to see the end of *Saint Joan*. I remember a man rushing past me saying in English, 'My God, that girl's wonderful!' I was so happy I nearly hugged him, though when I was actually watching Ann act I didn't remember she was my daughter. I had seen her Joan in Bristol. That was the first time I had ever seen the play, and I was absolutely enthralled. She was better than me as the Saint, I think—Clemence Dane thought her trial scene better than mine. And Ann was a real warrior too—we've got the same kind of drive. We're more alike on the stage than in life. On the stage your real self comes out more because you're not 'behaving'. In life you're always behaving. Shaw said, 'Don't interfere with the girl', just as Galsworthy had said, years before, when Ann played in *The Roof*."

"I think I was lucky," Ann says, "in seeing Mother's Saint Joan when I was young enough [she was in fact nine] to be captured by the character of Joan herself, rather than impressed by Mother's performance, and it was long enough ago for me to forget about it. Otherwise I'd have been bound to be too impressed, and either followed Mother or tried to be different, which would have been equally bad. As it was I read the documents of course, and all sorts of things that had happened to me helped me to understand Joan. Just a year before I had become a Catholic, so of course I was captured by Joan's faith in God and her voices.

"I wrote to Shaw before I started rehearsals and told him I was a Catholic but a Protesting one. He wrote back, 'You are in exactly the right mood for it, for Joan was a volcano of energy from beginning to end and never the snivelling Cinderella born to be burnt . . .'

"So I think, with all these inspirations, in spite of shortcomings I was able to go straight to Joan myself, and Father wisely directed me without reference to Mother either, but, as with her, to get what Shaw wanted, which he knew so well. It is very difficult to explain how, in a theatrical family, you can be quite detached from family feeling where work is concerned. It is the same thing that made Father, on occasion, address Mother as Miss Thorndike at rehearsal.

"I am a tremendous admirer of Mother and Father in their work. That has nothing whatever to do with their being relations. Father was always extremely hard to please, so if he thought anything good at all about one's performance it was most deeply valued. Now Mother's a marvellous mother first of all, and completely biassed in our favour. She sees the good in people first, in everyone, but in her own family most of all.

"It must have been an extraordinary experience for her to see *Saint Joan*. I remember very well her coming round after the show at Bristol. She was quite speechless, for her *Saint Joan* had been one of the great experiences of her life. She is quite marvellously generous in her appreciation of other people, and even if there was one scene or one little bit of a scene that was true enough for her to really think it was good—well, that would be enough to make me deeply thankful.

"I have been very lucky to have the two things—Mother's praise and encouragement, and Father's penetrating and sometimes devastating criticism. Mother is a great person and a great actress, and, as I suppose people of genius are, full of superhuman energy. I am not any of these things, but in *Saint Joan* I had the advantage of being fairly young and having plenty of energy. I had my own identification with Joan, and first-class direction. I had to face the challenge of Father's hurricane force as a director, and if you can survive that you must get *somewhere*."

After this immensely successful season at the Comédie, the Old Vic Company returned to London. Sybil wanted to stay on in Paris with Lewis and Ann, but in order to be allowed to remain in France she had to work. Robert Speaight made this possible for her by asking her to give some recitals with him at Lille University and the Sorbonne. Then, when the others were free, the three Cassons went back to England together, and thence to Bron-y-garth for a holiday.

CHAPTER XVIII

NO END*

(1945–1953)

THE NEW OLD VIC bill of fare began for Sybil with the ribaldry of Mistress Quickly in both parts of Olivier's *Henry IV*, a splendid opportunity for her to wear her mouth all on one side in that inimitable way she has.

"I love the bawdy old bitch and the way she tells off Falstaff. She's like the old toughs I used to know in Westminster. John Burrell produced it. He had a good over-all view, but not being an actor himself he left us pretty much to our own devices."

Roger Furse contributed fine décor and costumes, and altogether this *Henry IV* was a good opening for the new season. To follow, Laurence Olivier had decided on an astonishing double bill—Sophocles' *Oedipus Rex* and Sheridan's *The Critic* in one programme. Yeats's translation of *Oedipus* was used, which the poet had made twenty years before and called *A Version for the Modern Stage*. Sybil does not like this rendering. She misses Gilbert Murray's lyricism in Yeats's "plain" dialogue, but to some Yeats's version seems closer to the austere Greek than Murray's rhymed verse.

"I like flights," Sybil, who played Jocasta, explains. "And Gilbert Murray was always in flight. If Yeats's translation were stark—or even bleak—I should like it, but I find it just

---

* Julian: "There's really no end to what we might do—there's no end . . ." (the last line of *A Day By the Sea* by N. C. Hunter).

pedestrian, except for the choruses, which are most beautiful. I also very much admire the translation of the American scholar Edith Hamilton, whom I enjoyed meeting when I was in New York. Larry played Oedipus magnificently, with startling realism, and Michel Saint-Denis' production was straightforward and down to earth, making of the play a good detective story, the first of the who-dunnits, but just missing its symbolic heights of tragedy. The sets by John Piper were very striking. It is a pity he didn't design the costumes too. They were good in themselves, but out of tone with the decor."

It was hard enough for the audience to leap from this tragedy to Sheridan's burlesque, and it was certainly a *tour de force* for the actors. Miles Malleson produced *The Critic* with great sensitivity, and Olivier gave full rein to his gift for comedy as Puff, while Sybil made a brief appearance as the justice's lady in elaborate eighteenth-century costume, patched and bewigged, "the only time," she characteristically observes, "that I've really looked stunning."

"My father dwelt in Rochester," the long-lost son declares, and the justice's lady exclaims, "How loudly nature whispers to my heart!"

It always has whispered to Sybil's heart, and Rochester and Aylesford have remained ever dear to her. She still visits them frequently, and is still very completely and consciously the daughter of her beloved father.

These plays carried on well into 1946, and were the end of Sybil's long and successful reign with Laurence Olivier in the Old Vic Company, which then left for America. Sybil declined Olivier's warm invitation to go with them, partly because she did not want to leave Lewis and partly because she had set her heart on playing Clytemnestra to Ann's Electra, which Lewis was directing for Basil Langton, a fine actor and a good manager, at the King's Theatre, Hammersmith. During this season Lewis and Sybil also played Mr and Mrs Woodrow Wilson in *Time to Come*.*

* By Howard Koch and John Huston.

"I was delighted to do this play because Woodrow Wilson had been so kind to Russell and me in those old days when we stayed with them in Princeton. Lewis made a marvellous portrait of Wilson with a false nose. He loved making noses —he was frightfully good at it—his most famous ones were for Socrates and Shylock.

"Ann was splendid—just the way I would have liked to play Electra myself. Basil Langton was an excellent Orestes, and it was lovely to be doing Gilbert Murray again. The notices were very stupid, saying that Ann copied my style of acting. It was the obvious thing to say, and the critics characteristically all said it. Ann never has copied me, but you can't help certain family likenesses."

In the spring of 1947 Clemence Dane brought Sybil a new play. The title was *Call Home the Heart*, and its theme is love and war-time love affairs, with a touch of clairvoyance in its conception. In fact, different as the two plays are, the atmosphere of the hallucinatory scene at the beginning of *Call Home the Heart* recalls Susan Glaspell's strange piece *The Verge*. However, though Clemence Dane was successful elsewhere in evoking the super-natural, this aspect of *Call Home the Heart* was not altogether effective, although in other ways this is an interesting play. While it was in rehearsal Clemence Dane was in America, and when she returned it was on tour, before coming to the St James's Theatre, where it ran for several months. Clemence Dane was not pleased with the production and insisted on various changes in the cast. Gifted and delightful woman though she was, she was not the easiest playwright to work with, possibly because of her almost possessive love of theatre. Among other things she could hardly bear to have a word of her scripts altered. Lewis Casson had a difficult time with her, for he seldom considered the text of a play final until it had come to life in rehearsal, a view which is of course debateable.

"Then one evening during the run Jack Priestley brought *The Linden Tree* to my dressing-room. 'There's nothing in it for you,' he said, 'but I want you to read it because of Lewis.' So that night I read it in bed, before Lewis ever saw it. I was immensely moved, for here *was* Lewis. More than anything he'd ever done, except *Socrates*.* Here he was as the Professor, with all his integrity and his devotion—his complete dedication to work. Personal things just didn't exist for Lewis where work was concerned. And here too were his philanthropy and his gentleness and understanding, in spite of the fierceness of his nature. Even his deep love of music was there. It just *was* Lewis. I was terribly moved, and I knew at once that I must play his wife, though she filled me with misery—that poor, empty-minded woman, so tired of poverty and unable to live up to her husband, and to resist the temptation of 'being nicely looked after'."

Lewis was thrilled when Sybil handed him the script. It was a long time since he had played such a star part.

The Linden Tree was produced by Michael MacOwan for the London Mask Theatre—the management which had run at the Westminster Theatre from 1936, but had come to an end when war broke out. Now Priestley, with whom MacOwan had always had a close understanding, chose this fertile moment to suggest the rebirth of the London Mask Theatre in association with the Arts Council. "I'll write you a play to start it off," he said. *The Linden Tree* was the result. When it was published the following year Priestley wrote in the dedication to J. P. Mitchell-hill:

"So far as the play has any virtue, it was a virtue plucked out of necessity. The heaviest snowfall the Isle of Wight had known for about a hundred years found me down at Billing-ham, in a house hard to warm and then desperately short of fuel. Besieged by this cruellest of Februarys, I ate, toiled and slept in one small room, and there the Lindens were born; and for ten days or so, while I worked at the play, they were almost my sole company and the people I seemed to know best.

* By Clifford Bax (Incorporated Stage Society, 1930).

And then—what luck!—I was back with you, back with the others, back at the Duchess, and all went miraculously well.

"That really was the marvellous thing," J. B. Priestley comments. "Lewis could just be this character not unlike himself, for there really was something a bit professorial about him, but Sybil had to act a woman utterly unlike herself and so give a *performance*, and that's when she's at her best."

MacOwan was deeply impressed with the play, and his opinion was strongly endorsed, for it won the Ellen Terry Award as the best play of 1947. He knew the Cassons well, and, though he and Lewis disagreed passionately over many issues, particularly politics, they liked one another greatly and admired each other's work. Before long MacOwan had assembled an excellent company.

"I remember at that first reading," Sybil says, "when Jack Priestley read it aloud to us—we were all simply struck dumb. Then Jack said, 'That's a bloody good play', and we all laughed and wholeheartedly agreed. He came to many of the later rehearsals and we all worked very happily together."

Michael MacOwan has vivid memories of those rehearsals:

"Lewis tended to overplay it a bit at first and would invent extraordinary things to do, like coming in bent double. To suggest Linden's age, he would explain—the professor being sixty-five and Lewis himself seventy-two. In fact, he needed confidence just to be himself, and Sybil was a fine ally. She was nervous and excited for him and watched him like a lynx, urging me to tell him when I thought anything should be changed.

"Each of them was a joy to direct because of their great intelligence, sensitivity and perception. Lewis had that astonishing precision in all his work which had one danger—that occasionally the so-to-speak 'construction' line would show—or again he would over-react in jerks. Of course, as he was such a splendid producer himself I discussed everything with him, though when he told me to tell the actors how to say their lines, I simply said, 'No, Lewis, you know that is not how I produce'. It was safe to feed Sybil anything, knowing that everything would be absorbed. 'Let me do it. Let me try it,' she would say the moment I suggested anything. Producing her was rather like a lighting rehearsal. 'Bring up No 3 full. Now take it down to half. Up a third. Now set.' The only thing I had to do was to stop her making faces.

"Although I think that Sybil's performance as Mrs Linden led to a new quietude in some later parts, it also linked up with her Jane Clegg of so many years earlier, which she had played with such impressive reserve. Because of her relationship with Lewis she could not be exactly the character that Jack Priestley wrote, and this deepened the play's tragedy. One could see how much the Lindens had once loved one another and had shared a happy life. One could feel the sadness of the changes life brings in people's relationships. The play is in fact compounded of hope and sadness. Hope for the future and sadness for the passing of the past."

They took *The Linden Tree* on tour for several weeks before bringing it in to the Duchess, and Michael MacOwan went off to other jobs. Suddenly he got a telegram from his manager, Thane Parker, "Take the next plane to Aberdeen."

"I found the company having a wonderful time playing for laughs, which the author—let alone I myself—had specified must not be done, and also Lewis was in tears during his final lines of the play. 'He looks down smilingly for a moment,' Priestley wrote, but Lewis loved to cry at this point, although I warned him that if *he* did, the audience wouldn't."

In any case the play was "a smash hit", and put the Mask Theatre firmly on its new feet. After the long London run the Cassons left the company and went to Glasgow, where John redirected the play for the Citizens' Theatre, with his parents in the lead.

Next Sybil went into St John Hankin's *The Return of the Prodigal*, directed by Peter Glenville at the Globe Theatre.

"It's a brilliant play," she maintains, "but although we had a fine company at the Globe, including John Gielgud as the Prodigal and Walter Hudd, Irene Browne, Rachel Kempson and Nora Nicholson, it wasn't as good as it was when we did it in the old Manchester days.* Somehow in this production it got too smart, too over-dressed, and it should be just ordinary middle-class northern people."

While she was playing in *The Return of the Prodigal* Sybil read Margery Sharp's novel *The Foolish Gentlewoman*, and wrote to her to say what a good play it would make. Margery Sharp replied that she was at that moment making a play from the book, and had intended to send it to Sybil.

"Now we can work together again, which will be lovely," Sybil said to Michael MacOwan. "And I can make all the faces I like."

This time Mary Merrall played opposite Sybil, and the rehearsals and even the performances were not without their private drama, for "Lewis and Mary had rows even when they were acting".

Mrs Brocken was an enchanting part for Sybil, made doubly pleasant by the fact that Lewis was playing her solicitor brother-in-law; for, while she never cared how alien to her nature her own roles were, she loved it when Lewis could play a character close to his own. Simon Brocken was not, of course, Lewis in the complete way that distinguished Professor Linden, but he had something of Lewis's attributes.

"I adored it in that play when he was huffy with me for being so vague. I am often vague in life, and it always made Lewis huffy."

The next play was even more fun—*Treasure Hunt*,† in which

* Gaiety, March 1913.   † By M. J. Farrell and John Perry.

Sybil looked enchanting with a great seagull, which holds the solution to the plot, perched on the brim of her hat, while she played the deliciously crazy Aunt Anna Rose. John Gielgud directed, Lewis portrayed a cultured business man, as interested in human nature as in antiques, and Sybil very much enjoyed playing opposite Marie Löhr.

During this period, 1947–50, Sybil also made a number of films, though she still never really liked film technique or thought herself good at it. There was Mrs Squeers in *Nicholas Nickleby* and Mrs Mouncey in *Britannia Mews*, based on another book by Margery Sharp, in which Sybil, to her annoyance, was not allowed to wear the fearful make-up she had devised, Jean Negulesco, the director, considering it altogether too horrifying. The one she did wear was frightening enough.

"It was like playing charades and I looked like Russell."*
This comment of Sybil's carries one in imagination back to the vicarage days. Sometimes, watching her in a lighthearted play, one catches a glimpse of the young girl bent on capturing the audience in a parish hall, or hilariously playing charades with Russell. The support of the audience means even more to her than to most actors. Asked in an interview not long ago what was the greatest reward an actor could have, she replied, "There's no title or anything that is greater than an audience's appreciation."

In 1949 an important family event occurred—the sale of Bron-y-garth, Lewis having come to the conclusion that it was too difficult and expensive to keep up for the small amount of time any of the family were now able to spend there.

"I knew it had to go," Sybil said, "but I was broken-hearted. I loved that place even more than Lewis did, more than any of them except Christopher and John. It seemed awfully sad to me that our grandchildren shouldn't know Bron-y-garth."

Not long after this sale Lewis bought Cedar Cottage, an enchanting sixteenth-century building with ancient beams and a deep sloping roof. It was in lovely country at Fairseat on the top

* *The Word*, January 1965.

of Wrotham Hill in Kent, and it remained their country retreat for years.

"Lewis and Mary found Cedar Cottage, and I loved it the moment I saw it. We used to drive down on Saturday nights after the show. It had a beautiful garden—it's the only time I've ever enjoyed gardening. And we did lovely walks on the heath and round the farms. We had delightful neighbours, too. It was all charming, but somehow I had too much to do there, and always went back to town dead-beat."

For the Glasgow Citizens' Theatre's contribution to the 1950 Edinburgh Festival James Bridie chose three plays, one of them being the simple little tragedy *Douglas* or *The Noble Shepherd*, poignant in its sincerity. It had been written in the mid-eighteenth century by that strange Scottish divine John Home, who although he chose the kirk loved arms and had joined as a volunteer against the Pretender, and been taken prisoner at Falkirk. It was presented in 1756 in Edinburgh, in 1815 at the Theatre Royal, Drury Lane, and in 1819 at Covent Garden, with Mrs Siddons making her last appearance on the stage at a Benefit for Mr and Mrs Kemble.

Now Sybil played the part of Lady Randolph, with Lewis as her husband, directed by their son John.

"We played it as in Mrs Siddons' day," John Casson says. "Backdrop and wings, leaving the stage clear for action."

"Real old melodrama," Sybil adds. "They thought we were going to guy it, but we played it absolutely straight, and got away with it."

The Cassons had not long returned to London when Hugh Beaumont's partner, John Perry, brought Sybil the first of N. C. Hunter's immensely successful plays, *Waters of the Moon*, which Tennents were to present at the Haymarket, directed by Frith Banbury with Reece Pemberton sets. Sybil liked the play and was delighted to be acting with Edith Evans again after so many years.

England's two leading actresses were a fine foil for one another
—Dame Edith as Helen Lancaster, a rich and elegant woman in
her forties, demanding adoration, and Dame Sybil as Mrs
Whyte, an "aristocratic-looking woman of perhaps sixty, who
has known better days". Sybil loved her part—

"Though the knitting was a bit tiresome. I could see them all
watching me drop stitches. I hate all kinds of sewing, and the
only things I can knit are long, long scarves. But I'd always
wanted to play one of those widows, intelligent and slightly
soured. The whole idea was interesting and somehow of the
time—people who had been left in the lurch and were getting
on one another's nerves. Frith Banbury was an excellent
director. So decisive and critical, wouldn't let one do any of
one's tricks, but he was understanding, too."

Frith Banbury certainly helped Sybil to act with the impressive
quietude that had been growing with the years—but from which
it was still easy for her to lapse—and thus to portray, with very
few lines, the whole life of this woman, sadly putting up with her
predicament. "The winters here seem interminable . . . I don't
care to speak of what I did in the old days. All that—was another
life."
As Mrs Whyte, Sybil played exquisitely some Chopin pieces,
sitting up-stage at the piano at her most beautiful, with an unsentimental portrayal of sadness that could not fail to wring the
heart. At each performance when she stopped playing there was
a hushed silence and then a burst of applause. One night Myra
Hess was in front, and she went round to see Sybil and told her
that she was "a great artist". Possibly, of all the praise that Sybil
has received, this tribute from a pianist whom she so greatly
admired was the one that gave her the most joy.
One night an over-convivial party in the audience started to
laugh during Wendy Hiller's broken-hearted scene (as Evelyn)
with the champagne bottle. She was acting it beautifully, and
this was just thoughtless laughter at a drunken woman. Sybil
did not play louder for fear of drowning Wendy Hiller's words,

but she changed the phrasing of the Chopin in some magical way that stopped the laughter.

This is the only time that Wendy Hiller has played with Sybil, and she recalls Sybil's unfailing love of her fellow-beings with delighted amusement.

"All kinds of people came to her dressing-room, and she gave the needy not only her own husband's trousers but my husband's too. For that matter, when she was touring in Wales during the war, and I was just looking after my baby, she inspired me to open a canteen. One just had to help."

Sybil always remembers how Dame Edith came to her aid one night when she got something in her eye.

"It hurt horribly. After the scene Edith gave me some kind of silent healing. I suppose it was her Christian Science. Anyway, the pain suddenly went away.

"A delightful addition to our circle of friends at about this time was Mary Stocks,"* Sybil recalls. "I found her an original and lovable personality and a most entertaining talker."

In 1950 Mary Stocks became a governor of what had once been the Fogerty Central School of Speech and Drama, and in her autobiography† she wrote:

"Among the many debts I owe to the Central School was the fact that it involved contacts with Lewis Casson, who was an active member of its governing body. And one day—though in what year I cannot remember, but it seems a long time ago— I received a letter written from the Haymarket Theatre which said, 'Dear Mrs Stocks, Lewis says I must know you! And I want to! Can you come and lunch at 98 Swan Court . . . ? Yours very sincerely, Sybil Thorndike Casson.' Thus began the second of the two corporate loves of my life."

Waters of the Moon ran for nearly two years, and during this

---

* Since 1962 the Baroness Stocks.
† *My Commonplace Book* (Peter Davies, 1970).

period Sybil was, of course, swept into many other activities. One of them took place on July 13th, 1951, when the Queen, now the Queen Mother, laid the foundation stone of the National Theatre on the South Bank, and Sybil read the Poet Laureate's Ode—not acting now, but fully voicing her love of the theatre: "Men's passions made a plaything and sublime."

Another event during this period, particularly exciting to Sybil, was an invitation to give three speeches of Hecuba on the air, in Greek. A Greek professor came to her dressing-room during *Waters of the Moon* to rehearse her for this.

And so to the end of 1953 and the coming of *A Day by the Sea*, N. C. Hunter's equally successful play, directed by the recently knighted John Gielgud, who took the part of Julian Anson, the introvert Foreign Office son of Laura Anson, an extrovert county lady played by Sybil. Once again it was a splendid cast, with Ralph Richardson as an alcoholic doctor and Lewis, at the age of seventy-eight, making up elaborately to portray a man of eighty. Irene Worth was the girl with a past who refuses a future—the first and only time that she played with the Cassons, an enriching experience which she finds it impossible to overrate. She calls Sybil her guardian angel.

"She is a superb person—one of the very few artists who having been blessed with a great gift has repaid the debt by living up to it as a human being.

"Coming to know her well during *A Day by the Sea* gave me a great admiration for her courage. She was racked with rheumatism at this time, and being kept awake at night by cramps in her legs, but she never complained. She and Lewis would refuse all offers to fetch taxis for them, and go off home by bus—to have their favourite meal of bread and milk."

During the run of *A Day by the Sea*, in 1954, Sybil's sister Eileen died, a deep and lasting sorrow to her. Eileen had a stroke, was taken to hospital and never regained consciousness. The family kept watch by her bed, forcing Sybil to go home for a few hours' sleep at night. The end came one afternoon.

"It was an appalling shock. We were very close. If you do have that kind of close relationship with a sister there's nothing like it—except the same thing with a brother. It has been like that with Russell and me always, and so it was with Frank, our young brother who was killed in the first war. I cannot say too often how grateful I am for all the strong and beautiful family ties that have been mine all through my long life."

CHAPTER XIX

"THE TOP OF OUR LIVES"
(1954–1955)

THE CASSONS WERE still playing in *A Day by the Sea* when the enterprising New Zealand entrepreneur, Dan O'Connor, came over to ask them if they would tour Australia and New Zealand under the auspices of the British Council, giving recitals of poetry and "potted" drama. They accepted with alacrity. Dan O'Connor's invitation was specially timely because three years earlier John, with his parents' warm encouragement, had gone off to Australia with Patricia and the children, to be the resident producer of J. C. Williamson Theatres Ltd, the owners of a chain of theatres in Australia and New Zealand.

What finally made the prospect magical was the British Council's proposal that the Cassons should extend their tour to include India. This was to offer them their hearts' desire. They had grown passionately interested in India, and Indian theatre, ever since their meeting, nearly thirty years earlier, with Rabindranath Tagore. Later had followed their friendship with Krishna Menon, with whom they had shared many a platform in the cause of Freedom for India. Mahatma Gandhi had long been one of the strongest influences in their lives, and by now they also numbered among their friends Pandit Nehru and his sister Mrs Pandit, then the High Commissioner for India in London. In June 1954, shortly before they set off on this tour, Lewis and Krishna Menon, to their great pleasure, received together Honorary Doctorates of Law from Glasgow University.

Sybil and Lewis enjoyed preparing material for the recitals, making a wide selection of poems from the seventeenth century to the present day, and excerpts from many plays, finding it illuminating to reconstruct the latter through the eyes of only two characters.

"Whole plays in twenty-five minutes. And I'm still wearing some of the dresses I had made for that tour. They never wear out."

They went first to Perth, and were struck by its beauty even more strongly now than on their former visit.

"We gave our first recital in the fine Government House ballroom, but at the rehearsal the acoustics were quite awful. Nobody could hear a word. We were in agonies of nerves— only prayer got us there at all that night. Nerves get much worse as one grows older."

"I went round to warn them," Dan O'Connor says, "that owing to a full house and the arrival of the Governor there was bound to be a delay of about five minutes. I found Sybil pacing up and down the room.

" 'I suppose it would be worse if we were going to the scaffold,' she said, and a deep voice from an armchair interjected, 'I take leave to doubt it.'

"However, when the ballroom was full the acoustics were perfect and everything went swimmingly."

The recitals ranged, to mention only a few of the authors, from Euripides, Shakespeare, Shaw, Gerard Manley Hopkins and Browning to Edna St Vincent Millay. Lewis also read passages from *Under Milk Wood* in his beautiful Welsh diction, which was particularly moving as Dylan Thomas had recently died. The programmes were enthusiastically received—one reporter being acute enough to note a quality of Sybil's which is not often enough acclaimed. "She is a magnificent listener," he said; and this active participation of her listening while Lewis was speaking added greatly to the poignancy of the performance.

The Cassons flew next to Adelaide, where they were met by Patricia, who drove them to Melbourne on their next stage—the first time they had really seen the bush with its emus and kangaroos, the journey ending with the joy of staying in John's and Patricia's house and of being with their grand-children.

"It was an unprecedented season in Melbourne," Dan O'Connor says. "The side of theatre that interested me was always the literary one, but it hadn't been easy to find audiences for anything out of the ordinary, and I knew these recitals were a risk. Patricia had done splendid work preparing the way by writing innumerable letters and generally building up local interest, and the first night in the Assembly Hall was a splendid occasion. Even then we were not prepared for the sequel—twenty performances during the next two months, and never a seat to sell at the door. We then proceeded to Sydney, where the Cassons stayed with us at Vaucluse on the harbour, and gave six recitals in the huge Conservatorium Hall."

In Canberra they were the guests of Lord Slim, the Governor General, and Lady Slim, receiving "royal and festive" hospitality, and after briefly revisiting Sydney went on to New Zealand, once more amazed by the perfection of the country.

"At Rotorua we saw again that wonderful Maori woman, Guide Rangi, whom we had met on our first visit. She hadn't seen me for more than twenty years, but she knew me at once. I was so touched. In Auckland we met Edmund Hillary and his wife, which was a very great thrill. The Attlees were there too—dear Clem and Vi—which was jolly."

In Wellington the Cabinet adjourned in order that the Prime Minister and his colleagues could join their wives at a tea-party for the Cassons, who enjoyed the occasion thoroughly, while making it quite clear to their Conservative hosts that they were staunch members of the Labour Party.

They toured the length and breadth of the Islands, and by late October were back in Australia, Sybil to celebrate her seventy-second and Lewis his seventy-ninth birthday, after which they flew to Tasmania.

"In Hobart we played in a gem of a theatre that had been built by convicts. It had something about it of the convicts crying for home, and we kept on being reminded of the Tolpuddle martyrs."

Mid-November found them back in Melbourne to give a changed programme of recitals, to broadcast passages from *Ghosts* and *The Medea*, and to stay on for a delightful Christmas with their family.

And so came 1955, and what Sybil and Lewis both considered the greatest experience in their lives—India.

They flew from Sydney, staying one night in Singapore and characteristically visiting a night club before flying on to Bombay, where they were rapturously greeted and garlanded, and welcomed by the Chief Minister of Bombay State, Moraji Desai, a devoted follower of Gandhi. The audiences were wonderful, but the Cassons were horrified by the slums and the hovering vultures waiting to pick the bones of the dead at the Parsee burial ground, the Tower of Silence on the beautiful Malabar Hill.

Now came the highlight of the tour, the visit to New Delhi, where they stayed with the British High Commissioner, Sir Alexander Clutterbuck, and Lady Clutterbuck at the official Residence, a charming house set in a large garden. They could not have chosen a better time of year for their visit to upper India. The skies were blue, mornings and evenings cool, noons not uncomfortably hot, and the gardens gay with bougainvillaea and poinsettia, with the lovely jacarandas moving towards their new blossom and the whole place alive with birds.

"One of my vivid memories is of an old man sitting outside the gate under a tree chanting all night, and another of the charming little mongooses running about keeping the garden clear of snakes. Lewis and I used to pace up and down the long lawn, working out our parts—during this tour we went over our lines every single day, usually on a walk.

"Our hosts were enchanting, and so were Mr and Mrs Dundas and Mr and Mrs Clive Robinson, whom we came to know as 'Clivera'. What made the visit specially delightful was that everyone was so musical—Dorita Clutterbuck played the 'cello and Vera Robinson the viola, and I was frequently urged to play the piano—and nearly always chose Bach."

There were several gala recitals, widely attended, but their very first recital to the students of St Stephen's College in Old Delhi pleased the Cassons best.

"The audience was the most exciting we had ever had in our whole lives. The undergraduates were so quick—they got some comedy points in Shakespeare which I'd never known get over before. And Indian theatre is so thrilling too. Curiously, the actors reminded us of Irish players—particularly in the small parts and the crowd scenes. The Indians have the same natural gift of comedy. Here they were acting in Hindi; later on in Bengal we saw plays performed in Bengali and various other languages. It didn't matter not being able to understand the words because the acting was so expressive. There was a violence and a quiet and a change of pace that is also like the Welsh, as is the lilt of their beautiful English. They confirmed our view, which Lewis felt violent about, that we need far deeper study of speech in our theatre.

"The leading Indian actors played rather in the French tradition. There was one theatre in Madras where the company was all male—two hundred and fifty men—and they played the old classics, the mystery stories. They even did the old Christian story. It was most impressive. And the audiences were marvellous. Whole families sitting there all day, having brought their food with them. The children squatting for hours, perfectly quiet and happy. Everywhere those beautifully behaved audiences. They laughed and then they were quiet. They never coughed and they never fidgeted. I also remember an all-woman audience from the Women's College in Madras, sitting on the floor in every sort of exquisite colour and looking like a mass of sweet peas.

"We were never tired of watching the beauty and elegance of the Indians and the movements of their lovely hands. And I remember the wonderful way the women from the mountains walked—in strides, wearing swinging skirts. Everyone was so friendly, and I think too that Lewis and I were in a special and even more complete harmony during this time, which was the fulfilment of so much we had thought about and yearned for, and which was now completely shared. We were gloriously happy."

One evening, when they were playing in New Delhi, to their delight they were told that Dr Radakrishnan, the Vice-President of India (later Sir Sarvepalli Radakrishnan, the President), was sitting in the front row, and he sent a message inviting them to spend Sunday morning with him. He was Professor of Comparative Religion at Oxford and Mysore, and they had read his books, which gave them some insight into the religions of the world, and the unity there should be between them. They have been friends ever since.

And in New Delhi they once more met the beautiful Raj Kumari Amrit Kaur, then Minister of Health, whom Sybil had first known and admired with the Lester sisters in the Settlement at Bow. They lunched in her lovely home, and she went with them when they flew to Agra. There everyone knew her; she was greeted by the poorest people in the street.

"The Taj Mahal was a revelation. It doesn't look real—it looks as if it's floating, as if one's seeing a dream. That's my most vivid memory, and also of its vastness and of the exquisiteness of those tiny, tiny mosaic flowers, set into the marble. And the little monkeys scampering everywhere in the beautiful gardens."

In Madras they were entertained royally by Raja Gopalachais, the Governor of India who took over from Lord Mountbatten in 1948, and now they felt even more deeply that they were in the heart of India.

"We made trips to the old temples on the sea shore, feeling ourselves going back centuries into another century of thought, with a sense of other beings present.

"We were greatly entertained by the little lizards on the walls of our room at the hotel. They kept off the mosquitoes. Mosquitoes have very amusing faces when you study them, and as for the stillness of lizards—this is perfectly amazing. Contemplating that stillness helped me in the theatre to keep still and disappear unseen."

In Calcutta they had a little flat just off the great park, the Maidan in Theatre Street. They were horrified by the plight of whole families of people living on the wide pavements, but there were many pleasures too, among them the delight of giving recitals and watching the students act in the University of Bengal. The undergraduates performed scenes from *Macbeth* and *The Merchant of Venice*, and again the acting was outstanding.

"More than anything I want to see the sun rise on Everest," Sybil had said to Nehru before she and Lewis left England, and Nehru had replied with characteristic courtesy, "I will arrange the sunrise and everything for you". Now this promise was fulfilled: Nehru had planned for the Cassons to fly up to Bogdhara, and thence go by car seven thousand feet up to Darjeeling.

"We were almost delirious with excitement. One of the strongest wishes of our lives had been to get to the Himalayas and see the peak of Everest. We'd been on every journey that had been made, gone up foot by foot with the climbers. And now here we were—and not a mountain to be seen. Fog."

They were nearly in despair as they reached their hotel, fearing that they would have the same fate as the Huxleys, who had stayed at Darjeeling for six weeks and never seen a mountain. However, everyone assured them that it would be all right on the morrow, and the Cassons prayed and prayed that it would be. They were much comforted by going to tea that afternoon with Tensing, Sir Edmund Hillary's co-climber, who had a school for mountaineers at Darjeeling.

"The next morning we were called at four o'clock, and I looked out of the window and said, 'Oh, no, Lewis, it can't be! It must just be clouds.' But it was—the great range, a hundred miles of it, all over 21,000 feet rising to Kangchenjunga. We knew every crevice of Kangchenjunga, because we had read every book about those mountains that we could lay hands on."

An hour later a colonel of the Gurkhas called for them in an odd kind of car and drove them up to Tiger Hill. People were generally required to do that last bit of the journey on foot, but the colonel insisted on driving the Cassons, and brought hot coffee for them to drink as they waited in the intense cold of that frozen hillside.

"And then the sun rose. Kangchenjunga turned red, and soon in the far distance we saw three marshmallows turning pink— Everest, Lhotse and Makalu—the most marvellous sight in the world. We were speechless—Lewis just clutched my hand and we looked and looked. Then I said to him, 'I don't care if I never see anything beautiful again. We've reached the top.'"

On the way back they visited the Gom Monastery and were taken over it by the head Lama. He showed them the fine library, and took them into the room where an old Lama was turning the prayer wheel.

"We gave him some money to put in it. You felt you wanted to pray there—the wheel was like a rosary.

"As we were leaving I said to the head Lama, 'Father, I've only had one disappointment. I wanted to hear your great trumpets, but I know that's not possible.' At that moment there was an ear-splitting sound which made Lewis and me jump nearly sky-high. We turned round and there were two of the young Lamas with these enormously long trumpets—horns, I believe they call them. And this terrible wonderful sound resounded through the mountains. Then these young Lamas, who had the most lovely faces, rocked and rocked with laughter to see how they had frightened and amazed us, and we shouted with laughter too."

The colonel of the Gurkhas, who was an admirable guide and was determined that his passengers should miss nothing, took them into one of the many very poor houses that they passed. It was still early in the morning, and in all the houses people were at prayer. The Cassons were much impressed by the devoutness that they witnessed everywhere.

"One room in this small house was a chapel, and Lewis and I knelt down and said our prayers there just as if we were in a chapel at home. We felt then—we actually experienced for ourselves the oneness of religions."

Down, then, all those thousands of feet—"There's no ground floor in Darjeeling—the roads are all cut out of the mountains"—and up more thousands to Kalimpong and the Ranee Dorji. She was Tibetan, and was wearing beautiful Tibetan dress and long plaits. She had been educated in Paris and was a highly cultured woman. This was another memorable visit, and Sybil has never forgotten how she powdered her nose in the very room where the Dalai Lama had taken refuge when he was exiled from Tibet. Here they saw the Tibetan caravans coming in, and once again their wide reading and indefatigable study of explorations enabled them to savour to the full each experience that this magical journey brought.

They would have been sadder to leave India had not further

exploration awaited them—a series of recitals in Hong Kong. So now came another inspiring flight, "Hong Kong looking in the mist exactly like a Chinese painting", to stay on the top of the Peak with their friends Sir Michael and Lady Turner. The Turners were already friends of the Cassons'—indeed, Lady Turner was at school with Patricia, and had been one of her bridesmaids. One of her endearing memories of this visit is of Sybil playing duets on the grand piano with her small son Michael.

"We used to watch them from the minstrels' gallery. They were very intent and completely happy. Sybil treated Michael just as if he were her contemporary—and so did he her."

"This was our first contact with Chinese people," Sybil recollects, "and we loved them. Even more elegant than the Indians, with hands like flowers and such graciousness. The view from the Peak was marvellous. Every morning we looked out there seemed to be more islands, as if they had bred in the night."

Patricia had preceded them to Hong Kong with her daughter Penelope, to do the advance publicity and make the necessary arrangements for their visit. She proved herself a splendid manager and press relations officer; she has a sound and swift understanding of the problems involved, but also a sure sympathy with the people concerned—a perfect recipe for getting things done. In Hong Kong the Cassons gave several matinées for children and two evening performances for adults, and their other recital was at a Chinese college in Kowloon, on the mainland.

"The students were most responsive, but they did not laugh in the way the Indian students had. All our audiences here were very appreciative, but quieter than those in India. The children were entrancing, sitting there so still and so lovely, gazing at us and listening so intently."

The press was lyrical, finding Sybil's speech from *Saint Joan* the highlight of the programme. To quote *The South China Morning Post*:

"Her face changed quite obviously, and she was not the person she had appeared to be the moment before.

"When she did speak she was again the . . . young French girl who dared defend her vocation against the challenge of an interested Church.

"In those few and moving and simple words, Dame Sybil recreated the eternal and essential youth that only an actress needs and only a great actress may ever possess."

Now, fifteen years later, we are still acclaiming Sybil Thorndike's eternal youth. Once, when Lionel Harris asked her what her secret is, she said, "I think people forget that after a certain age you have to start generating your own electricity." If this is true, then the way Sybil generates her electricity, which charges not only herself but everyone with whom she has contact, is through her intense interest in and love for her fellow-beings. And also from her life-long habit of "looking forward", which she has often advised others to do.

The Casson family also paid a memorable visit to the Leper Colony on Hay Ling Chay Island, with the chairman of the Mission, Mr Osmond Skinner and his wife. Sybil had been interested in lepers and had maintained contact with them, ever since those early days at the Old Vic when she used to visit the Leper Colony in Essex with Lilian Baylis. She was deeply impressed by the way the lepers were treated here under the leadership of Dr Neil Fraser. All but a very few of the several hundred patients were expecting to be cured, and many were at work on the farms and building sites on the rocky island which the Cassons toured. They gave a recital, carefully chosen to entertain both young and old, and the leper children performed a mime and their elders a Chinese play in honour of their guests, a play which according to Chinese custom went on for hours after the visitors had been seen off by crowds, all waving until they were out of sight.

Sybil's chief memory is of "gay and laughing people and a strange and wonderful light bathing the island".

Their only real disappointment was that they were unable to visit Peking or to see the Great Wall of China. Not to speak of visiting Japan. Tempting invitations to continue their tour eastward had reached them, but they were committed not only to recitals in Singapore and Kuala Lumpur, but to returning immediately afterwards to Australia to join Ralph Richardson and his wife, Meriel Forbes, for a Terence Rattigan season.

They found Singapore oppressively hot whenever they had to be out of doors, but interest and enjoyment continued unabated. They stayed for several nights with Malcolm MacDonald,★ then Commissioner General for South East Asia. He was an inspired ornithologist, and Lewis, in particular, enjoyed his company. They used to watch him climbing a tall ladder against a swaying tree every day to examine an eagle's nest.

"I was enchanted by the Cassons' visit," Mr MacDonald says. "I had had many theatre friends since my earliest days in Government Office, and liked to spend my scanty leisure discussing things with them. Lewis and Sybil were extraordinary. They never talked about what they were doing themselves, but were genuinely and unflaggingly interested in our concerns. This was a critical time in Singapore, when Britain was doing her utmost to weld together the hostile factions— Chinese, Malay, Indians, Eurasians, Ceylonese—and the Cassons helped us, for about them at least there was a united opinion."

One day strolling round a street corner Sybil and Lewis ran into Lionel Harris, who was putting in a few enforced days in Singapore en route to Australia, where he was to direct the Rattigan plays. He was bored and lonely, and rather alarmed at the prospect of directing an actor and an actor-producer, both of such eminence as the Cassons.

★ The Right Hon. Malcolm MacDonald.

"I didn't know them well then," Lionel Harris says, "although I had met her first when she was playing with Ralph Richardson in *Peer Gynt* and I was making my début in London directing *The Duenna* for Nigel Playfair. But Russell Thorndike had joined my company in Swansea a few years later and we were good friends, and now in this boiling Singapore street Sybil and Lewis greeted me like a long-lost brother. I saw them performing to an audience of enraptured native children, and they roped me in to interview them on Radio Malaya. I've adored them ever since. Sybil wrote to me when Lewis died. She knew how awful it was for me being in Australia at such a time and unable to see her."

At the beginning of March they went on to Kuala Lumpur, where they gave one recital for adults and two for children, and as always saw everything that they could. The tapping of the rubber from the trees in the plantations, the delicious lingering smell of the cocoa berries as they were picked, the Rose of Sharon, with its single day of life, white in the morning and deep red at night—these things lingered in their memories as they flew back to Melbourne after three months of adventure, both physical and spiritual, which Sybil calls "The Top of our Lives".

CHAPTER XX

THERE AND BACK

(*1955–1958*)

"HUNDREDS OF MILES of nothingness—that's what I remember of our flight from Melbourne to Perth."

Early one morning the Cassons met the ship bringing Ralph Richardson and Meriel Forbes from England.

"We had known her—Mu, as she has always been called—ever since her father, Frank Forbes-Robertson, played with us in Manchester. Ralph and I have always been *en rapport*, and I was delighted at the prospect of acting with him again. The Richardsons are rather different from us, not such madly keen explorers of places and people. Actually, I think Ralph is rather shy. He considers an actor should display his feelings in his art, and off the stage be as private as he wishes. Mu understood this and backed him up in his unwillingness to meet people. And of course we respected his point of view, although we didn't share it."

Lionel Harris arrived with the Australian company, and rehearsals of *The Sleeping Prince* and *Separate Tables* began, with John's and Patricia's sixteen-year-old daughter Jane playing the little princess in *The Sleeping Prince*. Harris found it most interesting and challenging to direct four stars of such completely different temperaments, and he was fascinated by the strong likeness which Jane bore to her grandmother, although Jane would not have been pleased by this comparison at the time, concentrating as she was on "being herself".

They opened in Perth with *The Sleeping Prince*, the glamour of the première added to by the presence of Terence Rattigan.

"I had always liked his writing and was thrilled to meet him. He has a kind of witty sympathy. You never have to explain anything."

It was delightful for Sybil to play the resplendent and pre-posterous Grand Duchess one night and on the next the odious Mrs Railton-Bell in *Separate Tables*. According to Harris, as the Grand Duchess she caught the whole atmosphere of eccentric royalty, and in some extraordinary way the other actors too avoided theatricality, so that the audience had the impression that they were meeting real royal people about whom they had heard many peculiar stories.

As Mrs Railton-Bell Sybil played the part straight, making no bid for sympathy to excuse her dreadfulness.

"But I've always had a kind of feeling for that sort of old bitch, so it was interesting to act her. Moo gave an exquisite performance, almost too subtle for all but the most perceptive of audiences. But our audiences were very perceptive. Ralph was, as usual to me, perfect in both plays."

Lewis, as the diplomat in *The Sleeping Prince*, "quite frighten-ing in his perfect manners", became Mr Fowler in *Separate Tables*, the rather dim retired schoolmaster; and together the Richardsons brought to full life Terence Rattigan's finely drawn characters of the double parts.

During their time in Perth John Casson telephoned from Melbourne:

" 'Father,' I said, 'will you lend me two thousand pounds?'
" 'Yes,' said my father, without a moment's hesitation, adding as an afterthought, 'What for?'
"I have never forgotten that immediate response. It hurt my father to pay for a taxi instead of a bus, but he was ready to

lend me this large sum without waiting to know why I wanted it. It was in fact to pay a deposit on a new house."

In each city the plays were such a success and the stars so fêted that their progress came to be called the "royal tour". They continued through Australia and New Zealand for the rest of the year, and Christmas found the Cassons back with their family in Melbourne for a beautiful service of carols by candlelight—a congregation of hundreds, each one carrying a candle—at which Lewis and Sybil read the lessons from the New Testament. There were also, of course, all the old well-loved home festivities, and besides the children three Pekingese now shared in the family affection. There is a photograph in a Melbourne paper of Sybil holding one of the little dogs on her lap as she studies Greek.

In January they sailed to Durban with Dan O'Connor and his wife Shirley to resume their recitals. Thence they flew to Johannesburg, where Dan hired a station wagon in which the party journeyed far and wide. Shirley O'Connor did all the driving until Lewis, who had held one of the earliest English licences, now at the age of seventy-nine acquired a South African one so as to be able to take the wheel—which led to many adventures.

In Johannesburg the Cassons gave a fortnight of recitals in the Brooke Theatre, Brian and Petrina Brooke being an English couple who had done more than anyone to keep the legitimate theatre alive in South Africa, and whose supporters had built this theatre for them. Sybil and Lewis naturally found themselves involved in the colour problem, which had been close to their hearts ever since their first visit to South Africa in 1928. They were shown over Sophiatown, the African location, the only district in which the natives had been allowed to own property and from which they were now being moved, in order to be at a distance from the white residential suburbs. Sophiatown had no sanitation and no street lighting; it was a slum, but to its inhabitants it was home. The Cassons were struck by the fact that it was people who had their own problems in society, such as Jews and Communists, who were doing most to help the Negroes.

After Johannesburg they visited Kruger Park, seeing wild

animals in their natural state for the first time. Lewis, who was driving, ditched the car, so—against all regulations—everyone had to get out and push.

They drove hundreds of miles through Natal to Durban and resumed recitals in East London, Grahamstown and Port Elizabeth. In Johannesburg they gave a special performance for the natives which was also attended by many of their white friends. Next came recitals at Salisbury and Bulawayo, and then a few days in Greece—their first visit—on the way to Israel. They spent hours on the Acropolis, and Sybil has never forgotten the ethereal light which haloes it. They also went to Corinth, where they saw what they believed to be Medea's house, which inspired Sybil to declaim:

> Women of Corinth, I am come to show
> My face, lest ye despise me. For I know
> Some heads stand high and fail not, even at night
> Alone—far less like this, in all men's sight . . .

In Israel the Cassons were amazed to find how much had been done since they were there nearly a quarter of a century before. Miles of land that had been barren then were now fertile and blooming with orchards, and everywhere, all the way up the coast, there were trees.

"It was lovely to see the trees that had been planted for me outside Jerusalem, now fully grown. We had one of our best audiences ever in Jerusalem, again in an enormous cinema, and we gave some of our best performances, *Macbeth* particularly being a huge success."

Here, as in most places, they succeeded not only in seeing everything but in going to a large number of meetings, specially those concerned with the position of women and with Jewish problems.

"We were not able to go into any of the holy places, as these were in Arab hands. But in the Roman Catholic church we

went to between Jerusalem and Tel Aviv there was no un-
friendliness at all, and people of many different religions—
Christian, Mohammedan, Hindu—were praying side by side.
We found the rift between Israel and Arabia miserable and
crazy, when we could see how much each race had to give the
other.

"In Tel Aviv we saw Yadin, that actor from the Camera
Theatre who has such a beautiful deep bass voice. He drove us to
Haifa and Nazareth. 'You see we have plenty of taxis here,' he
said, pointing to a row of donkeys coming down the side of
the hill.

"At the last recital we gave at Tel Aviv, a special matinée
for artists and actors, we were presented by the Camera Theatre
with a most marvellous piece of glass that had been dug up
six months before. It was a goblet of the time of Christ, wonderful and of course immensely valuable. Now it is safely lodged
in the Victoria and Albert museum in London."

During the Australian tour the Cassons had received an invitation from "Binkie" Beaumont for Sybil to take the part of Amy,
the Dowager Lady Monchensey, and Lewis that of Dr Warburton
in T. S. Eliot's *The Family Reunion*. Tennents were about to
present the play as part of their Paul Scofield/Peter Brook season
at the Phoenix Theatre. So early in April the Cassons flew back
to England, happy to be home again, and as ever happy to
see the other members of their family. It was the first time they
had been seen on the London stage for nearly three years.

The Family Reunion had first been produced by Martin Browne
in 1939 at the Westminster Theatre. In 1946 it had been put on
at the Mercury, with Eileen Thorndike as Amy's sister Violet.
When, the following year, Martin Browne took his production
to the Gateway Theatre for the first Edinburgh Festival, Eileen
played Amy. The rehearsals were held at the Mercury Theatre
and Sybil regularly attended them, much admiring her sister's
performance, the first big role Eileen had played for some time.
For Sybil *The Family Reunion*, like *The Verge*, which had affected
her so deeply thirty years before, was a mystical exploration and

"broke the mould". Sybil based her own performance to a large extent on Eileen's and, knowing Martin Browne's production so well, she found it difficult to work under another director, although she was keenly interested in being produced by Peter Brook. Theatrically his production was very effective and the critics gave it high praise, but Sybil could not help feeling that Martin Browne, who was such an intimate friend of Eliot's, understood the spiritual music and haunting quality of the play more clearly than did the young Peter Brook. Gwen Ffrangçon-Davies, who was playing Agatha, also found Peter Brook difficult to work for, and both actresses had many an argument with him and were almost in despair at the dress rehearsal. Eliot, however, was very helpful in his quiet way, and the final product was an undoubted success.

In July, when *The Family Reunion* had been running for a month, Sybil and Lewis went down, as so often, to the Barn Theatre in the grounds of Ellen Terry's house at Smallhythe, Kent. Edith Craig, the creator of these memorable anniversary programmes, had died some years before, but the performances had gone on under the auspices of the Ellen Terry Fellowship. On this occasion Clemence Dane had written and assembled a commemoration of the centenary of Ellen Terry's first appearance on the stage. Many scenes were chosen from plays in which Ellen Terry had appeared, played as far as possible by actresses of the age she had been at the time, from Mamillius in *The Winter's Tale* at the age of eight to the *Romeo and Juliet* Nurse in old age. It was an all-star cast: almost every distinguished member of the profession was there on that tiny stage, the performance directed by Margaret Webster, with Sybil and Lewis, wearing their doctors' caps and gowns, speaking the narration that linked the scenes.

In this same year Sybil played the Grand Duchess in *The Prince and the Showgirl*, the film based on Terence Rattigan's *The Sleeping Prince*, directed by Laurence Olivier, who also took the part of the prince to Marilyn Monroe's showgirl.

"Dear sweet Marilyn, whom I loved and admired so much.

Sybil, Lewis
and Elizabeth,
at work on the
book, 1968

Topping Out
at Leatherhead

The first day I was going through some little bits of scenes with Larry and a funny, rather shabby girl who was just saying some of the words without any expression. I thought she was the stand-in and that it was rather stupid of her not to make something of her appearance in front of us all. No make-up, her hair not combed and not even particularly clean. 'Isn't Marilyn coming today?' I asked as we went down on to the set. 'That *is* Marilyn,' they said.

"Oh, but she was the most lovely person! She could never be in time and we were all hung up waiting for her, but she was a darling and we loved her. She had no leading lady frills at all. She was as nice to the small boy who brought her coffee as she was to the stars.

"She was lovely to work with too, although you couldn't always hear what she said. When I did the first shots with her I couldn't hear a word and I thought it was frightful under-acting. I said so to Larry afterwards and he said, 'Come and look at the rushes, duckie'. Marilyn was perfect and I was old ham. I thought I was playing quite gently, but I was old ham. She knew her medium perfectly.

"Her husband, Arthur Miller, was around all the time we were making the film and I liked him so much. It was a tragedy the way that marriage had to come to an end.

"I remember one wonderful party, with two great hostesses, Marilyn Monroe and Vivien Leigh. One fair and the other dark —both in white and so lovely."

During the six-month run of *The Family Reunion* the young American director Carmen Capalbo brought the Cassons Graham Greene's *The Potting Shed*, which Robert Flemyng had agreed to do in New York. This was another work of religious experience, although it could not have been more different from Eliot's. The theme fascinated Sybil and Lewis—the miracle that spoilt the certainties—and she was eager to play Mrs Callifer. One speech she always remembers:

"It was all right to doubt the existence of God as your grandfather did in the time of Darwin. Doubt—that was human

K

liberty. But my generation, we didn't doubt, we knew. [Knew God didn't exist.] I don't believe in this miracle—but I'm not sure any longer. We are none of us sure. When you aren't sure you are alive."

There is an echo here of lines which Sybil has always loved, and which have been a constant help to her. Her vicar once found them in a dentist's waiting-room and sent them to her:

Our highest truths are but half-truths,
Think not to settle down for ever in any truth,
Make use of it as a tent to pass a summer's night,
But build no house on it or it will be your tomb.
When you first have an inkling of its insufficiency,
And begin to descry a dim counter-truth looming up beyond,
Then weep not but give thanks, it is the Lord's voice whisper-
ing:
"Take up thy bed and walk."*

In spite of her life-long faith she has always welcomed an openness to conjecture, and so did Lewis. In fact, his own faith was tempered with humanism, and both Bernard Shaw and Bertrand Russell had an influence on his mind. And he was always obsessed by the need to understand other people's points of view.

"The biggest plays don't offer a solution," Sybil reflects. "They say 'what about it?'"

She was particularly interested in Graham Greene's conversion to Roman Catholicism, Christopher and Ann both having joined this Church.

Graham Greene joined the company in New York for the rehearsals, during which, according to his own account, he re-wrote the last scene unsatisfactorily against time. He was distressed by the play's lack of unity, but unwilling to let any director have the job of putting it together.

"I don't want a producer's play—I want an author's play, and

* Author unknown.

anyway there is a fascination in unity, in trying to work in what Wordsworth called 'the sonnet's narrow room'".*

Carmen Capalbo had stage-managed for Emlyn Williams as Dickens in New York, and he and his partner, Stanley Chase, ran the tiny Bijou Theatre, a non-commercial off-Broadway enterprise in the heart of Broadway. The Cassons liked the set-up, although Lewis fought fiercely with Capalbo over his direction of *The Potting Shed*. On one occasion he even let the sun go down upon his wrath, which was strictly against his principles and upset him greatly. Sybil also used to get bored by the number of "conferences" that Capalbo liked to hold with the cast—a somewhat American custom.

The play did well, although the title puzzled the Americans, as they do not have the expression "potting shed" for a place where the gardening tools, seedlings and so forth are kept. But it was enjoyed as a spiritual and intellectual detective story, and the setting was much admired. The Cassons told the press that after their long absence they now found more kinship between the American and English theatre. "The exchange of plays and players is very healthy, and English audiences are becoming more alert, like yours." When Lewis was asked his views he said there was too much dependence now, especially by young players, on television and films to get a reputation. "They pull speech down and make the theatre too like ordinary life."

The Bijou Theatre restricted its programmes to three-month runs, so as *The Potting Shed* was still doing well it continued in New York, moving to the Golden Theatre. Meanwhile the Cassons did a recital at the Theatre de Lys, and also for a pleasant spree judged a Beauty Contest of Veteran American and British cars. They chose a gleaming white Rolls Royce, built in 1910, Dame Sybil admitting to a little bias in its favour, as they had borrowed just such a car for their honeymoon fifty years ago, and she had spent many hours sitting at the roadside while her husband was happily stretched out beneath the car. Lewis never lost his enthusiasm for cars, and his greatest pleasure of a Sunday,

* Graham Greene: from the preface to *Three Plays* (Mercury Books, 1961).

in his younger days, had been to take the engine to bits and strew the pieces over the road at Carlyle Square.

Their next engagement was in Australia, where they were under contract to J. C. Williamson to do Enid Bagnold's *The Chalk Garden*. They had seen the play before they left London for New York, directed by John Gielgud and with Edith Evans and Peggy Ashcroft in the leading parts. Sybil, although admiring the beauty and wit of the dialogue, did not then think of the play as much more than a stylish Haymarket comedy. It was Irene Mayer Selznick who made her see it when she put it on in New York. "This distraught, gifted, raging personality", as Enid Bagnold describes Irene Selznick, had at her own insistence worked with the author on *The Chalk Garden*—"Nobody has ever got so near writing without writing"*—and presented it in America with Gladys Cooper and Siobhan McKenna, Cecil Beaton doing the decor.

"Irene Selznick read it to us in her New York office," says Sybil. "She gave orders that she was not to be interrupted, and acted the whole play from start to finish. I found it extremely interesting and exciting. I don't think Enid knew what a profound play she had written—she draws on her instinct and it takes over—nor do I think John [Gielgud] really understood what he was directing. Irene was an immense help to me in working out my performance."

This production in New York had in fact been a landmark in theatre history, weakening the prejudice against English plays on Broadway.

Sybil and Lewis were delighted to be produced once more by Lionel Harris, and to have in their company the first-class Australian actress Patricia Kennedy, who had not yet had the recognition she deserved and who has recently been working at the Bristol Old Vic, and also their old friend Gordon Chater. With some difficulty Harris, whole-heartedly backed by Sybil and Lewis, persuaded Sir Frank Tait, the managing director of

---

* *Enid Bagnold's Autobiography.*

J. C. Williamson, to allow the Australian stars to be billed with Dame Sybil Thorndike and Sir Lewis Casson, a privilege reserved by contract for them alone. Strangely enough, the Australian managements did not wish to create stars of their own nationality. They preferred them as visitors from other countries who would not become liabilities. Now, of course, there are many fully recognised indigenous stars.

Sybil was once more in her element, in a gayer part now as Mrs St Maugham, "an old, overpowering, once beautiful, ex-hostess of London society". Her grandchild, the sixteen-year-old Laurel, was played by her own grand-daughter Jane Casson, now eighteen. Lionel Harris auditioned many other girls before Jane was given the part, Lewis and Sybil both insisting that she should be given no preference on account of her relationship with them.

"It was really rather a remarkable performance," Sybil says. "She wasn't in the least a stage ingénue. She played it with great reality. She gave me a new view of the character, and in a way dominated the play. It was frightening. You felt Laurel's future was at stake—she had been spoiled by her grandmother and was a child rotting like a plant that can't grow in the wrong soil. You felt she was a potential murderer. Patricia Kennedy was tremendously interesting as the strange ex-convict governess—she had a kind of veiled look—you knew there was something hidden. Strangely enough, at times she looked almost saintly. She was bent on saving the plants in the chalk garden and leading her young charge away from crime.

"Gordon Chater was splendid as the manservant, looking after his mistress and the child. He and Jane had a wonderful relationship, both on and off the stage. Playing those parts of grandmother and grandchild had an effect on Jane's and my personal relationship too. We're both very violent and we had tremendous rows, but our rows always ended not in tears but in uncontrollable laughter."

Sybil's mention of violence brings to mind a passage in Enid Bagnold's autobiography:

"At breakfast in Oxford the other day, Dame Sybil said [this was during the run of Enid Bagnold's play *Call Me Jacky*], 'Lewis,' she said, 'is a very violent man.' (Pause.) 'But I am a violent woman.'

"I looked at those serene blue eyes. 'You really are?'

"'Yes,' she said, and I believed her. That marriage has lasted sixty years."

The whole company was greatly excited about the production of *The Chalk Garden*. The original setting had been based on Enid Bagnold's own house in a Sussex village and gave no impression of spaciousness, but as Lionel Harris studied the play he got a sense of decay on the grand scale, and so he and the designer, Tom Lingwood, invented an enormous conservatory —an addition to the mansion with its numerous rooms shrouded in dust sheets—filled with furniture and ornaments carefully chosen in the antique shops of Melbourne and Sydney to illustrate the taste of the lady of the house. Here all the action took place, and here Mrs St. Maugham (Sybil very glamorous in her Victor Stiebel clothes) tried to relive a dead past through her young grand-daughter and the old butler dying upstairs.

"I think we brought out what was between the lines, which made our production more significant than the Haymarket one," Sybil says, and at least one Australian critic, who saw both versions, agreed with her.

Lewis was admirable as the judge, but a side of his nature which one is apt to forget, in one's image of him as a serious and critical perfectionist, was his quite preposterous sense of humour —or should it be more aptly called love of the absurd? He adored jokes. He liked shops that sold cushions which made rude noises, glasses that dribbled when you drank from them, ridiculous hats and comic noses. He chose this sombre play for an outburst of boyish high spirits. His arrival at the front door as the judge in *The Chalk Garden* could not be seen by the audience, but only by Gordon Chater, who as the manservant ushered him in. Lewis would appear at the door wearing a flower pot on his head or carrying Sybil's handbag and wearing a grotesque nose, only to assume his proper appearance at the last possible second.

On one occasion worse mischief took charge. Discussing the play with his colleagues during an overnight train journey, Lewis said he thought he was playing the judge a little young. That night he gave a completely different performance: the judge had become a slow, decrepit, almost unintelligible old man. At a reception after the play one of the guests asked Gordon Chater if he did not think Sir Lewis was "a little old to be doing it still".

In the morning Chater, knowing that Sybil was the only person who could deal with this situation, told her what had been said. That afternoon at the matinée, when Gordon Chater went to the door to let the judge in, he nearly collapsed. A dapper young man stood there with fair hair, blue eye shadow, pink cheeks and cherry lips. Gordon had painfully suppressed giggles, Jane had a nose-bleed, the imperturbable Patricia Kennedy quivered from head to foot and Sybil was struck dumb.

She was absolutely furious and did not hide her wrath, although it is only fair to record that she herself was capable of mild unprofessionalism. For example, Jane tells of her grandmother crossing her eyes at her just as they were to play a scene together, or tickling the palm of the hand she was holding, making it an ordeal for Jane not to giggle. However, Sybil would never have behaved as outrageously as this. Even if she had not protested, Lewis would have made amends in his own incomparable way. Before the evening performance he called on the management to apologise for his lapse, and then at each dressing-room in turn.

"I should have shown you what I was going to look like before I came on," he said to Gordon Chater, but in spite of the whimsy his apology was humble and sincere. This was one of Lewis's high qualities: he never minded admitting that he was in the wrong or apologising. Very early in their relationship Sybil had incurred some disapproval by taking on another job while under contract to Ben Greet.

" 'You had better go and apologise,' Lewis said as they got off a bus.

" 'Why? It doesn't interfere. It just fills up my week.'

" 'All the same, I think you'd better go and apologise,' Lewis advised. 'Don't have any dignity.' "

A remarkable phrase from one so blessed with dignity as Lewis—the natural dignity of superb human quality, which Sybil shares. What neither of them ever had was any false pride.

The need to fill up the week that this story recalls has never left Sybil. The years, the days and the hours play games for her, enabling her to fit more into them than would be possible by any ordinary time-table.

In those days of *The Chalk Garden* Lewis rehearsed the company in *King Lear* just as an exercise—to Gordon Chater's special joy, as it was his one chance of being directed by Lewis. "I learnt such an enormous amount from him and Sybil. They knew everything there was to be known about theatre." Gordon Chater was also much impressed by the generosity of Sybil towards her fellow actors. "This is their scene," she would say. "I should really play with my back turned and not too well lit."

Sybil regretted that Lewis never played Lear, which she is right in thinking he would have done magnificently. His great gifts as an actor had come to be overshadowed by his fame as a director and Sybil's fame as an actress. This was largely his own doing. There was something in his nature that made him want to hide his light under a bushel, but at the same time regret that it should be hidden.

One very exciting event, during the beginning of the run in Melbourne, was the appearance of the first sputnik sent up by the Russians. The company had been warned that it was due at about seven-thirty in the evening, just when they would be dressing for the performance, so up they all went to the roof of the theatre in their dressing-gowns and various degrees of costume and make-up. Sybil stood with Patricia Kennedy quite high up, but Lewis went even higher. Sybil's voice, Patricia Kennedy says, rose tenderly to the heavens, greeting the newcomer, and afterwards Gordon Chater heard her say, "O Lewis, if only we could be the first ones to play on the moon!"

Besides going everywhere, seeing everybody and lending their services wherever they were needed, Sybil made a film *Smiley Gets a Gun*, directed by Anthony Kimmins, in which she played an old woman of the Australian backwoods. She would be on the set at eight in the morning, work in blazing heat, do a matinée, and fulfil whatever other engagements she had without demur.

In Perth the Cassons stayed with their friends Alec and Catherine King—Alec being a professor at the University and Catherine head of a women's programme on the Australian Broadcasting Commission.

"We slept in a hut in their garden. Delicious. Every night we went down from the house in our dressing-gowns and lingered to gaze at the stars. They were so marvellous—different from anywhere else. It was as if one could see behind them."

Just before they left for New Zealand Patricia Kennedy, to the joy of all the company, won the Erik Kuttner Award for Acting for her performance as Miss Madrigal.

They had a rough passage to Auckland, which did not trouble Sybil and Lewis, and were met by Patricia, who had flown down to act as their social secretary. Dan and Shirley O'Connor now had a beautiful home in Auckland, and here Sybil and Lewis stayed, happily renewing their old friendship. Whilst here they saw *The Prince and the Show Girl*, the film in which Sybil had starred with Laurence Olivier and Marilyn Monroe. She had only seen a preview until now, and although she thought the film far less good than the Rattigan play she was as impressed as ever with Marilyn Monroe's performance.

And so, after a splendid tour, they came home again, stopping in Canada to visit Ann and her husband, who were living in Ontario.

CHAPTER XXI

ACTRESS TO SAINT
(1958–1962)

FOR A LONG time now Sybil and Lewis had known that Clemence Dane had written a play to celebrate their golden wedding. This had the enchanting title, so inappropriate to the brilliant light which haloed Sybil, of *Eighty in the Shade*. The play was directed by Lionel Harris with a first-class cast, including the Cassons, Robert Flemyng and Valerie Taylor, and opened at Blackpool. On the day of their golden wedding, December 22nd, 1958, they were playing in Brighton, so it was here, with members of the family and the company, that the celebrations took place. The play was presented by Tennents at the Globe Theatre, London, on January 8th, and Sybil received an ovation which wholeheartedly expressed the affection and admiration she had won for herself over the years, with the unfailing help and support of her husband.

Eighty in the Shade is far from being Clemence Dane's best play, although it has a very effective middle act, and when they first read it the Cassons and Lionel Harris were all disappointed. Rehearsal time was not of the happiest; the second act played itself, but the rest of the play was hard to stage and, as always, Clemence Dane resented and resisted any change in her script. She was furious with Lewis when she discovered that at Blackpool he had added a few words "to clarify the action". Fortunately Lionel Harris understood her temperament well and had his own subtle way of getting over difficulties. Even so, although Sybil came to like the first scene, which gave her fine scope for acting, Lionel Harris was never really satisfied except by the second act.

In the autumn of this year Stephen Mitchell asked Sybil to go on tour in *The Seashell*,* playing the part of Mrs Kittridge, the elderly mother of a British Columbia family. Sybil accepted the engagement, as the idea of playing such a Canadian woman interested her, and her co-players were to include Patience Collier, Heather Sears and the as yet little known Sean Connery. Just before they went into production the B.B.C. requested her to play Maurya, another elderly mother, in J. M. Synge's classic *Riders to the Sea*. In this Sean Connery was to be her son, and Sybil welcomed the opportunity of working with him before going into *The Seashell*.

She had been in Dublin fairly recently for the making of two films. The first was *Shake Hands with the Devil*, a picture about the Dublin rising set around 1920. In this James Cagney played the lead, Sybil was an aristocratic rebel-sympathiser, Lewis a judge and Christopher a general. Work on the film was begun just as Christopher and his family were moving into the charming house which Lewis had bought for them at Sandymount, outside Dublin. Sybil's next visit had been in 1960 for the last part of *The Big Gamble*.

Now she decided to return to stay with Christopher once more and work with a member of the Abbey Theatre so as to perfect the accent and intonation of Synge's melodious Anglo-Irish language, which uses so much Gaelic and idiom. Lewis also helped her with her speeches. Her copy of the play is marked all through by him, and as one follows these markings, which were always like a musical notation, one can hear his voice wordlessly speaking the lines, as was his custom, in order to get their tune.

With *Riders to the Sea* beautifully realised, Sybil went happily to work on *The Seashell* with the very lively director Henry Kaplan. The play opened early in October in Edinburgh, Sybil much enjoying acting with Sean Connery.

On October 10th she appeared on B.B.C. television in *This is Your Life*, the programme which, unknown to the protagonist, invites people to meet on the screen the celebrity in whose life they have played a part. Sybil was invited to the studio, as she

* By the American writer Jess Gregg.

thought, simply to record the moving Prologue to *Henry VIII* and the heartbreaking speeches of Queen Katharine. This she did superbly. Hearing those speeches, delivered with consummate grace, at a recent replay of the programme, viewers and technicians were as moved as the original audience. On this evening in 1960, Eamonn Andrews suddenly appeared.

"Hullo," said Sybil, friendly and surprised.

Eamonn Andrews congratulated her on her performance, then explained that it was not the real reason for her being there, and handed her a large volume entitled *This is Your Life*.

"Oh crikey!" Sybil exclaimed, words that are joyfully remembered by the planners of the programme. But it really was a shock to her, and she could scarcely forgive Lewis, who soon appeared to talk of their happy life and endless arguments, for having kept the secret so well. Her brother Russell came to recall older memories, with Jenny Hyman of those early musical days, a postmistress from the Rhondda Valley, Joseph Kirby, who had taught Sybil to fly in *Alice*, and a member of the staff from the Leper Colony near Hong Kong. Fellow actors came to add their tributes, John Casson broadcast from Melbourne and a film showed Ann's children in Canada, after which she herself dramatically appeared, flown over for the occasion. The programme had a dream-like quality with its anachronistic dives into the past, the young old and the old young again.

One evening Noël Coward and Margaret Webster went round to Swan Court.

"Please read this play," they said to Sybil. "We want to do it at once, and you must play the part."

Sybil and Lewis were both delighted with *Waiting in the Wings*, Noël Coward's play about the home for old actresses.*

"I always enjoyed speaking Noël's words. They are so true to character. It's very seldom you don't have to manœuvre dialogue, but with Noël's you don't. It's a lovely play. Noël has such compassion for the old and such understanding of, for

---

* Produced by F.E.S. (Plays) Ltd. in association with Michael Redgrave Productions Ltd.

instance, an actress's relationship with her dresser. That scene between Lotta and her faithful Dora is terribly moving, and the unsentimental scene between mother and son so good. Noël seems to get right to the heart of things without any effort. I loved my part, and Lewis was both very amusing and pathetic as the faithful old beau still bringing violets every Sunday to his old love. Of course, with his feeling for words he adored Noël's writing. I was delighted to be playing again with Marie Löhr—I had that subtle scene of reconciliation with her, all the things we really felt we never said—and there were so many other old friends, including Nora Nicholson, my first pal at the Old Vic, and Norah Blaney, who was such a fine pianist—she and I used to love playing together on two pianos.

"I've never enjoyed a play more. There we were, a pack of old pros all on the verge of going to old actors' homes, so we didn't have any difficulty in portraying them.

"Noël worked splendidly with Peggy Webster, to whom I'm so close that she's practically a member of my family, and the rehearsals were a joy. Whenever Noël was in front at a performance I used to fluff in the first act. Since then he's always called me 'Fluffy Damesie'.

"We took the play to Dublin, where they simply loved it, and we had a riotous party at Christopher's. The end of the run was rather tragic: two of the company died—Molly Lumley, the grand-daughter of that famous actress Mrs John Wood, and Maureen Delaney, who played the old Irish actress so charmingly and died in the play, and actually did die just after it came off."

The "unsentimental scene between mother and son" of which Sybil speaks was one of her triumphs. The son, played by William Hutt, turns up unexpectedly from Canada—she has not even heard from him for seventeen years—and brings her a letter from his wife. She does not read it aloud, but from Sybil's expression and quiet movements, as she sat reading in silence, one heard the letter's tone of kindly patronage as the daughter-in-law invites her husband's mother to go out and live with them.

An invitation which, of course, she quietly and firmly refuses.

Just as she had always wished to portray the character of Saint Joan, Sybil had long wanted to portray Saint Teresa of Avila, whom she saw as a kind of mature Joan. Teresa's personality—nun, mystic, aristocrat, woman of inflexible will, of irresistible charm and preposterous humour—enthralled Sybil. She had read and studied the autobiography and letters and many books by the saint and about her, including V. Sackville West's *The Eagle and the Dove*, which she found more helpful than anything in her understanding of Teresa's character.

"Perhaps because it was written by someone outside the Church, and unorthodox, it gave a spice to the interpretation of her character, which somehow I missed in the orthodox Catholic view. And of course I was fascinated by Gertrude Stein's play, in which she says, 'St. Teresa, half in and half out of doors', which is really what she was."

Now, to their pleasure, the Cassons' dear friend Hugh Ross Williamson had completed his play *Teresa of Avila*, dedicating it "For Sybil and Lewis with love". So in 1961 Sybil gave herself up heart and soul to becoming a living portrait of Teresa. Canon Alfonso de Zulueta, Canon of Westminster Cathedral and Rector of the Chelsea Church of the most Holy Redeemer and St Thomas More, who is an authority on Saint Teresa and a friend of the Cassons', arranged to take Sybil and Lewis—who was to play the Father-General—to the Carmelite monastery at Ware in Hertfordshire.

"And so I met these dear women behind the grill who have been my friends ever since. It did something wonderful for me, and the grill made no separation between us. I met one very old nun who had seen Lewis play before I even knew him. She quoted lines from *Prunella*. And there was Sister Mary of the Holy Trinity who is still my special friend, and of course Mother Margaret herself, so human and warm—I fell for her at once.

"Then an extern sister dressed me in one of their holy habits, and when I came back to the grill the whole community were there and they all clapped and said, 'It is our Holy Mother!'

" 'I can't wear the undershirt, it tickles so,' I said.

"They all laughed, and the Reverend Mother said, 'You'd soon get used to it.'

" 'Not while I was acting I wouldn't,' I assured her.

" 'Then you'd better leave it off,' the Reverend Mother said, 'but it seems a pity.'

"And so we left, having gained this new blessedness of friendship. Lewis and I often went down to the monastery after that—they used to call him 'our darling Father-General'."

Studying the character of Teresa took Sybil back to thinking about Dame Laurentia, the Benedictine nun who was such a fine musician and whom Shaw called "an enclosed nun with an unenclosed mind". She and Lewis visited the Benedictines near Worcester, where they were shown the unpublished correspondence between Dame Laurentia and Bernard Shaw. This invitation was the result of the nuns' joy in hearing Sybil say on the air that her "book of the year" was their own tribute to Dame Laurentia, *In a Great Tradition*.* Sybil still says, "I've often felt I'd rather have been Dame Laurentia than anyone I've ever heard of."

The production of *Teresa of Avila* was altogether unusual. Hugh Ross Williamson, having been a well-known editor and press director in his early days, besides writing a great many books and plays, had for twelve years been an Anglican priest. In 1955 he and his family had converted to Roman Catholicism. Nevertheless he chose Norman Marshall, with whom he had so often worked before,† to direct *Teresa of Avila*. Marshall is not a Catholic, or even a convinced believer. "I'll leave all the religious side to you," he told the Cassons and the author, who under the name of Ian Rossiter was playing a small part as one of the monks.

* A Collection of Essays by the Benedictines of Stanbrook (John Murray, 1956).

† One of these occasions was in the production of Ross Williamson's *The Seven Deadly Virtues* at the Gate Theatre in 1935, in which he wrote the part of Chastity for the nineteen-year-old Ann Casson.

It was an admirable cast, with Nicholas Hannen as Teresa's brother, Rachel Kempson and Betty Hardy as her devoted nuns, and Ernest Milton wonderfully regal as King Philip. Lewis was staunchly convincing as the Father-General, whom the author describes as "a man of great weight—judicious but kindly, worldly-wise but holy", and Sybil, by an act of will and an act of love, recreated the astonishing character of Teresa.

Some of Teresa's constant self-criticism might indeed be Sybil's, for Teresa described herself as subject to bursts of ill-temper, and Sybil frequently speaks of her own irritability and does not subscribe to the general impression that she is compounded of sweetness. Teresa, we know, had her acerbity even with those whom she loved, even at times with "His Majesty Our Lord Himself. The Devil sends so offensive a spirit of bad temper I think I could eat people up."

Without wanting to draw ridiculous comparisons between the sixteenth-century nun of Avila and Sybil Thorndike, the two women have certain things in common that made the playing of the saint natural for Sybil. Teresa's unfailing devotion to her family and interest in people; her delight in children; her boundless humour and gay approach to religion in spite of fearful agonies, including those of her ecstasies ("God deliver me from sullen saints!"); her love of travel, even in the most appalling conditions —"restless gad-about", as an angry Papal Nuncio had called her, although sometimes ill-health "prevented her adventures from amusing her as much as they should"—all these attributes appealed to Sybil. And it so happened—again let it be emphasised that no comparison is intended here between her and the woman she was portraying—that during this play Sybil suffered greatly from the arthritic pains which later were to become excruciating. A curvature of the spine had developed—"my husband used to say I was crooked from the start"—and indeed, although the condition had been exacerbated by the fall in *Hippolytus* and by too much climbing in Wales and on her travels, she does seem to have been born off the straight. Betty Hardy says that, when Sybil was playing St Teresa, off-stage she would sometimes exclaim with pain and irritation at her difficulty in rising from a

low seat, but when she was on the stage she moved as if winged.
In fact, until recently, although sciatica was racking her, when
performing she never had a twinge.

Teresa of Avila opened for the Dublin Festival in September and
then went to Liverpool, where Cardinal Heenan, at that time
Archbishop of Liverpool and an old friend of the Cassons, took
the theatre for a special matinée to which he invited priests and
nuns and monks, for whom the theatre was usually forbidden,
and treated them to lollies and ice-creams in the intervals.

"They were the best audience we ever had. They got the
comedy in a way no secular audience did, and Teresa's humorous speeches, such as when she makes up a verse to rid the nuns'
habits of 'those evil gentry' the fleas, or when she retorts, after
Our Lord has told her that to make them suffer is the way He
treats His friends, 'That, Your Majesty, must be why You
have so few of them', were greeted by roars of laughter such
as we never got from ordinary audiences. It was the most
exhilarating experience. I wish we could have had a similar
audience for *Saint Joan*."

In October *Teresa of Avila* opened in London at the Vaudeville Theatre. "I don't think people wanted a play about God,"
Sybil gives as a reason for its lack of success, but perhaps also the
play, although so authentic, lacks the drama of its subject.
Teresa's life was so fantastic—one sees her holding on to railings to
stop the embarrassment of levitating in public, and carrying on
her wide human cares and responsibilities while engaged in a
desperate war between God and the Devil. How could a play
give scope to such a personality unless perhaps by sheer poetry?

"Being in close touch with the Carmelite and Benedictine
nuns has made me think so much about discipline," Sybil says.
"And music too. To be an instrumentalist you have to have such
discipline. And such dedication to be a musician at all—more
than to be an actor. Music requires a far higher technical
standard, and doesn't depend so directly on personality. I

wonder if there is enough discipline in the theatre today. Outside discipline, of course, there is—in rehearsal—but there isn't the same inner discipline that we used to have, that made one work and work and live one's work."

At the beginning of January Sybil and Lewis left by sea for the last of their always successful recitals in Australia, organised this time by the Australian Elizabethan Theatre Trust. Once again they visited old friends and loved places, and gave old favourites and new choices in their dramatic and poetic programmes, among the latter several extracts from Clemence Dane's brilliant but ill-fated play *The Lion and the Unicorn*.* This had been written some years before, and its production would have fulfilled one of Sybil's dearest ambitions—to portray Elizabeth the First. Charles Cochran had planned to present it with Sybil as Elizabeth and Lewis as Burleigh. Everything was ready for a brilliant production—and then Cochran tragically died, and the show was cancelled. The play never had a professional stage production, although it has been performed in schools and, as on this present tour, Sybil and Lewis gave many excerpts from it in their recitals. But not to have played the part of Elizabeth the First in full has been the greatest disappointment of her professional life.

They were still away when a telegram reached them from Laurence Olivier asking them to join him in *Uncle Vanya* for the first Chichester Festival.

* William Heinemann (Limited Edition, 1943).

CHAPTER XXII

EIGHTY IN THE LIGHT
(1962–1968)

"BRITAIN'S REPUTATION IN music, drama and the visual arts has never been higher," wrote Jennie Lee* when she congratulated the Chichester Festival Theatre on the success of its first two seasons. The opening night, on July 3rd 1962, was a festival for theatre enthusiasts. Christopher Fry wrote a prologue for the occasion which began:

> A theatre, speaking for the age
> We live in, has an ancient need;
> The link between audience and stage
> For which I come to intercede.
>
> The Romans met, as you today,
> Long ago in this old city
> To share the laughter, fear and pity,
> On summer evenings, listening to a play.
>
> Though now we know a great unrest,
> Men of another world almost,
> The mortal heart is still the guest,
> The human story still the host . . .

The building of the theatre was a landmark in theatre history, and stemmed from Tyrone Guthrie's productions at the Stratford Festival Theatre, Ontario, which presented the Chichester Theatre with its open stage of Canadian maple. The outstanding success of the season was *Uncle Vanya*, directed by Laurence

* *Baroness Lee of Asheridge*, then Minister for the Arts.

Olivier, who adapted Tchekhov's intimate domestic drama to the wide spaces of the Chichester stage, with a single set serving alike for indoor and outdoor scenes. The illusion was skilfully aided by the lighting, which appeared to flow inward or outward through the windows as the scenes required; but none the less one missed the close interior in which Tchekhov's characters are so mournfully enclosed, and the wide outside world, symbolised by the swing, in which Ilyena will eventually swing free.

Sybil's Marina was perfect—who could forget the scenes in which she wound the wool from the hands of Lewis's pathetic old Telyegin or tenderly comforted the broken-hearted Sonya, so beautifully played by Joan Plowright? Laurence Olivier was Astrov, the doctor, and Michael Redgrave Uncle Vanya. In February 1970 Sybil watched Paul Scofield's Uncle Vanya at the Royal Court Theatre with undiminished appreciation of the art of the players and the play. "Uncle Vanya is an actor-proof part," she says. "I mean for a top actor."

Sybil celebrated her eightieth birthday on tour with Frances Cuka at the Bristol Hippodrome, playing a musical comedy part for the first time since her teens, as Thackeray's preposterous Miss Crawley in Julian Slade's and Robin Miller's version of *Vanity Fair*. This she did with characteristic gusto, particularly enjoying the chance to perform a solo dance and song, and in November the show opened in London for a run at the Queen's Theatre.

When this came off the Cassons toured with a dramatic recital, *Some Men and Some Women*, which they subsequently presented for a series of matinées at the Haymarket. The programmes were selected from a wide field of interest and were beautifully delivered. Sybil continued with them after Lewis's death, and in August 1970 gave two long and warmly received recitals at Stratford-upon-Avon.

The Sybil of poetry and reading and music, particularly when she is playing Bach, differs in some subtle way from the Sybil of the stage, perhaps because on such occasions she unconsciously reveals her innermost self instead of whole-heartedly presenting the character she has assumed. There is a sensitivity and control of a very high order. And although she declares that on occasion she likes to over-act, "to act big", she "detests acting being just a personal show-off".

The melancholy of *Uncle Vanya* was followed by another burst of frivolity with a revival of *Queen B.*, first at the Theatre Royal, Windsor, and then on tour, with Sybil as Lady Beatrice Cuffe and Lewis, now about to be eighty-eight, playing the butler.

One cannot exaggerate the sense of absurdity shared by this remarkable couple. However serious the situation, however profound their thoughts, the ludicrous aspect of human existence was never long absent, and they loved the opportunity to express it in their work. The sheer nonsense of *Queen B.* gave them full scope.

They were still on the road when Sybil was invited to play the Dowager Countess of Lister in William Douglas-Home's political farce, *The Reluctant Peer*.

"A brilliant play, a perfect comedy part and a delight to be playing with Naunton Wayne who underplayed with such largeness—not like the underplaying of slackness which is such a bore—and under Charles Hickman's delicious comical direction.

"To add to my pleasure William Douglas-Home and his delightful family became close friends of ours. I have the greatest admiration for his brother, Sir Alec, in spite of our political disagreements."

Before *The Reluctant Peer* opened Sybil had promised H. M. Tennent to play Anne Storch in *Season of Goodwill.** The production was put off for six months, but in the autumn she had to hand over her perfect part of Molly Lister to Athene Seyler, and make another big change from the sparkle of *The Reluctant Peer* to the greyness of *Season of Goodwill*. In this play she and Gwen Ffrangçon-Davies appeared as a pair of strange old sisters.

---

* By Arthur Marshall, based on the novel by Dorothy Malm.

"Gwen was wonderful. We really did play like a pair of absurd sisters, with Paul Rogers as our brother. We cut the beginning so as to give me the marvellous first line: 'I have excellent peripheral vision.' "

Season of Goodwill is about three old mid-Westerners who are trying to celebrate Christmas in the time-honoured way—"that lovely, lovely snow . . . and our lovely, lovely tree twinkling away"—but whose home is invaded by a pair of young relatives, a quarrelsome married couple. It is a somewhat dim play, ending in a sordid tragedy, but Sybil liked it—she would not otherwise have agreed to be in it.

"It was significant. I have never played in a play that I did not like. They all had some significance. But the critics didn't like it, and as the public always follows the critics it came off after a meagre run. The critics often don't like what I like—but Lewis and I saw eye to eye in the choice of plays, although our approach was different. I get the atmosphere at once, before I start criticising, Lewis criticised from the word go."

Curiously enough, the very next production that Sybil went into, *Return Ticket*★ (originally called *O.U.T. Spells Out*), which opened at the Duchess in March 1965, was the only play in which she remembers not feeling happy.

"I don't know what it was. I admired the author. I liked playing an old north country woman again and I loved Megs Jenkins' peformance. But I wasn't happy."

This is not really surprising, for in this rather murky version of the eternal triangle, Sybil was a pretty beastly old woman who spends her time unknotting old bits of string, but does nothing to help untangle the muddle her son-in-law has brought into her family. Not that Sybil ever minded playing a beastly character, but there was nothing there to build on, no violence, no drama.

★ By William Corlett.

The next play, the revival of *Arsenic and Old Lace*, was sheer bliss, but before it reached the stage one of the greatest tragedies in the Cassons' lives occurred: their beloved friend Susan Holmes, who had been their secretary for over forty years, died. Her death was a shock, for although she had been ill for some time she had made little of it, and had continued to work.

"We all loved Sukey, as we called her, and I miss her to this day. She managed everything for us. She had a very unusual personality which remained strong, although she could be perfectly selfless in the way she submitted to the demands of other people. She went on working for Lilian Braithwaite after she came to us, and she did this for Johnny* and Larry too, and they all loved her. We wanted her to come on tour with us, but in those days her father was still alive, so she couldn't. We were tremendously lucky to have her all those years, and I am very lucky now to have her great friend Marjorie Forsyth to help me—the widow of our dear Matthew, who managed so many of our productions and died so tragically. Margie is a darling and has been my right hand for a long time now. She is a very able actress. She understudied me in that play *There Was an Old Woman* at the Thorndike Theatre in 1969, and always hears my lines."

It was fortunate for Sybil to have the distraction of *Arsenic and Old Lace*, with Athene Seyler as her sister in the fantastic partnership of those two elderly ladies who in the goodness of their hearts murder old gentlemen by the dozen, in order to save them from living out their last years in lonely melancholy—and with Lewis as their final victim.

"It was gorgeous. We were *awful*, Athene and I. We kept on having terrific arguments in the wings and had to be pushed on to the stage. And twice we got the giggles. It was agony. I can pull myself together with anyone in the world except Athene."

The next play was a complete contrast. This was *The Viaduct*,†

---

* Gielgud.   † By Marguerite Duras, translated by Barbara Bray.

an extremely strange reconstruction of a mysterious crime that had been committed in France about ten years before. Human remains were discovered at different railway stations all over France, and proved on analysis all to be parts of the same female body. Further research revealed that these pieces of body had all passed beneath the same viaduct. Finally the authors of this gruesome crime were discovered to be a retired railway employee and his wife, a quiet old couple of blameless character, and their victim a deaf and dumb cousin who had lived on good terms with them for many years. The theme of the play is the complete devotion of this old couple and their utter inability to discover a motive for their own crime—which the law, while convicting them, also failed to do.

Harold Hobson brought the play to the notice of the Cassons, and Sybil said at once, "I don't understand it, but it's something I want to express." A production was therefore arranged at the Yvonne Arnaud Theatre in Guildford.

Lewis longed to play the part of the old railway man, but, although his memory was excellent in other respects, his ability to memorise many lines had gone, so the part was taken by Max Adrian. "He was very good," Sybil says, and adds wistfully, "but it should have been Lewis."

Sybil liked *The Viaduct* so much that she even said that she did not mind if it ended her acting career. And she tried hard to fathom the mystery.

"She was a very strange woman who had always hidden something in her life, who had smothered her deep longing, far deeper than anything I can express, to show off. That's what she was, a simple railwayman's wife with this overpowering desire to be somebody. Underneath the quietness she was a very violent character, and had suppressed her violence all her life. It was she who had incited her husband to commit the murder, and she was looking forward to the drama of the trial. She had music in her mind all the time—*La Traviata*—it was inexplicable, but I knew the play must be done."

Once again the critics, apart from Harold Hobson, did not share Sybil's high opinion of the play. For her *The Viaduct* had something of the strangeness of *The Verge*, something of an attempt to break the mould, but for them it was simply a thriller that had misfired, with Sybil Thorndike waking faint echoes of Grand Guignol.

A project which was now greatly interesting the Cassons was the building of the new theatre at Leatherhead in Surrey, particularly as early on in the proceedings Sybil had been asked if she would agree to its being named after her—the Thorndike Theatre. She and Lewis were delighted, and to their great pleasure it was decided that one large room, in which particularly the Young Stagers would work, should be named the Casson Room.

The Leatherhead Theatre had been in existence for some years, and done well in difficult circumstances. Early in the sixties the owners of the property, which included Leatherhead's Crescent Cinema, decided that the cinema should close and the site be redeveloped for offices and shops and a better theatre for the Leatherhead Company. The well-known architect Roderick Ham accepted the invitation of Hazel Vincent Wallace, the manager, and her colleagues to design the new theatre, and they worked in close co-operation over the whole scheme. In May 1967 Sybil and Lewis first saw the model of the new Thorndike Theatre, and in October of the same year she wielded a hammer to break through the back wall of the Crescent Cinema and signed her name for a foundation stone.

At the "Break-through Ceremony" Lewis Casson made an impromptu speech in which he said:

"Every play that you see is an opportunity to create for yourself a work of art. It is the duty of the actors to encourage the audience to use their own imaginations to create together a great work of art."

A year later Sybil attended the "Topping-Out Ceremony", and drank beer with the workmen on the site.

Sybil's next play was *Call Me Jacky* by Enid Bagnold, which opened at the Playhouse, Oxford, in February 1968. Although it never reached London it was stimulating for Sybil, both because she liked the play and because its author is herself so stimulating. Enid Bagnold had never seen Sybil in *The Chalk Garden*, as she only played it on the Australian tour. Now she was able to see Sybil working in a part which was not dissimilar from Mrs St Maugham of *The Chalk Garden*—as Mrs Basil, a wealthy left-over of the gentry, grandmother and gardener, living in the ruin of her ancestral home.

From watching her in *Call Me Jacky*, Enid Bagnold observes that she could have said almost in her sleep how Sybil did Mrs St Maugham:

"For I know its pitfalls; the greatest of all being over-emphasis. My peculiar language has to be undercooked to make sense. If it is flourished it becomes absurd. I am sure Sybil knew this and I am sure Lewis demanded it of her if, in temptation, she ever slipped."

How right Enid Bagnold is! All through the years of working together Lewis protected Sybil from the slippery slopes of her own impetuousness.

Of Sybil at work in this play Enid Bagnold says:

"She was then much older [than when she had acted in *The Chalk Garden*], and the rehearsal-time much shorter, and the character perhaps more nebulous. But in spite of these difficulties I recognised with what immense care she learned it, what a stickler she was (as I am) for every comma of meaning, and with what gusto she inhabited the part . . . Gusto and humour and intelligence all came to her aid; and above all understanding. And then again, if there was anything she hadn't understood she immediately asked, and pressed for an answer.

"What amazed me about Sybil was what seemed like humility but which was, in fact, a delight in co-operation. She is one of the rare stars in that profession of temperament who does not want anything for herself, but puts that self beautifully as the servant of the character.

"Also she is truthful. When she says 'I love your play' she loves it and will fight for it.

"All arts upset the temperament, but at least in writing one upsets oneself. On the stage a temperament upsets everyone. Whatever Sybil has—of Celtic impetuousness, of sentiment, of a quick rise to anger—she watches over it like someone who owns a lion and must keep it in order."

The notices were Sybil's. "Miss Thorndike has all the best lines and never wastes one," said *The Times*. "Her diction is a constant joy." But *Call Me Jacky* was not well enough received for the management to risk London, so, to quote its author again, it "lay upside down at Oxford like a dog with its paws in the air. Even in failure Sybil was perfection."

Still at Oxford, though this time at the New, at the end of April a revival of Emlyn Williams' *Night Must Fall* began its tour. This was Lewis Casson's last appearance on the stage, and it was a fitting one. With a little contriving he managed the single long speech with which the play opens. To quote the author's instructions:

"The orchestra plays light tunes until the house lights are turned down; the curtain rises in darkness, accompanied by solemn music; the opening chords of Holst's *The Perfect Fool*. A small light grows in the middle of the stage, and shows the LORD CHIEF JUSTICE sitting in judgment, wearing wig and red robes of office, in the Court of Criminal Appeal. His voice . . . gradually swells up with the light as he reaches his peroration."

Dame Sybil Thorndike played the part of Mrs Bramson—whom Dame May Whitty, when she created the part thirty-three years earlier, called "an old beast in a wheelchair"*—with the same fine professionalism as her predecessor, while Dan, the disarming young murderer, whom the author had originally

* *The Same Only Different.*

played himself, was taken by the popular singer Adam Faith, who gave, Sybil says, a most sympathetic performance, less wildly mad than Emlyn's, but perhaps more human.

This production of *Night Must Fall* never reached London, but it toured for some months, moving from Oxford to Cambridge, then going up north and coming back south again.

Comparatively quiet days followed at Swan Court, with many visits from the family. John and Patricia Casson were back from Australia and planning to live in Chelsea. Glad as Sybil was to have them close to her, she wept for the sale of their Melbourne house, which had been so dear a home to her and Lewis. A new thrill had occurred there during the last years—the birth of their first great-grandchildren Randal Lewis and Thomas Walter, the children of John's and Patricia's son Anthony and his wife Janekke. There was rejoicing in the family that its latest members were boys, so that the name of Casson was safely carried on into the new generation. Not long ago Sybil took them to see Russell. They stood—Thomas under two and Randal Lewis just three—gazing at him enraptured. "You are our great-great-uncle Russell," Randal observed, and then added to his great-grand-mother, "He is my friend."

In October came Lewis's ninety-third and Sybil's eighty-sixth birthday, and on December 22nd they celebrated their diamond wedding, which fell on a Sunday, so that their closest theatrical friends were free to attend. They had two parties. The first was held in the large flat that John and Patricia had been lent in Kensington. Lewis and Sybil were in wonderful form. They sat on a dais, almost as if enthroned, Sybil resplendent in a golden dress, and enjoyed their friends to the full, Ellaline Terriss, in her ninety-ninth year, and Cardinal Heenan shining stars amid the galaxy. The second party was given in Owen Reed's house at Hampton-on-Thames and was for close relatives only, a heart-warming gathering of the clan.

A few days later came Christmas.

"The whole family went to midnight Mass—even the Roman Catholics came. In the evening we had a wonderful dinner at

John and Patricia's, a Christmas tree and beautiful presents, with the children and grandchildren.

"This was Lewis's last Christmas, our last Christmas all together. It could not have been more happy and joyous."

CHAPTER XXIII

HERNE'S OAK HAS FALLEN*
(1969)

HOW WELSH HE was! Everywhere in that magical strip of north Wales, railwaymen, farmers, labourers and taximen all gaze at you with the same penetrating yet kindly blue eyes set deeply into a thinker's brow. A Welsh face which Lewis inherited from his mother, but which was carved too out of the countryside which bred him.

His nature was deep and fierce, and, if he was critical and expected high standards from others, he was ruthless in what he demanded of himself. Nobody ever had a stronger conscience, and although he would argue a point fiercely he was always convinced that it was his duty to see the other man's point of view. All his life Lewis was subject to depressions, largely stemming from his hyper-sensitive conscience. In spite of his sense of humour and his taste for outright folly, the failings and sorrows of humanity weighed upon him. He seemed to feel a kind of remorse that impelled him to share its burdens. Young actors, young directors, might be in awe of him and even find him forbidding, but he approached anyone in trouble—in sickness or in grief— with deep and understanding compassion. The wounds of others were his wounds. "He had healing in his voice," Sybil says, "and in his hands."

He bore the decline of old age—the gradual loss of hearing, of eyesight, of memory—with fortitude and dignity, but he resented these failings. He never, for instance, came to terms with his

* Title of obituary notice by Sir John Gielgud in *Plays and Players* (July 1969). *The Merry Wives of Windsor* (IV, 4).

hearing-aid, and poor sight gave him a sense of helplessness; he could no longer, as he loved to do, make and mend.

It was an accident during the 1962 tour that started the deterioration of his eyesight. The Cassons had been lunching with friends near Melbourne, and afterwards went for a walk along a narrow cliff path. Lewis fell, cutting his head and injuring an eye. He was advised to stay in bed, but refused even to lie down. Shortly after this he began to have difficulty in reading, and a few years later the ability left him altogether. Sybil became his eyes.

Lewis had also been suffering for some time from anaemia, which was not too alarming, as it at least guarded his fiery temperament from high blood pressure. He had regular injections for the anaemia, which was contributing to his depressions, but he refused to take any form of "pep" pills. A jab he could tolerate, but tablets of any kind were anathema.

In spite of these disabilities he maintained his physical and mental vitality.

"At his diamond wedding party . . . [John Gielgud wrote], I put my hand on his arm in saying goodbye, and said to someone, 'How amazingly strong he is—he feels like Herne's Oak!'"

How strong his mind was, too. He continued, as was his wont, to think constructively and challengingly on all manner of subjects, and to take a creative interest in other people, particularly in all the members of his family. Every Sunday he and Sybil went to lunch with their daughter Mary and her husband, Ian Haines, and then they would all go back to Swan Court and Mary would sing to him—songs of the Hebrides and other old favourites. This was one of his greatest joys.

The last time he appeared as head of the Casson family was at "Penny's" (Penelope Casson's) marriage to her second cousin once removed, the writer Tom Pocock. Lewis was in good form at the wedding, but after it he was very tired and in low spirits, for all his fortitude. In those last weeks the words of his countryman came to mind:

Do not go gentle into that good night,
Old age should burn and rave at close of day;
Rage, rage against the dying of the light.*

A fortnight after that wedding party, one evening after dinner, Mary sang to Lewis for the last time. In the week beginning May 12th his doctors began to be worried about him. Sybil was due to give a Dickens reading at Rochester that evening. She asked Lewis if she should cancel it, but he said, "No, we never do", and she went. Patricia kept him company, but he was very restless and refused to stay in bed until Sybil came home. On Tuesday he went into the Nuffield Nursing Home. Sybil was expected at Aylesford to give a recital to school-children. Once again Lewis would not hear of her missing the engagement, and the children, who had been told by the vicar of Sir Lewis's illness and Dame Sybil's gallantry in coming down to Aylesford, gave her a rousing ovation.

All Wednesday and Thursday she was with Lewis, but he was very weak. Early on the Friday morning Patricia drove Sybil to the hospital, the rush-hour traffic seeming in some miraculous way to vanish from their path. Lewis was having an examination, and soon after the specialist left he collapsed. He was given oxygen but he did not rally, and with Sybil holding his hand the curtain dropped.

The many long obituary notices by actors and drama critics all paid wide homage to Lewis as a human being and as a man of the theatre. Michael MacOwan expresses the feeling shared by so many of his colleagues:

"The shock of grief with which I heard of Lewis Casson's death has taught me a lot about him. I learnt that his achievements, and his vital part in most of what is best in theatre history for the past seventy years, were equalled in importance by the man."

H. B. Marriott wrote in *The Stage*:†

* Dylan Thomas.   † May 22nd, 1969.

The Family Reunion

There Was an Old Woman, 1969

"He once declared that his ambition was to be a 'good work-man' and to 'serve rather than score off the theatre'".

Marriott speaks of his complete freedom from the snares of petty jealousy, from any jealousy at all, in fact. To him, as to Shaw, the theatre was a temple of life, and therein he worked like a faithful servant of his Creator.

It was a joy to see him act, he brought such delicacy and sincerity to his performances. His charming personality was deployed for a part when this was helpful, but was instantly subdued, put out of mind, when it would have got in the way of his interpretation. This quality of integrity is far more un-common than might be suspected.

On May 19th he was cremated privately at Golders Green, and on June 3rd came *A Service of Thanksgiving for Sir Lewis Casson, M.C., D.Litt., LL.D* at Westminster Abbey. Casson is the only actor, other than Henry Irving, to be accorded this honour.

The Abbey is completely filled, and so is the street outside. People—not in mourning, as it is understood that this would not be appropriate—are ushered to their seats by leading members of the profession. A great quietness reigns, broken at last by the organ in the perfection of Bach's *Prelude in G*. After Parry's *Andante* more Bach follows, during which the congregation rises and Sybil Thorndike Casson comes up the aisle and through the chancel on the arm of her son John, with other members of the family following. She is dressed in creamy white, her pale face and her white hair framed in white, and her expression is that of a visionary. Although there are tears in very many eyes, no heart can fail to be uplifted.

Then, as the Dean of Westminster's procession enters, the service begins with the choir singing sentences from the Bible. The order of this *Service of Prayer and Praise* has been chosen by Sybil with a clear memory of the discussions she often had with Lewis about the music and the words they would have to see them off on their last journey. The result is pure and perfect beauty.

A prayer, a hymn, a superb reading of Henley's poem* by John Casson, hundreds holding their breath as he ends, his voice giving that last word "death" the ecstasy of the poet's "shining peace".

A psalm, a heartbreaking reading by John Gielgud from *The Tempest*, a Spenser anthem, a reading of a Revelation by the Archdeacon of Westminster, again Bach, and the final prayer spoken by the Precentor of the Abbey.

The bells are rung, half-muffled, the procession withdraws to the strains of Bach's *Fantasia in G major*, and the glorious valediction is over.

One famous actor, Laurence Olivier, has not been present in the Abbey, and before many minutes have passed Sybil is at his bedside in the Nuffield Nursing Home.

* W. E. Henley: *Margaritae Sorori.*

CHAPTER XXIV

COMPANION OF HONOUR
(1969–1970)

NOT A SINGLE one of the hundreds of letters of sympathy which Sybil received remained unanswered for long, and very many of the replies were in her own handwriting. It was hard at first to realise her loss—"I can't take it in yet" was a constant refrain. The close love of her family and the wide love of her friends supported her, and of course her steadfast faith, and she went staunchly on fulfilling her promises to give recitals in aid of one cause and another.

On September 17th 1969 Princess Margaret, Lord Snowdon and Jennie Lee were among those who were with her at Leatherhead for the eagerly awaited opening of the Thorndike Theatre. The play chosen for the occasion was James Goldman's *The Lion in Winter*, and the invited audience included many relatives and friends of Sybil's, among whom were celebrities from every walk of life.

After the performance Dame Sybil went up on to the stage, the whole audience rising to applaud her, and congratulated the architect, the manager and other people connected with the building and launching of the beautiful theatre. It was a wonderfully friendly occasion, only shadowed by Sybil's sorrow, shared by so many of those present, at the absence of Sir Lewis Casson.

Sybil had already agreed to play the lead in John Graham's *There Was an Old Woman* for the next production at her theatre.

"As soon as I read the first line I knew I wanted to do it. I always wonder about those old girls you see sitting around on steps and benches—what's happened to them. What they're thinking about. I read the play aloud to Lewis and he said, 'This is you, you must do it'. But by the time I did it he had gone.

"John Graham came to see me and I liked him. His writing was so fine, but perhaps the shape of the play was less good. It didn't quite work in production."

For the three weeks' run there was never an empty seat, and at each performance Sybil was given a great ovation. Her performance was remarkable—she was scarcely recognisable as the shapeless old woman in a bundle of coats, her head tied up in an old scarf, tugging along a couple of bulging carrier bags.

From her bench—"a merry octogenarian", as Philip Hope-Wallace called her,[*] rough, tough, matey, funny and moving— she takes the audience into her confidence with a swig from her bottle of gin. "You've got to keep warm."

"I thoroughly enjoyed myself. It's my favourite sort of play. At the end of the final performance me knicks came down, which brought the house down too."

During those three weeks Sybil stayed with old friends, the Blowers, living near Leatherhead, and she greatly enjoyed the beauty of the Surrey countryside, miles of woods and heath in ever changing weather. Its capricious climate is one of the things she loves best about England. She found her long part tiring, however; she was on the stage throughout the play, although there were scenes, during flash-backs to her youth, in which she scarcely spoke.

She was back in Swan Court for a quiet Christmas with the family, and then at the beginning of 1970 she resumed her life of recitals and broadcasts, seeing her relatives and friends and quite often going to the theatre. Among these beautiful recitals were several with John Casson for the Apollo Society, one with Sir Hugh Casson on television, one for the Royal Society of

* *The Guardian* (October 15th, 1969).

Literature, one with Léon Goossens at the Thorndike Theatre, one at the new theatre at Bryanston School in Dorset, one at St Albans, and one for the Indian people at the Royal Commonwealth Institute in London. Besides these recitals she read with Emlyn Williams in a Dickens programme at Westminster Abbey at which Queen Elizabeth the Queen Mother was present, and presented an appreciation of Mrs Pankhurst, written by herself, at the National Portrait Gallery. At the beginning of June she went to Plymouth to read pilgrim poetry during the week celebrating the Pilgrim Fathers, and later that month read a passage from the *Pilgrim's Progress* at the Memorial Service for the writer Vera Brittain. All the time she continued to visit and to welcome at Swan Court her family and close friends, and every day she still played the piano, although she was now greatly troubled by arthritis.

In the Birthday Honours of June 1970 Dame Sybil Thorndike, Lady Casson, received the high distinction of being made a Companion of Honour. The only other recipient of the C.H. on this occasion was her friend Sir Frederick Ashton, Director of the Royal Ballet, who accompanied her to Buckingham Palace for a private investiture by the Queen.

In the same Honours List Sir Laurence Olivier was raised to the peerage, to become the first lord of the theatre. He and Sybil exchanged telegrams of congratulation, and in Larry's message he said, "I can't imagine the Queen having a nicer Companion."

Who can?

INDEX

INDEX